In memory of my beloved parents, who, after having faced monumental adversities, provided me with the guidance to develop a love for mathematics, and chiefly to Barbara, without whose support and encouragement this book would not have been possible.

MATH WONDERS

to Inspire Teachers and Students

Alfred S. Posamentier

Association for Supervision
and Curriculum Development

Alexandria, Virginia USA

Association for Supervision and Curriculum Development
1703 N. Beauregard St. * Alexandria, VA 22311-1714 USA
Telephone: 800-933-2723 or 703-578-9600 * Fax: 703-575-5400
Web site: http://www.ascd.org * E-mail: member@ascd.org

Gene R. Carter, *Executive Director*; Nancy Modrak, *Director of Publishing*; Julie Houtz, *Director of Book Editing & Production*; Darcie Russell, *Project Manager*; Technical Typesetting, Inc., *Typesetting*; Tracey Smith, *Production*

Printed in the United States of America.

s/April 2003

ISBN: 0-87120-775-3 ASCD product no.: 103010
ASCD member price: $22.95 Nonmember price: $27.95

Library of Congress Cataloging-in-Publication Data

Posamentier, Alfred S.
  Math wonders to inspire teachers and students / [Alfred S.
  Posamentier].
    p. cm.
Includes bibliographical references and index.
  ISBN 0-87120-775-3 (alk. paper)
1. Mathematics–Study and teaching. 2. Mathematical recreations. I.
Title.
QA11.2 .P64 2003
510—dc21

                                           2003000738

12 11 10 09 08 07 06 05 04 03   12 11 10 9 8 7 6 5 4 3 2 1

Math Wonders to Inspire Teachers and Students

Foreword

Bertrand Russell once wrote, "Mathematics possesses not only truth but supreme beauty, a beauty cold and austere, like that of sculpture, sublimely pure and capable of a stern perfection, such as only the greatest art can show."

Can this be the same Russell who, together with Alfred Whitehead, authored the monumental *Principia Mathematica*, which can by no means be regarded as a work of art, much less as sublimely beautiful? So what are we to believe?

Let me begin by saying that I agree completely with Russell's statement, which I first read some years ago. However, I had independently arrived at the same conviction decades earlier when, as a 10- or 12-year-old, I first learned of the existence of the Platonic solids (these are perfectly symmetric three-dimensional figures, called polyhedra, where all faces, edges, and angles are the same—there are five such). I had been reading a book on recreational mathematics, which contained not only pictures of the five Platonic solids, but patterns that made possible the easy construction of these polyhedra. These pictures made a profound impression on me; I could not rest until I had constructed cardboard models of all five. This was my introduction to mathematics. The Platonic solids are, in fact, sublimely beautiful (as Russell would say) and, at the same time, the symmetries they embody have important implications for mathematics with consequences for both geometry and algebra. In a very real sense, then, they may be regarded as providing a connecting link between geometry and algebra. Although I cannot possibly claim to have understood the full significance of this relationship some 7 decades ago, I believe it fair to say that this initial encounter inspired my subsequent 70-year love affair with mathematics.

Our next meeting is shrouded in the mists of time, but I recall with certainty that it was concerned with curves. I was so fascinated by the shape and mathematical description of a simple curve (cardioid or cissoid perhaps) that I had stumbled across in my reading that again I could not rest until I had explored in depth as many curves as I could find in the encyclopedia during a 2-month summer break. I was perhaps 13 or 14 at the time. I found their shapes, infinite variety, and geometric properties to be indescribably beautiful.

At the beginning of this never-to-be-forgotten summer, I could not possibly have understood what was meant by the equation of a curve that invariably appeared at the very beginning of almost every article. However, one cannot spend 4 or 5 hours a day over a 2-month period without finally gaining an understanding of the relationship between a curve and its equation, between geometry and algebra, a relationship itself of profound beauty. In this way, too, I learned analytic geometry, painlessly and effortlessly, in fact, with pleasure, as each curve revealed its hidden treasures—all beautiful, many profound. Is it any wonder, then, that this was a summer I shall never forget?

Now, the cycloid is only one of an infinite variety of curves, some planar, others twisted, having a myriad of characteristic properties aptly described by Russell as "sublimely beautiful" and capable of a stern perfection. The examples given here clearly show that the great book of mathematics lies ever open before our eyes and the true philosophy is written in it (to paraphrase Galileo); the reader is invited to open and enjoy it. Is it any wonder that I have never closed it?

I would like to tell you about one of these beautiful curves, but it is more appropriate that the discussion be relegated to a unit of this wonderful book. So if you wish to see the sort of thing that turned me on to mathematics in my youth, see Unit 8.13.

Why do I relate these episodes now? You are about to embark on a lovely book that was carefully crafted to turn you, the reader, and ultimately your students, on to mathematics. It is impossible to determine what an individual will find attractive. For me, it was symmetrically shaped solid figures and curves; for you, it may be something entirely different. Yet, with the wide variety of topics and themes in this book, there will be something for everyone and hopefully much for all. Dr. Alfred S. Posamentier and I have worked on several writing projects together, and I am well acquainted with his eagerness to demonstrate mathematics' beauty to the uninitiated. He does this with an admirable sense of enthusiasm. This is more than evident in this book, beginning with the selection of topics, which are fascinating in their own right, and taken through with his clear and comfortable presentation. He has made every effort to avoid allowing a possibly unfamiliar term or concept to slip by without defining it.

You have, therefore, in this book all the material that can evoke the beauty of mathematics presented in an accessible style—the primary goal of this book. It is the wish of every mathematician that more of society would share these beautiful morsels of mathematics with us. In my case, I took this early love for mathematics to the science research laboratories, where it provided me with insights that many scientists didn't have. This intrinsic love for mathematical structures allowed me to solve problems that stifled the chemical community for decades. I was surprisingly honored to be rewarded for my work by receiving the Nobel Prize for Chemistry in 1985. I later learned that I was the first mathematician to win the Nobel Prize. All this, as a result of capturing an early love for the beauty of mathematics. Perhaps this book will open new vistas for your students, where mathematics will expose its unique beauty to them. You may be pleasantly surprised in what ways this book might present new ideas or opportunities for them. Even you will benefit from having a much more motivated class of students to take through the beauties and usefulness of mathematics.

Herbert A. Hauptman, Ph.D.
Nobel Laureate 1985
CEO and President
Hauptman-Woodward Medical Research Institute
Buffalo, New York

Preface

This book was inspired by the extraordinary response to an Op-Ed article I wrote for *The New York Times*.* In that article, I called for the need to convince people of the beauty of mathematics and not necessarily its usefulness, as is most often the case when trying to motivate youngsters to the subject. I used the year number, 2,002,** to motivate the reader by mentioning that it is a palindrome and then proceeded to show some entertaining aspects of a palindromic number. I could have taken it even further by having the reader take products of the number 2,002, for that, too, reveals some beautiful relationships (or quirks) of our number system. For example, look at some selected products of 2,002:

$$2,002 \cdot \quad 4 = 8,008$$
$$2,002 \cdot \ 37 = 74,074$$
$$2,002 \cdot \ 98 = 196,196$$
$$2,002 \cdot 123 = 246,246$$
$$2,002 \cdot 444 = 888,888$$
$$2,002 \cdot 555 = 1,111,110$$

Following the publication of the article, I received more than 500 letters and e-mail messages supporting this view and asking for ways and materials to have people see and appreciate the beauty of mathematics. I hope to be able to respond to the vast outcry for ways to demonstrate the beauty of mathematics with this book. Teachers are the best ambassadors to the beautiful realm of mathematics. Therefore, it is my desire to merely open the door to this aspect of mathematics with this book. Remember, this is only the door opener. Once you begin to see the many possibilities for enticing our youth toward a love for this magnificent and time-tested subject, you will begin to build an arsenal of books with many more ideas to use when appropriate.

---

* January 2, 2002.

** Incidentally, 2,002 is the product of a nice list of prime numbers: 2, 7, 11, and 13.

This brings me to another thought. Not only is it obvious that the topic and level must be appropriate for the intended audience, but the teacher's enthusiasm for the topic and the manner in which it is presented are equally important. In most cases, the units will be sufficient for your students. However, there will be some students who will require a more in-depth treatment of a topic. To facilitate this, references for further information on many of the units are provided (usually as footnotes).

When I meet someone socially and they discover that my field of interest is mathematics, I am usually confronted with the proud exclamation: "Oh, I was always terrible in math!" For no other subject in the curriculum would an adult be so proud of failure. Having been weak in mathematics is a badge of honor. Why is this so? Are people embarrassed to admit competence in this area? And why *are* so many people really weak in mathematics? What can be done to change this trend? Were anyone to have the definitive answer to this question, he or she would be the nation's education superstar. We can only conjecture where the problem lies and then from that perspective, hope to repair it. It is my strong belief that the root of the problem lies in the inherent unpopularity of mathematics. But *why* is it so unpopular? Those who use mathematics are fine with it, but those who do not generally find it an area of study that may have caused them hardship. We must finally demonstrate the inherent beauty of mathematics, so that those students who do not have a daily need for it can be led to appreciate it for its beauty and not only for its usefulness. This, then, is the objective of this book: to provide sufficient evidence of the beauty of mathematics through many examples in a variety of its branches. To make these examples attractive and effective, they were selected on the basis of the ease with which they can be understood at first reading and their inherent unusualness.

Where are the societal shortcomings that lead us to such an overwhelming "fear" of mathematics, resulting in a general avoidance of the subject? From earliest times, we are told that mathematics is important to almost any endeavor we choose to pursue. When a young child is encouraged to do well in school in mathematics, it is usually accompanied with, "You'll need mathematics if you want to be a _____." For the young child, this is a useless justification since his career goals are not yet of any concern to him. Thus, this is an empty statement. Sometimes a child is told to do better in mathematics or else_____." This, too, does not have a lasting effect on the child, who does just enough to avoid punishment. He will give mathematics attention only to avoid further difficulty from his parents. Now with the material in this book, we can attack the problem of enticing youngsters to love mathematics.

To compound this lack of popularity of mathematics among the populace, the child who may not be doing as well in mathematics as in other subject areas is consoled by his parents by being told that they, too, were not too good in mathematics in their school days. This negative role model can have a most deleterious effect on a youngster's motivation toward mathematics. It is, therefore, your responsibility to counterbalance these mathematics slurs that seem to come from all directions. Again, with the material in this book, you can demonstrate the beauty, not just tell the kids this mathematics stuff is great.* Show them!

For school administrators, performance in mathematics will typically be the bellwether for their schools' success or weakness. When their schools perform well either in comparison to normed data or in comparison to neighboring school districts, then they breathe a sigh of relief. On the other hand, when their schools do not perform well, there is immediate pressure to fix the situation. More often than not, these schools place the blame on the teachers. Usually, a "quick-fix" in-service program is initiated for the math teachers in the schools. Unless the in-service program is carefully tailored to the particular teachers, little can be expected in the way of improved student performance. Very often, a school or district will blame the curriculum (or textbook) and then alter it in the hope of bringing about immediate change. This can be dangerous, since a sudden change in curriculum can leave the teachers ill prepared for this new material and thereby cause further difficulty. When an in-service program purports to have the "magic formula" to improve teacher performance, one ought to be a bit suspicious. Making teachers more effective requires a considerable amount of effort spread over a long time. Then it is an extraordinarily difficult task for a number of reasons. First, one must clearly determine where the weaknesses lie. Is it a general weakness in content? Are the pedagogical skills lacking? Are the teachers simply lacking motivation? Or is it a combination of these factors? Whatever the problem, it is generally

---

* For general audiences, see *Math Charmers: Tantalizing Tidbits for the Mind* (Prometheus, 2003).

not shared by every math teacher in the school. This, then, implies that a variety of in-service programs would need to be instituted for meeting the overall weakness of instruction. This is rarely, if ever, done because of organizational and financial considerations of providing in-service training on an individual basis. The problem of making mathematics instruction more successful by changing the teachers' performance is clearly not the entire solution. Teachers need ideas to motivate their students through content that is appropriate and fun.

International comparative studies constantly place our country's schools at a relatively low ranking. Thus, politicians take up the cause of raising mathematics performance. They wear the hat of "education president," "education governor," or "education mayor" and authorize new funds to meet educational weaknesses. These funds are usually spent to initiate professional development in the form of the in-service programs we just discussed. Their effectiveness is questionable at best for the reasons outlined above.

What, then, remains for us to do to improve the mathematics performance of youngsters in the schools? Society as a whole must embrace mathematics as an area of beauty (and fun) and not merely as a useful subject, without which further study in many areas would not be possible (although this latter statement may be true). We must begin with the parents, who as adults already have their minds made up on their feelings about mathematics. Although it is a difficult task to turn on an adult to mathematics when he or she already is negatively disposed to the subject, this is another use for this book—provide some parent "workshops" where the beauty of mathematics is presented in the context of changing their attitude to the subject matter. The question that still remains is how best to achieve this goal.

Someone not particularly interested in mathematics, or someone fearful of the subject, must be presented with illustrations that are extremely easy to comprehend. He or she needs to be presented with examples that do not require much explanation, ones that sort of "bounce off the page" in their attractiveness. It is also helpful if the examples are largely visual. They can be recreational in nature, but need not necessarily be so. Above all, they should elicit the "Wow!" response, that feeling that there really is something special about the nature of mathematics. This specialness can manifest itself in a number of ways. It can be a simple problem, where mathematical reasoning leads to an unexpectedly simple (or elegant) solution. It may be an illustration of the nature of numbers that leads to a "gee whiz" reaction. It may be a geometrical relationship that intuitively seems implausible. Probability also has some such entertaining phenomena that can evoke such responses. Whatever the illustration, the result must be quickly and efficiently obtained. With enough of the illustrations presented in this book, you could go out and proselytize to parents so that they can be supportive in the home with a more positive feeling about mathematics.

At the point that such a turnaround of feelings occurs, the parents usually ask, "Why wasn't I shown these lovely things when I was in school?" We can't answer that and we can't change that. We can, however, make more adults goodwill ambassadors for mathematics and make teachers more resourceful so that they bring these mathematics motivators into their classrooms. Teaching time isn't lost by bringing some of these motivational devices into the classroom; rather, teaching time is more effective since the students will be more motivated and therefore more receptive to new material. So parent and teacher alike should use these mathematics motivators to change the societal perception of mathematics, both in the classroom and outside it. Only then will we bring about meaningful change in mathematics achievement, as well as an appreciation of mathematics' beauty.

1 The Beauty in Numbers

We are accustomed to seeing numbers in charts and tables on the sports or business pages of a newspaper. We use numbers continuously in our everyday life experiences, either to represent a quantity or to designate something such as a street, address, or page. We use numbers without ever taking the time to observe some of their unusual properties. That is, we don't stop to smell the flowers as we walk through a garden, or as it is more commonly said: "take time to smell the roses." Inspecting some of these unusual number properties provides us with a much deeper appreciation for these symbols that we all too often take for granted. Students too often are taught mathematics as a dry and required course of instruction. As teachers, we have an obligation to make it interesting. To show some of the number oddities brings some new "life" to the subject. It will evoke a "gee whiz" response from students. That's what you ought to strive for. Make them curious about the subject. Motivate them to "dig" further.

There are basically two types of number properties, those that are "quirks" of the decimal system and those that are true in any number system. Naturally, the latter gives us better insight into mathematics, while the former merely points out the arbitrary nature of using a decimal system. One might ask why we use a decimal system (i.e., base 10) when today we find the foundation of computers relies on a binary system (i.e., base 2). The answer is clearly historical, and no doubt emanates from our number of fingers.

On the surface, the two types of peculiarities do not differ much in their appearance, just their justification. Since this book is intended for the average student's enjoyment (of course, presented appropriately), the justifications or explanations will be kept simple and adequately intelligible. By the same token, in some cases the explanation might lead the reader to further research into or inspection of the phenomenon. The moment you can bring students to the point where they question *why* the property exhibited occurred, they're hooked! That is the goal of this chapter, to make students want to marvel at the results and question them. Although the explanations may leave them with some questions, they will be well on their way to doing some individual explorations. That is when they really get to appreciate the mathematics involved. It is during these "private" investigations that genuine learning takes place. Encourage it!

Above all, they must take note of the beauty of the number relationships. Without further ado, let's go to the charming realm of numbers and number relationships.

1.1 Surprising Number Patterns I

There are times when the charm of mathematics lies in the surprising nature of its number system. There are not many words needed to demonstrate this charm. It is obvious from the patterns attained. Look, enjoy, and spread these amazing properties to your students. Let them appreciate the patterns and, if possible, try to look for an "explanation" for this. Most important is that the students can get an appreciation for the beauty in these number patterns.

$$
\begin{aligned}
1 \cdot 1 &= 1 \\
11 \cdot 11 &= 121 \\
111 \cdot 111 &= 12{,}321 \\
1{,}111 \cdot 1{,}111 &= 1{,}234{,}321 \\
11{,}111 \cdot 11{,}111 &= 123{,}454{,}321 \\
111{,}111 \cdot 111{,}111 &= 12{,}345{,}654{,}321 \\
1{,}111{,}111 \cdot 1{,}111{,}111 &= 1{,}234{,}567{,}654{,}321 \\
11{,}111{,}111 \cdot 11{,}111{,}111 &= 123{,}456{,}787{,}654{,}321 \\
111{,}111{,}111 \cdot 111{,}111{,}111 &= 12{,}345{,}678{,}987{,}654{,}321
\end{aligned}
$$

$$1 \cdot 8 + 1 = 9$$
$$12 \cdot 8 + 2 = 98$$
$$123 \cdot 8 + 3 = 987$$
$$1{,}234 \cdot 8 + 4 = 9{,}876$$
$$12{,}345 \cdot 8 + 5 = 98{,}765$$
$$123{,}456 \cdot 8 + 6 = 987{,}654$$
$$1{,}234{,}567 \cdot 8 + 7 = 9{,}876{,}543$$
$$12{,}345{,}678 \cdot 8 + 8 = 98{,}765{,}432$$
$$123{,}456{,}789 \cdot 8 + 9 = 987{,}654{,}321$$

Notice (below) how various products of 76,923 yield numbers in the same order but with a different starting point. Here the first digit of the product goes to the end of the number to form the next product. Otherwise, the order of the digits is intact.

$$76{,}923 \cdot \ \ 1 = 076{,}923$$
$$76{,}923 \cdot 10 = 769{,}230$$
$$76{,}923 \cdot \ \ 9 = 692{,}307$$
$$76{,}923 \cdot 12 = 923{,}076$$
$$76{,}923 \cdot \ \ 3 = 230{,}769$$
$$76{,}923 \cdot \ \ 4 = 307{,}692$$

Notice (below) how various products of 76,923 yield different numbers from those above, yet again, in the same order but with a different starting point. Again, the first digit of the product goes to the end of the number to form the next product. Otherwise, the order of the digits is intact.

$$76{,}923 \cdot \ \ 2 = 153{,}846$$
$$76{,}923 \cdot \ \ 7 = 538{,}461$$
$$76{,}923 \cdot \ \ 5 = 384{,}615$$
$$76{,}923 \cdot 11 = 846{,}153$$
$$76{,}923 \cdot \ \ 6 = 461{,}538$$
$$76{,}923 \cdot \ \ 8 = 615{,}384$$

Another peculiar number is 142,857. When it is multiplied by the numbers 2 through 8, the results are astonishing. Consider the following products and describe the peculiarity.

$$142,857 \cdot 2 = 285,714$$
$$142,857 \cdot 3 = 428,571$$
$$142,857 \cdot 4 = 571,428$$
$$142,857 \cdot 5 = 714,285$$
$$142,857 \cdot 6 = 857,142$$

You can see symmetries in the products but notice also that the same digits are used in the product as in the first factor. Furthermore, consider the order of the digits. With the exception of the starting point, they are in the same sequence.

Now look at the product, $142,857 \cdot 7 = 999,999$. Surprised?

It gets even stranger with the product, $142,857 \cdot 8 = 1,142,856$. If we remove the millions digit and add it to the units digit, the original number is formed.

It would be wise to allow the students to discover the patterns themselves. You can present a starting point or a hint at how they ought to start and then let them make the discoveries themselves. This will give them a sense of "ownership" in the discoveries. These are just a few numbers that yield strange products.

1.2 Surprising Number Patterns II

Here are some more charmers of mathematics that depend on the surprising nature of its number system. Again, not many words are needed to demonstrate the charm, for it is obvious at first sight. Just look, enjoy, and share these amazing properties with your students. Let them appreciate the patterns and, if possible, try to look for an "explanation" for this.

$$12345679 \cdot 9 = 111,111,111$$
$$12345679 \cdot 18 = 222,222,222$$
$$12345679 \cdot 27 = 333,333,333$$
$$12345679 \cdot 36 = 444,444,444$$
$$12345679 \cdot 45 = 555,555,555$$
$$12345679 \cdot 54 = 666,666,666$$
$$12345679 \cdot 63 = 777,777,777$$
$$12345679 \cdot 72 = 888,888,888$$
$$12345679 \cdot 81 = 999,999,999$$

In the following pattern chart, notice that the first and last digits of the products are the digits of the multiples of 9.

$$987654321 \cdot 9 = 08\ 888\ 888\ 889$$
$$987654321 \cdot 18 = 17\ 777\ 777\ 778$$
$$987654321 \cdot 27 = 26\ 666\ 666\ 667$$
$$987654321 \cdot 36 = 35\ 555\ 555\ 556$$
$$987654321 \cdot 45 = 44\ 444\ 444\ 445$$
$$987654321 \cdot 54 = 53\ 333\ 333\ 334$$
$$987654321 \cdot 63 = 62\ 222\ 222\ 223$$
$$987654321 \cdot 72 = 71\ 111\ 111\ 112$$
$$987654321 \cdot 81 = 80\ 000\ 000\ 001$$

It is normal for students to want to find extensions of this surprising pattern. They might experiment by adding digits to the first multiplicand or by multiplying by other multiples of 9. In any case, experimentation ought to be encouraged.

1.3 Surprising Number Patterns III

Here are some more charmers of mathematics that depend on the surprising nature of its number system. Again, not many words are needed to demonstrate the charm, for it is obvious at first sight. Just look, enjoy, and spread these amazing properties to your students. Let them appreciate the patterns and, if possible, try to look for an "explanation" for this. You might ask them why multiplying by 9 might give such unusual results. Once they see that 9 is one less than the base 10, they might get other ideas to develop multiplication patterns. A clue might be to have them consider multiplying by 11 (one greater than the base) to search for a pattern.

$$0 \cdot 9 + 1 = 1$$
$$1 \cdot 9 + 2 = 11$$
$$12 \cdot 9 + 3 = 111$$
$$123 \cdot 9 + 4 = 1,111$$
$$1,234 \cdot 9 + 5 = 11,111$$
$$12,345 \cdot 9 + 6 = 111,111$$
$$123,456 \cdot 9 + 7 = 1,111,111$$
$$1,234,567 \cdot 9 + 8 = 11,111,111$$
$$12,345,678 \cdot 9 + 9 = 111,111,111$$

A similar process yields another interesting pattern. Might this give your students more impetus to search further?

$$0 \cdot 9 + 8 = 8$$
$$9 \cdot 9 + 7 = 88$$
$$98 \cdot 9 + 6 = 888$$
$$987 \cdot 9 + 5 = 8,888$$
$$9,876 \cdot 9 + 4 = 88,888$$
$$98,765 \cdot 9 + 3 = 888,888$$
$$987,654 \cdot 9 + 2 = 8,888,888$$
$$9,876,543 \cdot 9 + 1 = 88,888,888$$
$$98,765,432 \cdot 9 + 0 = 888,888,888$$

Now the logical thing to inspect would be the pattern of these strange products.

$$
\begin{array}{rcr}
1 \cdot 8 & = & 8 \\
11 \cdot 88 & = & 968 \\
111 \cdot 888 & = & 98568 \\
1111 \cdot 8888 & = & 9874568 \\
11111 \cdot 88888 & = & 987634568 \\
111111 \cdot 888888 & = & 98765234568 \\
1111111 \cdot 8888888 & = & 9876541234568 \\
11111111 \cdot 88888888 & = & 987654301234568 \\
111111111 \cdot 888888888 & = & 98765431901234568 \\
1111111111 \cdot 8888888888 & = & 987654321791234568
\end{array}
$$

How might you describe this pattern? Let students describe it in their own terms.

1.4 Surprising Number Patterns IV

Here are some more curiosities of mathematics that depend on the surprising nature of its number system. Again, not many words are needed to demonstrate the charm, for it is obvious at first sight. Yet in this case, you will notice that much is dependent on the number 1,001, which is the product of 7, 11, and 13. Furthermore, when your students multiply 1,001 by a three-digit number the result is nicely symmetric. For example, $987 \cdot 1,001 = 987,987$. Let them try a few of these on their own before proceeding.

Now let us reverse this relationship: Any six-digit number composed of two repeating sequences of three digits is divisible by 7, 11, and 13. For example,

$$
\frac{643,643}{7} = 91,949
$$

$$\frac{643,643}{11} = 58,513$$

$$\frac{643,643}{13} = 49,511$$

We can also draw another conclusion from this interesting number 1,001. That is, a number with six repeating digits is always divisible by 3, 7, 11, and 13. Here is one such example. Have your students verify our conjecture by trying others.

$$\frac{111,111}{3} = 37,037$$

$$\frac{111,111}{7} = 15,873$$

$$\frac{111,111}{11} = 10,101$$

$$\frac{111,111}{13} = 8,547$$

What other relationships can be found that play on the symmetric nature of 1,001?

1.5 Surprising Number Patterns V

Here are some more charmers of mathematics that depend on the surprising nature of its number system. Again, not many words are needed to demonstrate the charm, for it is obvious at first sight. These depend on the property described in Unit 1.4 and the unusual property of the number 9.

$$999,999 \cdot 1 = 0,999,999$$
$$999,999 \cdot 2 = 1,999,998$$
$$999,999 \cdot 3 = 2,999,997$$
$$999,999 \cdot 4 = 3,999,996$$
$$999,999 \cdot 5 = 4,999,995$$
$$999,999 \cdot 6 = 5,999,994$$
$$999,999 \cdot 7 = 6,999,993$$
$$999,999 \cdot 8 = 7,999,992$$
$$999,999 \cdot 9 = 8,999,991$$
$$999,999 \cdot 10 = 9,999,990$$

Again, the number 9, which owes some of its unique properties to the fact that it is 1 less than the base 10, presents some nice peculiarities.

$$9 \cdot 9 = 81$$
$$99 \cdot 99 = 9,801$$
$$999 \cdot 999 = 998,001$$
$$9,999 \cdot 9,999 = 99,980,001$$
$$99,999 \cdot 99,999 = 9,999,800,001$$
$$999,999 \cdot 999,999 = 999,998,000,001$$
$$9,999,999 \cdot 9,999,999 = 99,999,980,000,001$$

While playing with the number 9, you might ask your students to find an eight-digit number in which no digit is repeated and which when multiplied by 9 yields a nine-digit number in which no digit is repeated. Here are a few correct choices:

$$81,274,365 \cdot 9 = 731,469,285$$
$$72,645,831 \cdot 9 = 653,812,479$$
$$58,132,764 \cdot 9 = 523,194,876$$
$$76,125,483 \cdot 9 = 685,129,347$$

1.6 Surprising Number Patterns VI

Here is another nice pattern to further motivate your students to search on their own for other patterns in mathematics. Again, not many words are needed to demonstrate the beauty of this pattern, for it is obvious at first sight.

$$
\begin{aligned}
1 &= 1 & &= 1 \cdot 1 = 1^2 \\
1+2+1 &= 2+2 & &= 2 \cdot 2 = 2^2 \\
1+2+3+2+1 &= 3+3+3 & &= 3 \cdot 3 = 3^2 \\
1+2+3+4+3+2+1 &= 4+4+4+4 & &= 4 \cdot 4 = 4^2 \\
1+2+3+4+5+4+3+2+1 &= 5+5+5+5+5 & &= 5 \cdot 5 = 5^2 \\
1+2+3+4+5+6+5+4+3+2+1 &= 6+6+6+6+6+6 & &= 6 \cdot 6 = 6^2 \\
1+2+3+4+5+6+7+6+5+4+3+2+1 &= 7+7+7+7+7+7+7 & &= 7 \cdot 7 = 7^2 \\
1+2+3+4+5+6+7+8+7+6+5+4+3+2+1 &= 8+8+8+8+8+8+8+8 & &= 8 \cdot 8 = 8^2 \\
1+2+3+4+5+6+7+8+9+8+7+6+5+4+3+2+1 &= 9+9+9+9+9+9+9+9+9 & &= 9 \cdot 9 = 9^2
\end{aligned}
$$

1.7 Amazing Power Relationships

Our number system has many unusual features built into it. Discovering them can certainly be a rewarding experience. Most students need to be coaxed to look for these relationships. This is where the teacher comes in.

You might tell them about the famous mathematician Carl Friedrich Gauss (1777–1855), who had superior arithmetic abilities to see relationships and patterns that eluded even the brightest minds. He used these uncanny skills to conjecture and prove many very important mathematical theorems. Give your students a chance to "discover" relationships. Don't discourage the trivial discoveries, for they could lead to more profound results later on.

Show them the following relationship and ask them to describe what is going on here.

$$81 = (8 + 1)^2 = 9^2$$

Then ask them to see if there is another number for which this relationship might hold true. Don't wait too long before showing them the following.

$$4,913 = (4 + 9 + 1 + 3)^3 = 17^3$$

By now the students should realize that the sum of the digits of this number taken to a power equals the number. This is quite astonishing, as they will see if they try to find other examples.

The list below will provide you with lots of examples of these unusual numbers. Enjoy yourself!

Number		(Sum of the digits)^n	Number		(Sum of the digits)^n
81	=	9^2	34,012,224	=	18^6
			8,303,765,625	=	45^6
512	=	8^3	24,794,911,296	=	54^6
4,913	=	17^3	68,719,476,736	=	64^6
5,832	=	18^3			
17,576	=	26^3	612,220,032	=	18^7
19,683	=	27^3	10,460,353,203	=	27^7
			27,512,614,111	=	31^7
2,401	=	7^4	52,523,350,144	=	34^7
234,256	=	22^4	271,818,611,107	=	43^7
390,625	=	25^4	1,174,711,139,837	=	53^7
614,656	=	28^4	2,207,984,167,552	=	58^7
1,679,616	=	36^4	6,722,988,818,432	=	68^7
17,210,368	=	28^5	20,047,612,231,936	=	46^8
52,521,875	=	35^5	72,301,961,339,136	=	54^8
60,466,176	=	36^5	248,155,780,267,521	=	63^8
205,962,976	=	46^5			

$$20,864,448,472,975,628,947,226,005,981,267,194,447,042,584,001 = 207^{20}$$

1.8 Beautiful Number Relationships

Who said numbers can't form beautiful relationships! Showing your students some of these unique situations might give them the feeling that there is more to "numbers" than meets the eye. They should be encouraged not only to verify these relationships, but also to find others that can be considered "beautiful."

Notice the consecutive exponents.

$$135 = 1^1 + 3^2 + 5^3$$
$$175 = 1^1 + 7^2 + 5^3$$
$$518 = 5^1 + 1^2 + 8^3$$
$$598 = 5^1 + 9^2 + 8^3$$

Now, taken one place further, we get

$$1,306 = 1^1 + 3^2 + 0^3 + 6^4$$
$$1,676 = 1^1 + 6^2 + 7^3 + 6^4$$
$$2,427 = 2^1 + 4^2 + 2^3 + 7^4$$

The next ones are really amazing. Notice the relationship between the exponents and the numbers.*

$$3,435 = 3^3 + 4^4 + 3^3 + 5^5$$
$$438,579,088 = 4^4 + 3^3 + 8^8 + 5^5 + 7^7 + 9^9 + 0^0 + 8^8 + 8^8$$

Now it's up to the class to verify these and discover other beautiful relationships.

---

* In the second illustration, you will notice that, for convenience and for the sake of this unusual situation, we have considered 0^0 as though its value is 0, when, in fact, it is indeterminate.

1.9 Unusual Number Relationships

There are a number of unusual relationships between certain numbers (as represented in the decimal system). There is not much explanation for them. Just enjoy them and see if your students can find others.

We are going to present pairs of numbers where the product and the sum are reversals of each other. Present them one at a time to your students so that they can really appreciate them.

The two numbers		Their product	Their sum
9	9	81	18
3	24	72	27
2	47	94	49
2	497	994	499

Ask students if they can find another pair of numbers that exhibits this unusual property. (They may have difficulty with this.)

Here's another strange relationship*:

$$1 = 1!$$
$$2 = 2!$$
$$145 = 1! + 4! + 5!$$
$$40,585 = 4! + 0! + 5! + 8! + 5!$$

(Remember that $0! = 1$.)

That appears to be all of this sort that exists, so don't bother having students search for more.

---

* The exclamation mark is called a factorial and represents the product of consecutive integers from 1 to the number before the factorial symbol. That is, $n! = 1 \cdot 2 \cdot 3 \cdot 4 \cdots (n-2)(n-1)n$.

1.10 Strange Equalities

There are times when the numbers speak more effectively than any explanation. Here is one such case. Just have your students look at these equalities and see if they can discover others of the same type.

$$1^1 + 6^1 + 8^1 = 15 = 2^1 + 4^1 + 9^1$$
$$1^2 + 6^2 + 8^2 = 101 = 2^2 + 4^2 + 9^2$$

$$1^1 + 5^1 + 8^1 + 12^1 = 26 = 2^1 + 3^1 + 10^1 + 11^1$$
$$1^2 + 5^2 + 8^2 + 12^2 = 234 = 2^2 + 3^2 + 10^2 + 11^2$$
$$1^3 + 5^3 + 8^3 + 12^3 = 2,366 = 2^3 + 3^3 + 10^3 + 11^3$$

$$1^1+5^1+8^1+12^1+18^1+19^1=63=2^1+3^1+9^1+13^1+16^1+20^1$$
$$1^2+5^2+8^2+12^2+18^2+19^2=919=2^2+3^2+9^2+13^2+16^2+20^2$$
$$1^3+5^3+8^3+12^3+18^3+19^3=15,057=2^3+3^3+9^3+13^3+16^3+20^3$$
$$1^4+5^4+8^4+12^4+18^4+19^4=260,755=2^4+3^4+9^4+13^4+16^4+20^4$$

Not much more one can say here. Your students will probably say Wow! If that is achieved, then you have met your goal.

1.11 The Amazing Number 1,089

This unit is about a number that has some truly exceptional properties. We begin by showing how it just happens to "pop up" when least expected. Begin by having your students, all working independently, select a three-digit number (where the units and hundreds digits are not the same) and follow these instructions:

1. Choose any three-digit number (where the units and hundreds digits are not the same).

> We will do it with you here by arbitrarily selecting **825.**

2. Reverse the digits of this number you have selected.

> We will continue here by reversing the digits of 825 to get **528**.

3. Subtract the two numbers (naturally, the larger minus the smaller).

> Our calculated difference is **825 − 528 = 297**.

4. Once again, reverse the digits of this difference.

> Reversing the digits of 297 we get the number **792**.

5. Now, add your last two numbers.

> We then add the last two numbers to get **297 + 792 = 1,089**.

Their result should be the same* as ours even though their starting numbers were different from ours.

They will probably be astonished that regardless of which numbers they selected at the beginning, they got the same result as we did, 1,089.

How does this happen? Is this a "freak property" of this number? Did we do something devious in our calculations?

---

* If not, then you made a calculation error. Check it.

Unlike other numerical curiosities, which depended on a peculiarity of the decimal system, this illustration of a mathematical oddity depends on the operations. Before we explore (for the more motivated students) why this happens, we want you to be able to impress your students with a further property of this lovely number 1,089.

Let's look at the first nine multiples of 1,089:

$$1,089 \cdot 1 = 1,089$$
$$1,089 \cdot 2 = 2,178$$
$$1,089 \cdot 3 = 3,267$$
$$1,089 \cdot 4 = 4,356$$
$$1,089 \cdot 5 = 5,445$$
$$1,089 \cdot 6 = 6,534$$
$$1,089 \cdot 7 = 7,623$$
$$1,089 \cdot 8 = 8,712$$
$$1,089 \cdot 9 = 9,801$$

Do you notice a pattern among the products? Look at the first and ninth products. They are the reverses of one another. The second and the eighth are also reverses of one another. And so the pattern continues, until the fifth product is the reverse of itself, known as a palindromic number.*

Notice, in particular, that $1,089 \cdot 9 = 9,801$, which is the reversal of the original number. The same property holds for $10,989 \cdot 9 = 98,901$, and similarly, $109,989 \cdot 9 = 989,901$. Students will be quick to offer extensions to this. Your students should recognize by now that we altered the original 1,089 by inserting a 9 in the middle of the number, and extended that by inserting 99 in the middle of the 1,089. It would be nice to conclude from this that each of the following numbers have the same property: 1,099,989, 10,999,989, 109,999,989, 1,099,999,989, 10,999,999,989, and so on.

---

* We have more about palindromic numbers in Unit 1.16.

As a matter of fact, there is only one other number with four or fewer digits where a multiple of itself is equal to its reversal, and that is the number 2,178 (which just happens to be $2 \cdot 1{,}089$), since $2{,}178 \cdot 4 = 8{,}712$. Wouldn't it be nice if we could extend this as we did with the above example by inserting 9s into the middle of the number to generate other numbers that have the same property? Your students ought to be encouraged to try this independently and try to come to some conclusion. Yes, it is true that

$$21{,}978 \cdot 4 = 87{,}912$$
$$219{,}978 \cdot 4 = 879{,}912$$
$$2{,}199{,}978 \cdot 4 = 8{,}799{,}912$$
$$21{,}999{,}978 \cdot 4 = 87{,}999{,}912$$
$$219{,}999{,}978 \cdot 4 = 879{,}999{,}912$$
$$2{,}199{,}999{,}978 \cdot 4 = 8{,}799{,}999{,}912$$

$$\vdots$$

As if the number 1,089 didn't already have enough cute properties, here is another one that (sort of) extends from the 1,089: We will consider 1 and 89 and notice what happens when you take any number and get the sum of the squares of the digits and continue the same way. Each time, you will eventually reach 1 or 89. Take a look at some examples that follow.

$n = 30$:

$$3^2 + 0^2 = 9 \rightarrow 9^2 = 81 \rightarrow 8^2 + 1^2 = 65 \rightarrow 6^2 + 5^2 = 61 \rightarrow$$
$$6^2 + 1^2 = 37 \rightarrow 3^2 + 7^2 = 58 \rightarrow 5^2 + 8^2 = \mathbf{89} \rightarrow$$
$$8^2 + 9^2 = 145 \rightarrow 1^2 + 4^2 + 5^2 = 42 \rightarrow 4^2 + 2^2 = 20 \rightarrow$$
$$2^2 + 0^2 = 4 \rightarrow 4^2 = 16 \rightarrow 1^2 + 6^2 = 37 \rightarrow 3^2 + 7^2 = 58 \rightarrow$$
$$5^2 + 8^2 = \mathbf{89} \rightarrow \ldots$$

Notice that, when we reached 89 for a second time, it is obvious that we are in a loop and that we will continuously get back to 89. For each of the following, we get into a loop that will continuously repeat.

$n = 31$: $3^2 + 1^2 = 10 \rightarrow 1^2 + 0^2 = \mathbf{1} \rightarrow 1^2 = \mathbf{1}$

$n = 32$: $3^2 + 2^2 = 13 \rightarrow 1^2 + 3^2 = 10 \rightarrow 1^2 + 0^2 = \mathbf{1} \rightarrow 1^2 = \mathbf{1}$

$n = 33$: $3^2 + 3^2 = 18 \rightarrow 1^2 + 8^2 = 65 \rightarrow 6^2 + 5^2 = 61 \rightarrow$
            $6^2 + 1^2 = 37 \rightarrow 3^2 + 7^2 = 58 \rightarrow 5^2 + 8^2 = \mathbf{89} \rightarrow$
            $8^2 + 9^2 = 145 \rightarrow 1^2 + 4^2 + 5^2 = 42 \rightarrow 4^2 + 2^2 = 20 \rightarrow$
            $2^2 + 0^2 = 4 \rightarrow 4^2 = 16 \rightarrow 1^2 + 6^2 = 37 \rightarrow$
            $3^2 + 7^2 = 58 \rightarrow 5^2 + 8^2 = \mathbf{89} \rightarrow \ldots$

$n = 80$: $8^2 + 0^2 = 64 \rightarrow 6^2 + 4^2 = 52 \rightarrow 5^2 + 2^2 = 29 \rightarrow$
            $2^2 + 9^2 = 85 \rightarrow 8^2 + 5^2 = \mathbf{89} \rightarrow 8^2 + 9^2 = 145 \rightarrow$
            $1^2 + 4^2 + 5^2 = 42 \rightarrow 4^2 + 2^2 = 20 \rightarrow 2^2 + 0^2 = 4 \rightarrow$
            $4^2 = 16 \rightarrow 1^2 + 6^2 = 37 \rightarrow 3^2 + 7^2 = 58 \rightarrow$
            $5^2 + 8^2 = \mathbf{89} \rightarrow \ldots$

$n = 81$: $8^2 + 1^2 = 65 \rightarrow 6^2 + 5^2 = 61 \rightarrow 6^2 + 1^2 = 37 \rightarrow$
            $3^2 + 7^2 = 58 \rightarrow 5^2 + 8^2 = \mathbf{89} \rightarrow 8^2 + 9^2 = 145 \rightarrow$
            $1^2 + 4^2 + 5^2 = 42 \rightarrow 4^2 + 2^2 = 20 \rightarrow 2^2 + 0^2 = 4 \rightarrow$
            $4^2 = 16 \rightarrow 1^2 + 6^2 = 37 \rightarrow 3^2 + 7^2 = 58 \rightarrow$
            $5^2 + 8^2 = \mathbf{89} \rightarrow \ldots$

$n = 82$: $8^2 + 2^2 = 68 \rightarrow 6^2 + 8^2 = 100 \rightarrow 1^2 + 0^2 + 0^2 = \mathbf{1} \rightarrow$
            $1^2 = \mathbf{1}$

$n = 85$: $8^2 + 5^2 = \mathbf{89} \rightarrow 8^2 + 9^2 = 145 \rightarrow 1^2 + 4^2 + 5^2 = 42 \rightarrow$
            $4^2 + 2^2 = 20 \rightarrow 2^2 + 0^2 = 4 \rightarrow 4^2 = 16 \rightarrow$
            $1^2 + 6^2 = 37 \rightarrow 3^2 + 7^2 = 58 \rightarrow 5^2 + 8^2 = \mathbf{89} \rightarrow \ldots$

Now let's return to the original oddity of the number 1,089. We assumed that any number we chose would lead us to 1,089. Ask students how they can be sure. Well, they could try all possible three-digit numbers to see if it works. That would be tedious and not particularly elegant. An investigation of this oddity is within reach of a good elementary algebra student. So for the more ambitious students, who might be curious about this phenomenon, we will provide an algebraic explanation as to why it "works."

We shall represent the arbitrarily selected three-digit number, htu, as $100h + 10t + u$, where h represents the hundreds digit, t represents the tens digit, and u represents the units digit.

Let $h > u$, which would be the case in either the number you selected or the reverse of it. In the subtraction, $u - h < 0$; therefore, take 1 from the tens place (of the minuend), making the units place $10 + u$.

Since the tens digits of the two numbers to be subtracted are equal, and 1 was taken from the tens digit of the minuend, then the value of this digit is $10(t - 1)$. The hundreds digit of the minuend is $h - 1$, because 1 was taken away to enable subtraction in the tens place, making the value of the tens digit $10(t - 1) + 100 = 10(t + 9)$.

We can now do the first subtraction:

$$
\begin{array}{lll}
100(h - 1) & + 10(t + 9) + (u + 10) \\
100u & + 10t & + h \\
\hline
100(h - u - 1) + 10(9) & + u - h + 10
\end{array}
$$

Reversing the digits of this difference gives us

$$100(u - h + 10) + 10(9) + (h - u - 1)$$

Now adding these last two expressions gives us

$$100(9) + 10(18) + (10 - 1) = 1{,}089$$

It is important to stress that algebra enables us to inspect the arithmetic process, regardless of the number.

Before we leave the number 1,089, we should point out to students that it has one other oddity, namely,

$$33^2 = 1{,}089 = 65^2 - 56^2$$

which is unique among two-digit numbers.

By this time your students must agree that there is a particular beauty in the number **1,089**.

1.12 The Irrepressible Number 1

This is not a trick. Yet mathematics does provide curiosities that appear to be magic. This is one that has baffled mathematicians for many years and still no one knows why it happens. Try it, you'll like it—or at least the students will!

Begin by asking your students to follow two rules as they work with any *arbitrarily* selected number.

> If the number is *odd*, then multiply by 3 and add 1.
> If the number is *even*, then divide by 2.

Regardless of the number they select, **they will always end up with 1**, after continued repetition of the process.

Let's try it for the *arbitrarily selected* number **12:**
12 is even; therefore, we divide by 2 to get 6.
6 is also even, so we again divide by 2 to get 3.
3 is odd; therefore, we multiply by 3 and add 1 to get $3 \cdot 3 + 1 = 10$.
10 is even, so we simply divide by 2 to get 5.
5 is odd, so we multiply by 3 and add 1 to get 16.
16 is even, so we divide by 2 to get 8.
8 is even, so we divide by 2 to get 4.
4 is even, so we divide by 2 to get 2.
2 is even, so we divide by 2 to get 1.

It is believed that, no matter which number we begin with (here we started with 12), we will eventually get to 1. This is truly remarkable! Try it for some other numbers to convince yourself that it really does work. Had we started with 17 as our arbitrarily selected number, we would have required 12 steps to reach 1. Starting with 43 will require 29 steps. You ought to have your students try this little scheme for any number they choose and see if they can get the number 1.

Does this really work for all numbers? This is a question that has concerned mathematicians since the 1930s, and to date no answer has been found, despite monetary rewards having been offered for a proof of this conjecture. Most recently (using computers) this problem, known in the literature as the "$3n + 1$" problem, has been shown to be true for the numbers up to $10^{18} - 1$.

For those who have been turned on by this curious number property, we offer you a schematic that shows the sequence of start numbers 1–20.

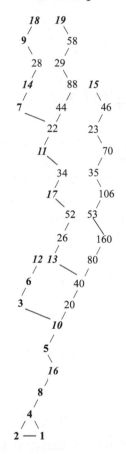

Notice that you will always end up with the final loop of 4–2–1. That is, when you reach 4 you will always get to the 1 and then were you to try to continue after having arrived at the 1, you will always get back to the 1, since, by applying the rule, $\boxed{3 \cdot 1 + 1 = 4}$ and you continue in the loop: 4–2–1.

We don't want to discourage inspection of this curiosity, but we want to warn you not to get frustrated if you cannot prove that it is true in all cases, for the best mathematical minds have not been able to do this for the better part of a century! Explain to your students that not all that we know or believe to be true in mathematics has been proved. There are still many "facts" that we must accept without proof, but we do so knowing that there may be a time when they will either be proved true for all cases, or someone will find a case for which a statement is not true, even after we have "accepted it."

1.13 Perfect Numbers

In mathematics, is there anything more perfect than something else? Most mathematics teachers constantly tell students that mathematics is perfect. Well, now we will introduce perfection in numbers—as it is defined by the mathematics community. According to tradition in number theory, we have an entity called a "perfect number." This is defined as a number equal to the sum of its proper factors (i.e., all the factors except the number itself). The smallest perfect number is 6, since $6 = 1 + 2 + 3$, which is the sum of all its proper factors.*

The next larger perfect number is 28, since again $28 = 1 + 2 + 4 + 7 + 14$. And the next one is $496 = 1 + 2 + 4 + 8 + 16 + 31 + 62 + 124 + 248$, which is the sum of all the proper factors of 496.

The first four perfect numbers were known to the Greeks. They are 6, 28, 496, and 8,128.

It was Euclid who came up with a theorem to generalize how to find a perfect number. He said that if $2^k - 1$ is a prime number, then $2^{k-1}(2^k - 1)$ is a perfect number. This is to say, whenever we find a value of k that gives us a prime for $2^k - 1$, then we can construct a perfect number.

---

* It is also the only number that is the sum and product of the same three numbers: $6 = 1 \cdot 2 \cdot 3 = 3!$ Also $6 = \sqrt{1^3 + 2^3 + 3^3}$. It is also interesting to notice that $\frac{1}{1} = \frac{1}{2} + \frac{1}{3} + \frac{1}{6}$. By the way, while on the number 6, it is nice to realize that both 6 and its square, 36, are triangular numbers (see Unit 1.17).

We do not have to use all values of k, since if k is a composite number, then $2^k - 1$ is also composite.*

Using Euclid's method for generating perfect numbers, we get the following table:

Values of k	Values of $2^{k-1}(2^k - 1)$ when $2^k - 1$ is a prime number
2	6
3	28
5	496
7	8,128
13	33,550,336
17	8,589,869,056
19	137,438,691,328

On observation, we notice some properties of perfect numbers. They all seem to end in either a 6 or a 28, and these are preceded by an odd digit. They also appear to be triangular numbers (see Unit 1.17), which are the sums of consecutive natural numbers (e.g., $496 = 1 + 2 + 3 + 4 + \cdots + 28 + 29 + 30 + 31$).

To take it a step further, every perfect number after 6 is the partial sum of the series: $1^3 + 3^3 + 5^3 + 7^3 + 9^3 + 11^3 + \cdots$. For example, $28 = 1^3 + 3^3$, and $496 = 1^3 + 3^3 + 5^3 + 7^3$. You might have your students try to find the partial sums for the next perfect numbers.

We do not know if there are any odd perfect numbers, but none has been found yet. Using today's computers, we have much greater facility at establishing more perfect numbers. Your students might try to find larger perfect numbers using Euclid's method.

---

* If $k = pq$, then $2^k - 1 = 2^{pq} - 1 = (2^p - 1)(2^{p(q-1)} + 2^{p(q-2)} + \cdots + 1)$. Therefore, $2^k - 1$ can only be prime when k is prime, but this does not guarantee that when k is prime, $2^k - 1$ will also be prime, as can be seen from the following values of k:

k	2	3	5	7	11	13
$2^k - 1$	3	7	31	127	2,047	8,191

where $2,047 = 23 \cdot 89$ is not a prime and so doesn't qualify.

1.14 Friendly Numbers

What could possibly make two numbers friendly? Your students' first reaction might be numbers that are friendly to them. Remind them that we are talking here about numbers that are "friendly" to each other. Well, mathematicians have decided that two numbers are considered friendly (or as often used in the more sophisticated literature, "amicable") if the sum of the proper divisors of one equals the second *and* the sum of the proper divisors of the second number equals the first number.

Sounds complicated? Have your students look at the smallest pair of friendly numbers: 220 and 284.

The proper divisors of 220 are 1, 2, 4, 5, 10, 11, 20, 22, 44, 55, and 110. Their sum is $1 + 2 + 4 + 5 + 10 + 11 + 20 + 22 + 44 + 55 + 110 = 284$.

The proper divisors of 284 are 1, 2, 4, 71, and 142, and their sum is $1 + 2 + 4 + 71 + 142 = 220$.
This shows the two numbers are friendly numbers.

The second pair of friendly numbers to be discovered (by Pierre de Fermat, 1601–1665) was 17,296 and 18,416:

$$17,296 = 2^4 \cdot 23 \cdot 47 \qquad \text{and} \qquad 18,416 = 2^4 \cdot 1,151$$

The sum of the proper factors of 17,296 is

$$1 + 2 + 4 + 8 + 16 + 23 + 46 + 47 + 92 + 94 + 184 + 188 + 368$$
$$+ 376 + 752 + 1,081 + 2,162 + 4,324 + 8,648 = 18,416$$

The sum of the proper factors of 18,416 is

$$1 + 2 + 4 + 8 + 16 + 1,151 + 2,302 + 4,604 + 9,208 = 17,296$$

Here are a few more friendly pairs of numbers:

1,184 and 1,210
2,620 and 2,924
5,020 and 5,564
6,232 and 6,368
10,744 and 10,856
9,363,584 and 9,437,056
111,448,537,712 and 118,853,793,424

Your students might want to verify the above pairs' "friendliness"!

For the expert, the following is one method for finding friendly numbers. Let

$$a = 3 \cdot 2^n - 1$$
$$b = 3 \cdot 2^{n-1} - 1$$
$$c = 3^2 \cdot 2^{2n-1} - 1$$

where n is an integer greater than or equal to 2 and a, b, and c are all prime numbers. Then $2^n ab$ and $2^n c$ are friendly numbers.

(Notice that for $n \leq 200$, the values of $n = 2, 4$, and 7 give us a, b, and c to be prime.)

1.15 Another Friendly Pair of Numbers

We can always look for nice relationships between numbers. Some of them are truly mind-boggling! Take, for example, the pair of numbers: 6,205 and 3,869.

Guide your students to do the following to verify these fantastic results.

$$6,205 = 38^2 + 69^2 \quad \text{and} \quad 3,869 = 62^2 + 05^2$$

Notice the pattern and then follow with these numbers:

$$5,965 = 77^2 + 06^2 \quad \text{and} \quad 7,706 = 59^2 + 65^2$$

Beyond the enjoyment of seeing this wonderful pattern, there isn't much. However, the manner in which this is presented to the class can make all the difference!

1.16 Palindromic Numbers

It is sometimes nice to show your class some amusing mathematics that parallels amusing word games. Think of it not as time wasted, but rather as time spent to motivate youngsters to like mathematics more. A palindrome is a word, phrase, or sentence that reads the same in both directions. Here are a few amusing palindromes:

RADAR

REVIVER

ROTATOR

LEPERS REPEL

MADAM I'M ADAM

STEP NOT ON PETS

NO LEMONS, NO MELON

DENNIS AND EDNA SINNED

ABLE WAS I ERE I SAW ELBA

A MAN, A PLAN, A CANAL, PANAMA

SUMS ARE NOT SET AS A TEST ON ERASMUS

Palindromic numbers are those that read the same in both directions. This leads us to consider that dates can be a source for some symmetric inspection. For example, the year 2002 is a palindrome, as is 1991.* There were several dates in October 2001 that appeared as palindromes when written in American style: 10/1/01, 10/22/01, and others. In February, Europeans had the ultimate palindromic moment at 8:02 P.M. on February 20, 2002, since they would have written it as 20.02, 20-02-2002. It is a bit thought provoking to have students come up with other palindromic dates. You might ask them to list the palindromic dates closest to one another.

Looking further, the first four powers of 11 are palindromic numbers:

$$11^1 = 11$$
$$11^2 = 121$$
$$11^3 = 1,331$$
$$11^4 = 14,641$$

A palindromic number can be either a prime number or a composite number. For example, 151 is a prime palindrome and 171 is a composite palindrome. Yet with the exception of 11, a palindromic prime must have an odd number of digits. Have your students try to find some palindromic primes.

It is interesting to show students how a palindromic number can be generated from any given number. All they need to do is to continually add a number to its reversal (i.e., the number written in the reverse order of digits) until a palindrome is arrived at.

---

* Those of us who have lived through 1991 and 2002 will be the last generation who will have lived through two palindromic years for over the next 1,000 years (assuming the current level of longevity).

For example, a palindrome can be reached with a single addition such as with the starting number 23:

$$23 + 32 = 55, \quad \text{a palindrome}$$

Or it might take two steps, such as with the starting number 75:

$$75 + 57 = 132 \qquad 132 + 231 = 363, \quad \text{a palindrome}$$

Or it might take three steps, such as with the starting number 86:

$$86 + 68 = 154 \quad 154 + 451 = 605 \quad 605 + 506 = 1111, \quad \text{a palindrome}$$

The starting number 97 will require six steps to reach a palindrome, while the number 98 will require 24 steps. Be cautioned about using the starting number 196; this one will go far beyond your capabilities to reach a palindrome.

There are some lovely patterns when dealing with palindromic numbers. For example, numbers that yield palindromic cubes are palindromic themselves.

Students should be encouraged to find more properties of palindromic numbers*—they're fun to play with.

---

* One source for more information on palindromic numbers is A. S. Posamentier and J. Stepelman, *Teaching Secondary School Mathematics: Techniques and Enrichment Units,* 6th ed. (Upper Saddle River, NJ: Prentice Hall/Merrill, 2002), pp. 257–258.

1.17 Fun with Figurate Numbers

How can numbers have a geometric shape? Well, although the numbers do not have a geometric shape, some can be represented by dots that can be put into a regular geometric shape. Let's take a look at some of these now.

Students should notice how the dots can be placed to form the shape of a regular polygon.

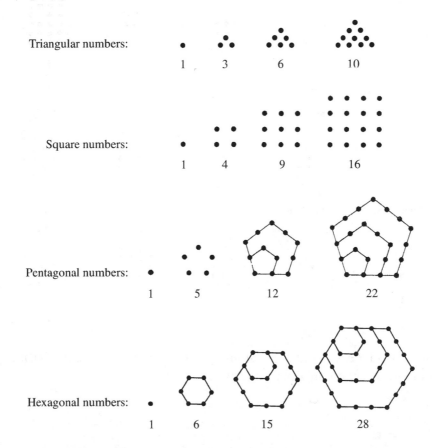

From the following arrangements of these figurate numbers, you ought to be able to discover some of their properties. It ought to be fun trying to relate these numbers to one another. For example, the nth square number is equal to the sum of the nth and the $(n-1)$th triangular numbers. Another example is that the nth pentagonal number is equal to the sum of the nth square number and the $(n-1)$th triangular number. There are lots of other such relationships to be found (or discovered!).

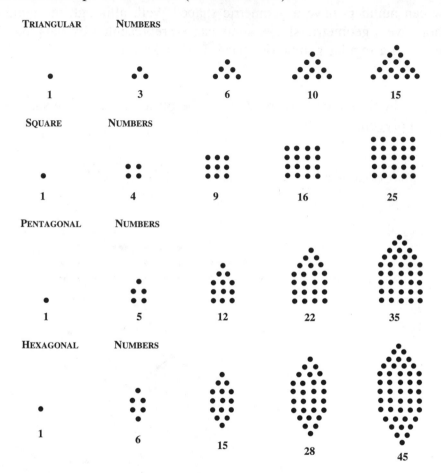

We can introduce students to *oblong numbers*, which look like $n(n+1)$, or rectangular arrays of dots such as

$1 \cdot 2 = 2$

$2 \cdot 3 = 6$

$3 \cdot 4 = 12$

$4 \cdot 5 = 20$

$5 \cdot 6 = 30$

$\vdots$

So here are some relationships involving oblong numbers; although examples are provided, your students should find additional examples to show these may be true. The more sophisticated can try to prove they are true.

An oblong number is the sum of consecutive even integers:

$$2 + 4 + 6 + 8 = 20$$

An oblong number is twice a triangular number:

$$15 \cdot 2 = 30$$

The sum of two consecutive squares and the square of the oblong between them is a square:

$$9 + 16 + 12^2 = 169 = 13^2$$

The sum of two consecutive oblong numbers and twice the square between them is a square:

$$12 + 20 + 2 \cdot 16 = 64 = 8^2$$

The sum of an oblong number and the next square is a triangular number:

$$20 + 25 = 45$$

The sum of a square number and the next oblong number is a triangular number:

$$25 + 30 = 55$$

The sum of a number and the square of that number is an oblong number:

$$9 + 81 = 90$$

Your students should now discover other connections between the various figurate numbers presented here.

1.18 The Fabulous Fibonacci Numbers

There aren't many themes in mathematics that permeate more branches of mathematics than the Fibonacci numbers. They come to us from one of the most important books in Western history. This book, *Liber abaci*, written in 1202 by Leonardo of Pisa, more popularly known as Fibonacci (1180–1250),* or son of Bonacci, is the first European publication using the Hindu–Arabic numerals that are the basis for our base 10 number system. This alone would qualify it as a landmark book. However, it also contains a "harmless" problem about the regeneration of rabbits. It is the solution of that problem that produces the Fibonacci numbers.

You might have your students try to set up a chart and solve the problem independently before progressing further. It may be stated as follows:

> **How many pairs of rabbits will be produced in a year, beginning with a single pair, if in every month each pair bears a new pair, which becomes productive from the second month on?**

It is from this problem that the famous *Fibonacci sequence* emerged. If we assume that a pair of baby (*B*) rabbits matures in one month to become

---

* Fibonacci was not a clergyman, as might be expected of early scientists; rather, he was a merchant who traveled extensively throughout the Islamic world and took advantage of reading all he could of the Arabic mathematical writings. He was the first to introduce the Hindu–Arabic numerals to the Christian world in his *Liber abaci* (1202 and revised in 1228), which first circulated widely in manuscript form and was first published in 1857 as *Scritti di Leonardo Pisano* (Rome: B. Buoncompagni). The book is a collection of business mathematics, including linear and quadratic equations, square roots and cube roots, and other new topics, seen from the European viewpoint. He begins the book with the comment: "These are the nine figures of the Indians 9 8 7 6 5 4 3 2 1. With these nine figures, and with the symbol 0, which in Arabic is called *zephirum*, any number can be written, as will be demonstrated below". From here on, he introduces the decimal position system for the first time in Europe. (Note: The word "zephirum" evolved from the Arabic word *as-sifr*, which comes from the Sanskrit word, used in India as early as the fifth century, "sunya," referring to *empty*.)

offspring-producing adults (*A*), then we can set up the following chart:

Month	Pairs	Number of pairs of adults (*A*)	Number of pairs of babies (*B*)	Total pairs
January 1	A	1	0	1
February 1	A B	1	1	2
March 1	A B A	2	1	3
April 1	A B A A B	3	2	5
May 1	A B A A B A B A	5	3	8
June 1	A B A A B A B A A B A A B	8	5	13
July 1		13	8	21
August 1		21	13	34
September 1		34	21	55
October 1		55	34	89
November 1		89	55	144
December 1		144	89	233
January 1		233	144	377

The number of pairs of mature rabbits living each month determines the Fibonacci sequence (column 1): 1, 1, 2, 3, 5, 8, 13, 21, 34, 55, 89, 144, 233, 377, ...

If we let f_n be the *n*th term of the Fibonacci sequence, then

$$f_1 = 1$$
$$f_2 = 1$$
$$f_3 = f_2 + f_1 = 1 + 1 = 2$$
$$f_4 = f_3 + f_2 = 2 + 1 = 3$$
$$f_5 = f_4 + f_3 = 3 + 2 = 5$$
$$\vdots \qquad \vdots$$
$$f_n = f_{n-1} + f_{n-2} \quad \text{for } n \text{ an integer} \geq 3$$

That is, each term after the first two terms is the sum of the two preceding terms.

Your students may (rightly) ask at this point, What makes this sequence of numbers so spectacular? For one thing, there is a direct relationship between (believe it or not) it and the Golden Section! Consider successive quotients of the Fibonacci numbers:

$\dfrac{f_{n+1}}{f_n}$	$\dfrac{f_{n+1}}{f_n}$
$\dfrac{1}{1} = 1.000000000$	$\dfrac{55}{34} = 1.617647059$
$\dfrac{2}{1} = 2.000000000$	$\dfrac{89}{55} = 1.6182181618$
$\dfrac{3}{2} = 1.500000000$	$\dfrac{144}{89} = 1.617977528$
$\dfrac{5}{3} = 1.666666667$	$\dfrac{233}{144} = 1.618055556$
$\dfrac{8}{5} = 1.600000000$	$\dfrac{377}{233} = 1.618025751$
$\dfrac{13}{8} = 1.625000000$	$\dfrac{610}{377} = 1.618037135$
$\dfrac{21}{13} = 1.615384615$	$\dfrac{987}{610} = 1.618032787$
$\dfrac{34}{21} = 1.619047619$	

Furthermore, you can refer students to Unit 4.8 to notice that successive powers of ϕ^* present us with the Fibonacci numbers.

$$\phi^2 = \phi + 1$$
$$\phi^3 = 2\phi + 1$$
$$\phi^4 = 3\phi + 2$$
$$\phi^5 = 5\phi + 3$$
$$\phi^6 = 8\phi + 5$$
$$\phi^7 = 13\phi + 8$$

$^*\phi$ represents the Golden Ratio.

If, by now, the students didn't see the connection, highlight the coefficients and the constants. This is quite incredible; two completely (seemingly) unrelated things suddenly in close relationship to one another. That's what makes mathematics so wonderful!

1.19 Getting into an Endless Loop

This unit demonstrates an unusual phenomenon that arises out of the peculiarities of our decimal number system. There isn't much you can do with it, other than to marvel at the outcome. This is not something we can prove true for all cases; yet no numbers have been found for which it won't work. That, in itself, suffices to establish that it is apparently always true. You may wish to have your students use a calculator, unless you want them to have practice in subtraction. Here is how this procedure goes:

Begin by having them select a four-digit number (except one that has all digits the same).

Rearrange the digits of the number so that they form the largest number possible. Then rearrange the digits of the number so that they form the smallest number possible.

Subtract these two numbers (obviously, the smaller from the larger).

Take this difference and continue the process, over and over and over, until you notice something disturbing happening. Don't give up before something unusual happens.

Eventually, you will arrive at the number 6,174, perhaps after one subtraction or after several subtractions. When you do, you will find yourself in an endless loop.

When you have reached the loop, remind students that they began with a randomly selected number. Isn't this quite an astonishing result? Some students might be motivated to investigate this further. Others will just sit back in awe. Either way, they have been charmed again with the beauty of mathematics.

Here is an example of this activity.

We will (randomly) select the number 3,203.

The largest number formed with these digits is 3,320.
The smallest number formed with these digits is 0,233.
The difference is 3,087.

The largest number formed with these digits is 8,730.
The smallest number formed with these digits is 0,378.
The difference is 8,352.

The largest number formed with these digits is 8,532.
The smallest number formed with these digits is 2,358.
The difference is 6,174.

The largest number formed with these digits is 7,641.
The smallest number formed with these digits is 1,467.
The difference is 6,174.

And so the loop is formed, since you keep getting 6,174 if you continue.

1.20 A Power Loop

Can you imagine that a number is equal to the sum of the cubes of its digits? Take the time to explain exactly what this means. This should begin to "set them up" for this most unusual phenomenon. By the way, this is true for only five numbers. Below are these five most unusual numbers.

$$1 \rightarrow 1^3 = 1$$
$$153 \rightarrow 1^3 + 5^3 + 3^3 = 1 + 125 + 27 = 153$$
$$370 \rightarrow 3^3 + 7^3 + 0^3 = 27 + 343 + 0 = 370$$
$$371 \rightarrow 3^3 + 7^3 + 1^3 = 27 + 343 + 1 = 371$$
$$407 \rightarrow 4^3 + 0^3 + 7^3 = 64 + 0 + 343 = 407$$

Students should take a moment to appreciate these spectacular results and take note that these are the *only* such numbers for which this is true.

Taking sums of the powers of the digits of a number leads to interesting results. We can extend this procedure to get a lovely (and not to mention, surprising) technique you can use to have students familiarize themselves with powers of numbers and at the same time try to get to a startling conclusion.

Have them select any number and then find the sum of the cubes of the digits, just as we did previously. Of course, for any other number than those above, they will have reached a new number. They should then repeat this process with each succeeding sum until they get into a "loop." A loop can be easily recognized. When they reach a number that they reached earlier, then they are in a loop. This will become clearer with an example.

Let's begin with the number 352 and find the sum of the cubes of the digits.

The sum of the cubes of the digits of 352 is $3^3 + 5^3 + 2^3 = 27 + 125 + 8 = 160$. Now we use this sum, 160, and repeat the process:

The sum of the cubes of the digits of 160 is $1^3 + 6^3 + 0^3 = 1 + 216 + 0 = 217$. Again repeat the process with 217:

The sum of the cubes of the digits of 217 is $2^3 + 1^3 + 7^3 = 8 + 1 + 343 = 352$. Surprise! This is the same number (352) we started with.

You might think it would have been easier to begin by taking squares. You are in for a surprise. Let's try this with the number 123.

Beginning with 123, the sum of the squares of the digits is $1^2 + 2^2 + 3^2 = 1 + 4 + 9 = 14$.

1. Now using 14, the sum of the squares of the digits is $1^2 + 4^2 = 1 + 16 = 17$.
2. Now using 17, the sum of the squares of the digits is $1^2 + 7^2 = 1 + 49 = 50$.
3. Now using 50, the sum of the squares of the digits is $5^2 + 0^2 = 25$.
4. Now using 25, the sum of the squares of the digits is $2^2 + 5^2 = 4 + 25 = 29$.
5. Now using 29, the sum of the squares of the digits is $2^2 + 9^2 = 85$.

6. Now using 85, the sum of the squares of the digits is $8^2 + 5^2 = 64 + 25 = 89$.
7. Now using 89, the sum of the squares of the digits is $8^2 + 9^2 = 64 + 81 = 145$.
8. Now using 145, the sum of the squares of the digits is $1^2 + 4^2 + 5^2 = 1 + 16 + 25 = 42$.
9. Now using 42, the sum of the squares of the digits is $4^2 + 2^2 = 16 + 4 = 20$.
10. Now using 20, the sum of the squares of the digits is $2^2 + 0^2 = 4$.
11. Now using 4, the sum of the squares of the digits is $4^2 = 16$.
12. Now using 16, the sum of the squares of the digits is $1^2 + 6^2 = 1 + 36 = 37$.
13. Now using 37, the sum of the squares of the digits is $3^2 + 7^2 = 9 + 49 = 58$.
14. Now using 58, the sum of the squares of the digits is $5^2 + 8^2 = 25 + 64 = 89$.

Notice that the sum, 89, that we just got in step 14 is the same as in step 6, and so a repetition will now begin after step 14. This indicates that we would continue in a loop.

Students may want to experiment with the sums of the powers of the digits of any number and see what interesting results it may lead to. They should be encouraged to look for patterns of loops, and perhaps determine the extent of a loop based on the nature of the original number.

In any case, this intriguing unit can be fun just as it is presented here or it can be a source for further investigation by interested students.

1.21 A Factorial Loop

This charming little unit will show an unusual relationship for certain numbers. Before beginning, however, review with your class the definition of $n!$.

$$n! = 1 \cdot 2 \cdot 3 \cdot 4 \cdots (n-1) \cdot n$$

Now that they have an understanding of the factorial concept, have them find the sum of the factorials of the digits of 145.

$$1! + 4! + 5! = 1 + 24 + 120 = 145$$

Surprise! We're back to 145.

Only for certain numbers, will the sum of the factorials of the digits equal the number itself.

Have your students try this again with the number 40,585:

$$4! + 0! + 5! + 8! + 5! = 24 + 1 + 120 + 40,320 + 120 = 40,585$$

At this point, students will expect this to be true for just about any number. Well, just let them try another number. Chances are that it will not work.

Now have them try this scheme with the number 871. They will get

$$8! + 7! + 1! = 40,320 + 5,040 + 1 - 45,361$$

at which point they will feel that they have failed again.

Not so fast. Have them try this procedure again with 45,361. This will give them

$$4! + 5! + 3! + 6! + 1! = 24 + 120 + 6 + 720 + 1 = 871$$

Isn't this the very number we started with? Again, we formed a loop.

If they repeat this with the number 872, they will get

$$8! + 7! + 2! = 40,320 + 5,040 + 2 = 45,362$$

Then repeating the process will give them

$$4! + 5! + 3! + 6! + 2! = 24 + 120 + 6 + 720 + 2 = 872.$$

Again, we're in a loop.

Students are usually quick to form generalizations, so they might conclude that if the scheme of summing factorials of the digits of a number doesn't get you back to the original number then try it again and it ought to work. Of course, you can "stack the deck" by giving them the number 169 to try. Two cycles do not seem to present a loop. So have them proceed through one more cycle. And sure enough, the third cycle leads them back to the original number.

Starting number	Sum of the factorials
169	$1! + 6! + 9! = 363,601$
363,601	$3! + 6! + 3! + 6! + 0! + 1!$
	$= 6 + 720 + 6 + 720 + 1 + 1 = 1,454$
1,454	$1! + 4! + 5! + 4!$
	$= 1 + 24 + 120 + 24 = 169$

Be careful about having students draw conclusions. These factorial oddities are not so pervasive that you should tell students to find others. There are "within reach" three groups of such loops. We can organize them according to the number of times you have to repeat the process to reach the original number. We will call these repetitions "cycles."

Here is a summary of the way our numbers behave in this factorial loop.

1 cycle	1, 2, 145, 40,585
2 cycle	871, 45,361 and 872, 45,362
3 cycle	169, 363,601, 1,454

The factorial loops shown in this charming little number oddity can be fun, but students must be cautioned that there are no other such numbers less than 2,000,000 for which this works. So let them not waste their time. Just appreciate some little beauties!

1.22 The Irrationality of $\sqrt{2}$

When we say that $\sqrt{2}$ is irrational, what does that mean? Students should be encouraged to inspect the word "irrational" to determine its meaning in English.

Irrational means not rational.
Not rational means it cannot be expressed as a ratio of two integers.
Not expressible as a ratio means it cannot be expressed as a common fraction.
That is, there is *no* fraction $\frac{a}{b} = \sqrt{2}$ (where a and b are integers).

If we compute $\sqrt{2}$ with a calculator we will get

$$\sqrt{2} = 1.41421356237309504880168872420969807856967187537694$$
$$80731766797379907324784621070388503875343 27641572 \cdots$$

Notice that there is no pattern among the digits, and there is no repetition of groups of digits. Does this mean that all rational fractions will have a period of digits*? Let's inspect a few common fractions.

$$\frac{1}{7} = 0.142857\underline{142857}142857\underline{142857}\cdots$$

which can be written as $0.\overline{142857}$ (a six-digit period).

Suppose we consider the fraction $\frac{1}{109}$:

$$\frac{1}{109} = 0.00917431192660550458715596330275229357798165 1376$$
$$14678899082568807339449541284403669724770642201834$$
$$8623\cdots$$

Here we have calculated its value to more than 100 places and no period appears. Does this mean that the fraction is irrational? This would destroy our previous definition. We can try to calculate the value a bit more

---

* A period of a sequence of digits is a group of repeating digits.

accurately, that is, say, to another 10 places further:

$$\frac{1}{109} = 0.0091743119266055045871559633027522935779816513761\,4$$
$$6788990825688073394495412844036697247706422018348623$$
$$8532110091$$

Suddenly it looks as though a pattern may be appearing; the 0091 also began the period.

We carry out our calculation further to 220 places and notice that, in fact, a 108-digit period emerges:

$$\frac{1}{109} = 0.009174311926605504587155963302752293577981651376\,1$$
$$46788990825688073394495412844036697247706422018348\,6$$
$$238532110091743119266055045871559633027522935779816$$
$$513761467889908256880733944954128440366972477706422\,0$$
$$18348623853211009174$$

If we carry out the calculation to 332 places, the pattern becomes clearer:

$$\frac{1}{109} = 0.\mathbf{009174311926605504587155963302752293577981651376}$$
$$\mathbf{1467889908256880733944954128440366972477064220183\,4}$$
$$\mathbf{86238532110}0917431192660550458715596330275229357\,79$$
$$816513761467889908256880733944954128440366972477\,06$$
$$42201834862385321\mathbf{1009174311926605504587155963302\,75}$$
$$\mathbf{2293577981651376146788990825688073394495412844036\,6}$$
$$\mathbf{9724770642201834862385321}1009174$$

We might be able to conclude (albeit without proof) that a common fraction results in a decimal equivalent that has a repeating period of digits.

Some common ones we are already familiar with, such as

$$\frac{1}{3} = 0.33333333\overline{3}$$

$$\frac{1}{13} = 0.076923076923076923076923\overline{769230}$$

To this point, we saw that a common fraction will result in a repeating decimal, sometimes with a very long period (e.g., $\frac{1}{109}$) and sometimes with a very short period (e.g., $\frac{1}{3}$). It would appear, from the rather flimsy evidence so far, that a fraction results in a repeating decimal and an irrational number does not. Yet this does not prove that an irrational number cannot be expressed as a fraction.

Here is a cute proof that $\sqrt{2}$ cannot be expressed as a common fraction and therefore, by definition is irrational.

Suppose $\frac{a}{b}$ is a fraction in lowest terms, which means that a and b do not have a common factor.
Suppose $\frac{a}{b} = \sqrt{2}$. Then $\frac{a^2}{b^2} = 2$, or $a^2 = 2b^2$, which implies that a^2 and a are divisible by 2; written another way, $a = 2r$, where r is an integer.
Then $4r^2 = 2b^2$, or $2r^2 = b^2$.
So we have b^2 or b is divisible by 2.
This contradicts the beginning assumption about the fact that a and b have no common factor, so $\sqrt{2}$ cannot be expressed as a common fraction.

Understanding this proof may be a bit strenuous for some students, but a slow and careful step-by-step presentation should make it understandable for most algebra students.

1.23 Sums of Consecutive Integers

Ask your students: Which numbers can be expressed as the sum of consecutive integers? You may have your students try to establish a rule for this by trying to express the first batch of natural numbers as the sum of consecutive integers. We will provide some in the following list.

$2 = $ not possible	$21 = 1 + 2 + 3 + 4 + 5 + 6$
$3 = 1 + 2$	$22 = 4 + 5 + 6 + 7$
$4 = $ not possible	$23 = 11 + 12$
$5 = 2 + 3$	$24 = 7 + 8 + 9$
$6 = 1 + 2 + 3$	$25 = 12 + 13$
$7 = 3 + 4$	$26 = 5 + 6 + 7 + 8$
$8 = $ not possible	$27 = 8 + 9 + 10$
$9 = 4 + 5$	$28 = 1 + 2 + 3 + 4 + 5 + 6 + 7$
$10 = 1 + 2 + 3 + 4$	$29 = 14 + 15$
$11 = 5 + 6$	$30 = 4 + 5 + 6 + 7 + 8$
$12 = 3 + 4 + 5$	$31 = 15 + 16$
$13 = 6 + 7$	$32 = $ not possible
$14 = 2 + 3 + 4 + 5$	$33 = 10 + 11 + 12$
$15 = 4 + 5 + 6$	$34 = 7 + 8 + 9 + 10$
$16 = $ not possible	$35 = 17 + 18$
$17 = 8 + 9$	$36 = 1 + 2 + 3 + 4 + 5 + 6 + 7 + 8$
$18 = 5 + 6 + 7$	$37 = 18 + 19$
$19 = 9 + 10$	$38 = 8 + 9 + 10 + 11$
$20 = 2 + 3 + 4 + 5 + 6$	$39 = 19 + 20$
	$40 = 6 + 7 + 8 + 9 + 10$

These consecutive number sum representations are clearly not unique. For example, 30 can be expressed in other ways such as $9 + 10 + 11$ or $6 + 7 + 8 + 9$. An inspection of the table shows that those where a consecutive number sum was not possible were the powers of 2.

This is an interesting fact. It is not something that one would expect. By making a list of these consecutive number sums, students will begin to see patterns. Clearly, the triangular numbers are equal to the sum of the first n natural numbers. A multiple of 3, say $3n$, can always be represented by the sum: $(n - 1) + n + (n + 1)$. Students will discover other patterns.

That's part of the fun of it (not to mention its instructional value—seeing number patterns and relationships).

For the more ambitious students, we now will provide a proof of this (until-now) conjecture. First, we will establish when a number can be expressed as a sum of at least two consecutive positive integers.

Let us analyze what values can be taken by the sum of (two or more) consecutive positive integers from a to b $(b > a)$

$$S = a + (a+1) + (a+2) + \cdots + (b-1) + b = \left(\frac{a+b}{2}\right)(b-a+1)$$

by applying the formula for the sum of an arithmetic series.* Then, doubling both sides, we get:

$$2S = (a+b)(b-a+1)$$

Calling $(a+b) = x$ and $(b-a+1) = y$, we can note that x and y are both integers and that since their sum, $x + y = 2b + 1$, is odd, one of x, y is odd and the other is even. Note that $2S = xy$.

Case 1 S is a power of 2.

Let $S = 2^n$. We have $2(2^n) = xy$, or $2^{n+1} = xy$. The only way we can express 2^{n+1} as a product of an even and an odd number is if the odd number is 1. If $x = a + b = 1$, then a and b cannot be positive integers. If $y = b - a + 1 = 1$, then we have $a = b$, which also cannot occur. Therefore, S cannot be a power of 2.

Case 2 S is not a power of 2.

Let $S = m2^n$, where m is an odd number greater than 1. We have $2(m2^n) = xy$, or $m2^{n+1} = xy$. We will now find positive integers a and b such that $b > a$ and $S = a + (a+1) + \cdots + b$.

The two numbers 2^{n+1} and m are not equal, since one is odd and the other is even. Therefore, one is bigger than the other. Assign x to be

---

* $S = \frac{n}{2}(a + l)$, where n is the number of terms and a is the first term and l is the last term.

the bigger one and y to be the smaller one. This assignment gives us a solution for a and b, as $x + y = 2b + 1$, giving a positive integer value for b, and $x - y = 2a - 1$, giving a positive integer value for a. Also, $y = b - a + 1 > 1$, so $b > a$, as required. We have obtained a and b.

Therefore, for any S that is not a power of 2, we can find positive integers a and b, $b > a$, such that $S = a + (a + 1) + \cdots + b$.

In conclusion, a number can be expressed as a sum of (at least two) consecutive positive integers if and only if the number is not a power of 2.

2 Some Arithmetic Marvels

Students often see arithmetic as a burden. They "have to" memorize the algorithms and don't have much chance to enjoy the nature of arithmetic. There are clever shortcuts around some arithmetic procedures and there are "tricks" for avoiding cumbersome arithmetic processes. For example, an almost visual inspection of numbers for divisors is a very useful technique, while some alternate forms of multiplication are more amusing than actually useful. In either case, they help to bring the topic of arithmetic to life.

This chapter also includes some recreational units that will strengthen students' understanding of the nature of arithmetic processes. For example, the unit on alphametics provides the student an opportunity to really work within the place value system, beyond the mere rote algorithms they learn.

The unit on the Rule of 72 is of particular use when dealing with compound interest and wanting to get some insight into the power of the compounding effect. The level at which this unit should be presented depends on the level of the students and their interests. It can be presented as an algorithm or presented as an investigation to discover why it works as it does.

There are several shortcuts for determining divisibility that can be used in everyday life, but in any case give students a more solid understanding of the nature of arithmetic. In each unit there are suggestions for using the unit. In some cases the enrichment provided is merely for entertainment, while in others there can be some rather helpful techniques to be learned.

Essentially, this chapter presents a variety of aspects of arithmetic applications, with the sole purpose of turning the students on to a subject that has been mostly tedious work for them.

2.1 Multiplying by 11

Here is a very nifty way to multiply by 11. This one always gets a rise out of students, because it is so simple—and, believe it or not, even easier than doing it on a calculator!

The rule is very simple: To multiply a two-digit number by 11, just add the two digits and place the sum between the two digits.*

For example, suppose you need to multiply 45 by 11. According to the rule, add 4 and 5 and place it between the 4 and 5 to get 495. It's as simple as that.

This can get a bit more difficult, as students will be quick to point out. If the sum of the two digits is greater than 9, then we place the units digit between the two digits of the number being multiplied by 11 and "carry" the tens digit to be added to the hundreds digit of the multiplicand. Let's try it with $78 \cdot 11$. Since, $7 + 8 = 15$, we place the 5 between the 7 and 8 and add the 1 to the 7, to get $[7 + 1][5][8]$ or 858.

Your students will next request that you extend this procedure to numbers of more than two digits. Let's go right for a larger number such as 12,345 and multiply it by 11.

Here we begin at the right-side digit and add every pair of digits going to the left:

$$1[1 + 2][2 + 3][3 + 4][4 + 5]5 = 135,795$$

If the sum of two digits is greater than 9, then use the procedure described before: Place the units digit appropriately and carry the tens digit. We will do one of these for you here. Multiply 456,789 by 11. We carry out the process step by step:

$$4[4 + 5][5 + 6][6 + 7][7 + 8][8 + 9]9$$
$$4[4 + 5][5 + 6][6 + 7][7 + 8][17]9$$
$$4[4 + 5][5 + 6][6 + 7][7 + 8 + 1][7]9$$

---

* With appropriate "causes" as explained later.

$4[4+5][5+6][6+7][16][7]9$

$4[4+5][5+6][6+7+1][6][7]9$

$4[4+5][5+6][14][6][7]9$

$4[4+5][5+6+1][4][6][7]9$

$4[4+5][12][4][6][7]9$

$4[4+5+1][2][4][6][7]9$

$4[10][2][4][6][7]9$

$[4+1][0][2][4][6][7]9$

$[5][0][2][4][6][7]9$

$5,024,679$

Students will be enthusiastic about this procedure, because it is so simple. They will go home and show it to their family and friends. By showing it and doing it, it will stay with them. Your goal is to maintain this enthusiasm.

2.2 When Is a Number Divisible by 11?

Try to convince your students that at the oddest times the issue can come up of a number being divisible by 11. If you have a calculator at hand, the problem is easily solved. But that is not always the case. Besides, there is such a clever "rule" for testing for divisibility by 11 that it is worth showing students just for its charm.

The rule is quite simple: **If the difference of the sums of the alternate digits is divisible by 11, then the original number is also divisible by 11**. It sounds a bit complicated, but it really isn't. Have your students take this rule a piece at a time. The sums of the alternate digits means you begin at one end of the number taking the first, third, fifth, etc. digits and add them. Then add the remaining (even placed) digits. Subtract the two sums and inspect for divisibility by 11.

It is probably best shown to your students by example. We shall test 768,614 for divisibility by 11. Sums of the alternate digits are

$$7 + 8 + 1 = 16 \quad \text{and} \quad 6 + 6 + 4 = 16$$

The difference of these two sums, $16 - 16 = 0$, which is divisible by 11.*

Another example might be helpful to firm up your students' understanding. To determine if 918,082 is divisible by 11, find the sums of the alternate digits:

$$9 + 8 + 8 = 25 \quad \text{and} \quad 1 + 0 + 2 = 3$$

Their difference is $25 - 3 = 22$, which is divisible by 11, and so the number 918,082 is divisible by 11.** Now just let your students practice with this rule. They will like it better with more practice, and they will love showing it to their family and friends.

---

* Remember that $\frac{0}{11} = 0$.

** For the interested student, here is a brief discussion about why this rule works as it does.

Consider the number ab,cde, whose value can be expressed as

$$N = 10^4 a + 10^3 b + 10^2 c + 10d + e$$
$$= (11 - 1)^4 a + (11 - 1)^3 b + (11 - 1)^2 c + (11 - 1)d + e$$
$$= [11M + (-1)^4]a + [11M + (-1)^3]b + [11M + (-1)^2]c + [11 + (-1)]d + e$$
$$= 11M[a + b + c + d] + a - b + c - d + e$$

which implies that divisibility by 11 of N depends on the divisibility of $a - b + c - d + e = (a + c + e) - (b + d)$, the difference of the sums of the alternate digits.

Note: $11M$ refers to a multiple of 11.

2.3 When Is a Number Divisible by 3 or 9?

The question of divisibility by 3 or 9 comes up quite often in everyday situations. Sometimes it's not too obvious, but you can put the question to your students and they will surely come up with examples. These examples should be ones where it becomes impracticable to take out a calculator to try the divisibility and where the actual quotient is not too important, just the question of divisible or not.

The rule, simply stated, is: **If the sum of the digits of a number is divisible by 3 (or 9), then the original number is divisible by 3 (or 9).***

Perhaps an example would best firm up an understanding of this rule. Consider the number 296,357. Let's test it for divisibility by 3 (or 9). The sum of the digits is $2 + 9 + 6 + 3 + 5 + 7 = 32$, which is not divisible by 3 or 9 and, therefore, neither is the original number, 296,357.

Another example: Is the number 457,875 divisible by 3 or 9? The sum of the digits is $4 + 5 + 7 + 8 + 7 + 5 = 36$, which is divisible by 9 (and then, of course, by 3 as well), so the number 457,875 is divisible by 3 and by 9.

A last example: Is the number 27,987 divisible by 3 or 9? The sum of the digits is $2 + 7 + 9 + 8 + 7 = 33$, which is divisible by 3 but not by 9; therefore, the number 27,987 is divisible by 3 and not by 9.

Students should be encouraged to practice this rule for a variety of numbers.

---

* For the interested student, here is a brief discussion about why this rule works as it does.

Consider the number ab,cde, whose value can be expressed as

$$N = 10^4 a + 10^3 b + 10^2 c + 10d + e$$
$$= (9+1)^4 a + (9+1)^3 b + (9+1)^2 c + (9+1)d + e$$
$$= [9M + (1)^4]a + [9M + (1)^3]b + [9M + (1)^2]c + [9 + (1)]d + e$$
$$= 9M[a + b + c + d] + a + b + c + d + e$$

which implies that divisibility by 9 of N depends on the divisibility of $a + b + c + d + e$, the sum of the digits.

Note: $9M$ refers to a multiple of 9.

2.4 Divisibility by Prime Numbers

In the previous unit, we presented a nifty little technique for determining if a number is divisible by 3 or by 9. Most students can determine when a number is divisible by 2 or by 5, simply by looking at the last digit (i.e., the units digit) of the number. That is, if the last digit is an even number (such as 2, 4, 6, 8, 0), then the number will be divisible by 2.* Similarly for 5: If the last digit of the number being inspected for divisibility is either a 0 or 5, then the number itself will be divisible by 5.** The question then is: Are there also rules for divisibility by other numbers? What about prime numbers?

With the proliferation of the calculator, there is no longer a crying need to be able to detect by which numbers a given number is divisible. You can simply do the division on a calculator. Yet, for a better appreciation of mathematics, divisibility rules provide an interesting "window" into the nature of numbers and their properties. For this reason (among others), the topic of divisibility still finds a place on the mathematics-learning spectrum and ought to be presented to students.

Most perplexing has always been to establish rules for divisibility by prime numbers. This is especially true for the rule for divisibility by 7, which follows a series of very nifty divisibility rules for the numbers 2 through 6.*** Students should be told up front that some of the divisibility rules for prime numbers are almost as cumbersome as the division

---

 * Incidentally, if the number formed by the last two digits is divisible by 4, then the number itself is divisible by 4. Also, if the number formed by the last three digits is divisible by 8, then the number itself is divisible by 8. You ought to be able to extend this rule to divisibility by higher powers of 2 as well.

 ** If the number formed by the last two digits is divisible by 25, then the number itself is divisible by 25. This is analogous to the rule for powers of 2. Have you guessed what the relationship here is between powers of 2 and 5? Yes, they are the factors of 10, the basis of our decimal number system.

 *** The rule for divisibility by 6 is simply to apply the rule for divisibility by 2 and by 3—both must hold true for a number to be divisible by 6.

algorithm, yet they are fun, and, believe it or not, can come in handy. You must present this unit as a "fun unit" so that students will not see this as something that they must memorize. Rather, they should try to understand the underpinnings of the rules.

Let us consider the rule for divisibility by 7 and then, as we inspect it, see how this can be generalized for other prime numbers.

Rule for Divisibility by 7   **Delete the last digit from the given number and then subtract twice this deleted digit from the remaining number. If the result is divisible by 7, the original number is divisible by 7. This process may be repeated if the result is too large for simple inspection of divisibility of 7.**

Let's try one as an example of how this rule works. Suppose we want to test the number 876,547 for divisibility by 7.

Begin with 876,547 and delete its units digit, 7, and subtract its double, 14, from the remaining number: $87,654 - 14 = 87,640$. Since we cannot yet visually inspect the resulting number for divisibility by 7, we continue the process.

Continue with the resulting number 87,640 and delete its units digit, 0, and subtract its double, still 0, from the remaining number; we get $8,764 - 0 = 8,764$. Since this did not change the resulting number, 8,764, as we seek to check for divisibility by 7, we continue the process.

Continue with the resulting number 8,764 and delete its units digit, 4, and subtract its double, 8, from the remaining number; we get $876 - 8 = 868$. Since we still cannot visually inspect the resulting number, 868, for divisibility by 7, we continue the process.

Continue with the resulting number 868 and delete its units digit, 8, and subtract its double, 16, from the remaining number; we get $86 - 16 = 70$, which is divisible by 7. Therefore, the number 876,547 is divisible by 7.

Before continuing with our discussion of divisibility of prime numbers, you ought to have students practice this rule with a few randomly selected numbers and then check their results with a calculator.

Now for the beauty of mathematics! Why does this rather strange procedure work? To see why it works is actually the wonderful thing about mathematics. It doesn't do things that for the most part we cannot justify.* This will all make sense to your students after they see what is happening with this procedure.

To justify the technique of determining divisibility by 7, consider the various possible terminal digits (that you are "dropping") and the corresponding subtraction that is actually being done by dropping the last digit. In the chart below, students will see how dropping the terminal digit and doubling it to get the units digit of the number being subtracted gives us in each case a multiple of 7. That is, they have taken "bundles of 7" away from the original number. Therefore, if the remaining number is divisible by 7, then so is the original number, because they have separated the original number into two parts, each of which is divisible by 7, and therefore the entire number must be divisible by 7.

Terminal digit	Number subtracted from original	Terminal digit	Number subtracted from original
1	$20 + 1 = 21 = 3 \cdot 7$	5	$100 + 5 = 105 = 15 \cdot 7$
2	$40 + 2 = 42 = 6 \cdot 7$	6	$120 + 6 = 126 = 18 \cdot 7$
3	$60 + 3 = 63 = 9 \cdot 7$	7	$140 + 7 = 147 = 21 \cdot 7$
4	$80 + 4 = 84 = 12 \cdot 7$	8	$160 + 8 = 168 = 24 \cdot 7$
		9	$180 + 9 = 189 = 27 \cdot 7$

Rule for Divisibility by 13 **This is similar to the rule for testing divisibility by 7, except that the 7 is replaced by 13 and instead of subtracting twice the deleted digit, we subtract nine times the deleted digit each time.**

Let's check for divisibility by 13 of the number 5,616.

---

* There are a few phenomena in mathematics that have not yet found an acceptable justification (or proof) but that doesn't mean we won't find one in the future. It took us 350 years to justify Fermat's conjecture! It was done by Dr. Andrew Wiles a few years ago.

Begin with 5,616 and delete its units digit, 6, and subtract it nine times, 54, from the remaining number: $561 - 54 = 507$. Since we still cannot visually inspect the resulting number for divisibility by 13, we continue the process.

Continue with the resulting number 507 and delete its units digit and subtract nine times this digit from the remaining number: $50 - 63 = -13$, which is divisible by 13; therefore, the original number is divisible by 13.

To determine the "multiplier," 9, we sought the smallest multiple of 13 that ends in a 1. That was 91, where the tens digit is 9 times the units digit. Once again, consider the various possible terminal digits and the corresponding subtractions in the following table.

Terminal digit	Number subtracted from original	Terminal digit	Number subtracted from original
1	$90 + 1 = 91 = 7 \cdot 13$	5	$450 + 5 = 455 = 35 \cdot 13$
2	$180 + 2 = 182 = 14 \cdot 13$	6	$540 + 6 = 546 = 42 \cdot 13$
3	$270 + 3 = 273 = 21 \cdot 13$	7	$630 + 7 = 637 = 49 \cdot 13$
4	$360 + 4 = 364 = 28 \cdot 13$	8	$720 + 8 = 728 = 56 \cdot 13$
		9	$810 + 9 = 819 = 63 \cdot 13$

In each case, a multiple of 13 is being subtracted one or more times from the original number. Hence, if the remaining number is divisible by 13, then the original number is divisible by 13.

Divisibility by 17 **Delete the units digit and subtract five times the deleted digit each time from the remaining number until you reach a number small enough to determine its divisibility by 17.**

We justify the rule for divisibility by 17 as we did the rules for 7 and 13. Each step of the procedure subtracts a "bunch of 17s" from the original number until we reduce the number to a manageable size and can make a visual inspection of divisibility by 17.

The patterns developed in the preceding three divisibility rules (for 7, 13, and 17) should lead students to develop similar rules for testing divisibility by larger primes. The following table presents the "multipliers" of the deleted digits for various primes.

To test divisibility by	7	11	13	17	19*	23	29	31	37	41	43	47
Multiplier	2	1	9	5	17	16	26	3	11	4	30	14

You may want to extend this table. It's fun, and it will increase their perception of mathematics. You may also want to extend their knowledge of divisibility rules to include composite (i.e., nonprime) numbers. Why the following rule refers to relatively prime factors and not just any factors is something that will sharpen their understanding of number properties. Perhaps the easiest response to this question is that relatively prime factors have independent divisibility rules, whereas other factors may not.

Divisibility by Composite Numbers   **A given number is divisible by a composite number if it is divisible by each of its relatively prime factors.**

The table below offers illustrations of this rule. You or your students should complete the chart to 48.

To be divisible by	6	10	12	15	18	21	24	26	28
The number must be divisible by	2, 3	2, 5	3, 4	3, 5	2, 9	3, 7	3, 8	2, 13	4, 7

At this juncture, your students have not only a rather comprehensive list of rules for testing divisibility, but also an interesting insight into elementary number theory. It is advisable to have students practice using these rules (to instill greater familiarity) and try to develop rules to test divisibility by other numbers in base 10 and to generalize these rules to other bases. Unfortunately, lack of space prevents a more detailed development here. Yet we have now whetted the appetites of this important population—our students!

---

* There is another curious rule for divisibility by 19. Delete the last digit of the number being tested for divisibility by 19 and *add* its double to the remaining number. Continue this process until you can recognize divisibility by 19.

2.5 The Russian Peasant's Method of Multiplication

You ought to begin the unit by mentioning to the students that it is said that the Russian peasants used a rather strange, perhaps even primitive, method to multiply two numbers. It is actually quite simple, yet somewhat cumbersome. Let's take a look at it.

Consider the problem of finding the product of $43 \cdot 92$. Let's work this multiplication together. We begin by setting up a chart of two columns with the two members of the product in the first row. Below you will see the 43 and 92 heading up the columns. One column will be formed by doubling each number to get the next, while the other column will take half the number and drop the remainder. For convenience, our first column will be the doubling column; the second column will be the halving column. Notice that by halving the odd number such as 23 (the third number in the second column) we get 11 with a remainder of 1 and we simply drop the 1. The rest of this halving process should now be clear. The process ends when the "halving" column is 1.

We make a list below each number. One list will be doubling the number; the other will take half the number (dropping the remainder).

43	92
86	46
172	**23**
344	**11**
688	**5**
1,376	2
2,752	**1**

Now have students locate the odd numbers in the halving column (here the right column). Then have them get the sum of the partner numbers in the doubling column (in this case the left column). These are highlighted in bold type. Therefore, $43 \cdot 92 = 172 + 344 + 688 + 2,752 = 3,956$.

This could also have been done by halving the numbers in the first column and doubling those in the second. See below.

43	92
21	184
10	368
5	736
2	1,472
1	2,944

Again, find the odd numbers in the halving column (in bold type), and then get the sum of their partner numbers in the second column (now the doubling column). Thus, $43 \cdot 92 = 92 + 184 + 736 + 2{,}944 = 3{,}956$.

Although this multiplication algorithm* is not efficient, it does allow students to inspect what goes on in the multiplication process. You might want to explain it with either of the following representations.

Here you see what was done in the above multiplication algorithm.

$$*43 \cdot 92 = (21 \cdot 2 + 1)(92) \quad = 21 \cdot 184 + \quad 92 = 3{,}956$$
$$*21 \cdot 184 = (10 \cdot 2 + 1)(184) \quad = 10 \cdot 368 + \quad 184 = 3{,}864$$
$$10 \cdot 368 = (5 \cdot 2 + 0)(368) \quad = 5 \cdot 736 \quad + \quad 0 = 3{,}680$$
$$*5 \cdot 736 = (2 \cdot 2 + 1)(736) \quad = 2 \cdot 1{,}472 + \quad 736 = 3{,}680$$
$$2 \cdot 1{,}472 = (1 \cdot 2 + 0)(1{,}472) = 1 \cdot 2{,}944 + \quad 0 = 2{,}944$$
$$*1 \cdot 2{,}944 = (0 \cdot 2 + 1)(2{,}944) = \quad 0 + 2{,}944 = 2{,}944$$
$$\overline{}$$
$$3{,}956$$

For those familiar with the binary system, one can also explain the Russian peasant's method with the following representation:

$$(43)(92) = (1 \cdot 2^5 + 0 \cdot 2^4 + 1 \cdot 2^3 + 0 \cdot 2^2 + 1 \cdot 2^1 + 1 \cdot 2^0)(92)$$
$$= 2^0 \cdot 92 + 2^1 \cdot 92 + 2^3 \cdot 92 + 2^5 \cdot 92$$
$$= 92 + 184 + 736 + 2{,}944$$
$$= 3{,}956$$

---

* Several years ago, I had a student in my class to whom I had shown this algorithm, who later mentioned that her mother multiplied numbers that way. Yes, she did emigrate from Russia.

The extent to which you choose to justify this method for the class is entirely up to you and the nature and level of the class. It is important that students get a chance to see that there is an alternate method to do multiplication, even though it is not more efficient. At least they will see that there is no universal way to multiply two numbers.

2.6 Speed Multiplying by 21, 31, 41

There are times when the multiplication algorithm gives you some shortcut multiplications if you just inspect what you are doing. Have your students perform various multiplications with the numbers 21, 31, 41, 51, ...

They will soon stumble on a neat little multiplication shortcut.

> **To multiply by 21: Double the number, then multiply by 10 and add the original number.**

For example: To multiply 37 by 21,

> Double 37 yields 74, multiply by 10 to get 740,
> and then add the original number 37 to get 777.

> **To multiply by 31: Triple the number, then multiply by 10 and add the original number.**

For example: To multiply 43 by 31,

> Triple 43 yields 129, multiply by 10 to get 1,290,
> and then add the original number 43 to get 1,333.

> **To multiply by 41: Quadruple the number, then multiply by 10 and add the original number.**

For example: To multiply 47 by 41,

> Quadruple 47 yields 188, multiply by 10 to get 1,880,
> and then add the original number 47 to get 1,927.

By now your students should be able to recognize the pattern. Have them extend the rule further to other numbers.

2.7 Clever Addition

One of the most popularly repeated stories from the history of mathematics is the tale of the famous mathematician Carl Friedrich Gauss (1777–1855) who at age 10 was said to have mentally added the numbers from 1 to 100 in response to a busy-work assignment given by the teacher.* Although it is a cute story and generally gets a very favorable reaction, its usefulness in the learning process is obtained when this scheme is used to develop a general formula for the sum of an arithmetic progression.

What Gauss did to get the sum of the first 100 natural numbers without writing a single number was not to add the numbers in the order in which they appear, but rather to add them in the following way: the first plus the last, the second plus the next to last, the third plus the third from last, and so on.

$$1 + 100 = 101$$
$$2 + 99 = 101$$
$$3 + 98 = 101$$
$$4 + 97 = 101$$
$$\vdots$$
$$50 + 51 = 101$$

The sum of these 50 pairs of numbers is $50 \cdot 101 = 5{,}050$.

It would be interesting to see if you have any prodigies in your class by giving the class the task of the addition before exposing the Gauss method. Remember, however, that Gauss was presumably 10 years old at the time.

---

* According to E. T. Bell in his book, *Men of Mathematics* (New York: Simon & Schuster, 1937), the problem given to Gauss was of the sort: $81{,}297 + 81{,}495 + 81{,}693 + \cdots + 100{,}899$, where the common difference between consecutive terms was 198 and the number of terms was 100. Today's lore uses the numbers to be summed from 1 to 100, which makes the point just as well, but in simpler form.

To get a general formula for an arithmetic series of n terms, where a is the first term and l is the last term, just use Gauss' method:

$$\text{Sum} = \frac{n}{2}(a + l)$$

2.8 Alphametics

One of the great strides made by Western civilization (which was learned from Arabic civilization) was the use of a place value system for our arithmetic. Working with Roman numerals was not only cumbersome but made many algorithms impossible. The first appearance of the Hindu–Arabic numerals, as mentioned earlier, was in Fibonacci's book, *Liber abaci*, in 1202. Beyond its usefulness, the place value system can also provide us with some recreational mathematics that can stretch our understanding and facility with the place value system.

Applying reasoning skills to analyzing an addition algorithm situation can be very important in training mathematical thinking. Be forewarned that some students may struggle with this for a while, but all will "get it" if the teacher is sensitive to the limited knowledge that many students have when it comes to analyzing algorithms. Begin by considering the following problem.

The following letters represent the digits of a simple addition:

$$
\begin{array}{r}
\text{S E N D} \\
+ \quad \text{M O R E} \\
\hline
\text{M O N E Y}
\end{array}
$$

Find the digits that represent the letters to make this addition correct, if each letter represents a unique digit and M is not equal to D.

Then have your students show that the solution is unique, that is, that there is only one possible solution. Most important in this activity is the analysis, and particular attention should be given to the reasoning used. We will do it step by step (in small increments) so that we can model a way it can be shown to students.

The sum of two four-digit numbers cannot yield a number greater than 19,999. Therefore, $M = 1$.

We then have MORE $< 2,000$ and SEND $< 10,000$. It follows that MONEY $< 12,000$. Thus, O can be either 0 or 1. But the 1 is already used; therefore, $O = 0.$

We now have

$$
\begin{array}{r}
S\,E\,N\,D \\
+\quad 1\,0\,R\,E \\
\hline
1\,0\,N\,E\,Y
\end{array}
$$

Now MORE $< 1,100$. If SEND were less than 9,000, then MONEY $< 10,100$, which would imply that $N = 0$. But this cannot be since 0 was already used; therefore, SEND $> 9,000$, so that $S = 9$.

We now have

$$
\begin{array}{r}
9\,E\,N\,D \\
+\quad 1\,0\,R\,E \\
\hline
1\,0\,N\,E\,Y
\end{array}
$$

The remaining digits from which we may complete the problem are $\{2, 3, 4, 5, 6, 7, 8\}$.

Let us examine the units digits. The greatest sum is $7 + 8 = 15$ and the least sum is $2 + 3 = 5$. If $D + E < 10$, then $D + E = Y$, with no carryover into the tens column. Otherwise, $D + E = Y + 10$, with a 1 carried over to the tens column.

Taking this argument one step further to the tens column, we get $N + R = E$, with no carryover, or $N + R = E + 10$, with a carryover of 1 to the hundreds column. However, if there is no carryover to the hundreds column, then $E + 0 = N$, which implies that $E = N$. This is not permissible. Therefore, there must be a carryover to the hundreds column. So $N + R = E + 10$, and $E + 0 + 1 = N$, or $E + 1 = N$. Substituting this value for N into the previous equation, we get $(E + 1) + R = E + 10$, which implies that $R = 9$. But this has already been used for the value of S. We must try a different approach.

We shall assume, therefore, that $D + E = Y + 10$, since we apparently need a carryover into the tens column, where we just reached a dead end.

Now the sum in the tens column is $1 + 2 + 3 < 1 + N + R < 1 + 7 + 8$. If, however, $1 + N + R < 10$, there will be no carryover to the hundreds column, leaving the previous dilemma of $E = N$, which is not allowed. We then have $1 + N + R = E + 10$, which ensures the needed carryover to the hundreds column. Therefore, $1 + E + 0 = N$, or $E + 1 = N$.

Substituting this in the above equation $(1 + N + R = E + 10)$ gives us $1 + (E + 1) + R = E + 10$, or $R = 8$.

We now have

```
      9 E N D
  +   1 0 8 E
    ───────────
    1 0 N E Y
```

From the remaining list of available digits, we find that $D + E < 14$.

So from the equation $D + E = Y + 10$, Y is either 2 or 3. If $Y = 3$, then $D + E = 13$, implying that the digits D and E can take on only 6 or 7.

If $D = 6$ and $E = 7$, then from the previous equation $E + 1 = N$, we would have $N = 8$, which is unacceptable since $R = 8$.

If $D = 7$ and $E = 8$, then from the previous equation $E + 1 = N$, we would have $N = 9$, which is unacceptable since $S = 9$. Therefore, $Y = 2$.

We now have

```
      9 E N D
  +   1 0 8 E
    ───────────
    1 0 N E 2
```

Thus, $D + E = 12$. The only way to get this sum is with 5 and 7. If $E = 7$, we once again get from $E + 1 = N$, the contradictory $N = 8$, which is not acceptable. Therefore, $D = 7$ and $E = 5$. We can now again use the equation $E + 1 = N$ to get $N = 6$.

Finally, we get the solution:

$$
\begin{array}{r}
9\,5\,6\,7 \\
+\quad 1\,0\,8\,5 \\
\hline
1\,0\,6\,5\,2
\end{array}
$$

This rather strenuous activity should provide your students with some important training and insight into mathematics.

2.9 Howlers

Students sometimes provide us with some ideas for exploring mathematical oddities. How often do we see students do something entirely mathematically incorrect and still end up with the correct answer? This could even lead students to justify their wrong work because it produced the right result. Let's consider the reduction of fractions.

In his book, *Fallacies in Mathematics*,* E. A. Maxwell refers to the following cancellations as howlers:

$$
\frac{1\cancel{6}}{\cancel{6}4} = \frac{1}{4} \qquad \frac{2\cancel{6}}{\cancel{6}5} = \frac{2}{5}
$$

Begin your presentation by asking students to reduce to lowest terms the following fractions: $\frac{16}{64}, \frac{19}{95}, \frac{26}{65}$, and $\frac{49}{98}$. After they have reduced to lowest terms each of the fractions in the usual manner, ask why they didn't simply do it in the following way:

$$
\frac{1\cancel{6}}{\cancel{6}4} = \frac{1}{4}
$$

$$
\frac{1\cancel{9}}{\cancel{9}5} = \frac{1}{5}
$$

$$
\frac{2\cancel{6}}{\cancel{6}5} = \frac{2}{5}
$$

$$
\frac{4\cancel{9}}{\cancel{9}8} = \frac{4}{8} = \frac{1}{2}
$$

* London: Cambridge University Press, 1959.

At this point, your students will be somewhat amazed. Their first reaction will probably be to ask if this may be done to any fraction composed of two-digit numbers of this sort. Challenge your students to find another fraction (composed of two-digit numbers) where this type of cancellation will work. Students might cite $\frac{55}{55} = \frac{5}{5} = 1$ as an illustration of this type of cancellation. Indicate to them that although this will hold true for all multiples of 11 yielding two-digit results, it is trivial, and our concern will be only with proper fractions (i.e., whose value is less than 1).

For a better class, or one that has a good working knowledge of elementary algebra, you may wish to "explain" this situation. That is, why are the four fractions above the only ones (composed of two-digit numbers) where this type of cancellation will hold true?

Have students consider the fraction $\frac{10x+a}{10a+y}$.

The above four cancellations were such that when cancelling the a's the fraction was equal to $\frac{x}{y}$.

Therefore,

$$\frac{10x + a}{10a + y} = \frac{x}{y}$$

This yields

$$y(10x + a) = x(10a + y)$$
$$10xy + ay = 10ax + xy$$
$$9xy + ay = 10ax$$

Therefore,

$$y = \frac{10ax}{9x + a}$$

At this point, have students inspect this equation. They should realize that it is necessary that x, y, and a are integers since they were digits in the numerator and denominator of a fraction. It is now their task to find the values of a and x for which y will also be integral.

To avoid a lot of algebraic manipulation, you might have students set up a chart that will generate values of y from $y = \frac{10ax}{9x+a}$. Remind them that x, y, and a must be single-digit integers. Below is a portion of the table they will construct. Notice that the cases where $x = a$ are excluded since $\frac{x}{y} = 1$.

X	1	2	3	4	5	6	$\cdots$	9
a (header spanning)								
1		$\frac{20}{11}$	$\frac{30}{12}$	$\frac{40}{13}$	$\frac{50}{14}$	$\frac{60}{15}=4$		$\frac{90}{18}=5$
2	$\frac{20}{19}$		$\frac{60}{21}$	$\frac{80}{22}$	$\frac{100}{23}$	$\frac{120}{24}=5$		
3	$\frac{30}{28}$	$\frac{60}{29}$		$\frac{120}{31}$	$\frac{150}{32}$	$\frac{180}{33}$		
4								$\frac{360}{45}=8$
$\vdots$								
9								

The portion of the chart pictured above generated the four integral values of y. Two of which are as follows: if $x = 1$, $a = 6$, then $y = 4$, and if $x = 2$, $a = 6$, then $y = 5$. These values yield the fractions $\frac{16}{64}$ and $\frac{26}{65}$, respectively. The remaining two integral values of y will be obtained when $x = 1$ and $a = 9$, yielding $y = 5$, and when $x = 4$ and $a = 9$, yielding $y = 8$. These yield the fractions $\frac{19}{95}$ and $\frac{49}{98}$, respectively. This should convince students that there are only four such fractions composed of two-digit numbers.

Students may now wonder if there are fractions composed of numerators and denominators of more than two digits where this strange type of cancellation holds true. Have students try this type of cancellation with $\frac{499}{998}$. They should find that

$$\frac{499}{998} = \frac{4}{8} = \frac{1}{2}$$

Soon they will realize that

$$\frac{49}{98} = \frac{499}{998} = \frac{4,999}{9,998} = \frac{49,999}{99,998} = \cdots$$

$$\frac{16}{64} = \frac{166}{664} = \frac{1,666}{6,664} = \frac{16,666}{66,664} = \frac{166,666}{666,664} = \cdots$$

$$\frac{19}{95} = \frac{199}{995} = \frac{1,999}{9,995} = \frac{19,999}{99,995} = \frac{199,999}{999,995} = \cdots$$

$$\frac{26}{65} = \frac{266}{665} = \frac{2,666}{6,665} = \frac{26,666}{66,665} = \frac{266,666}{666,665} = \cdots$$

Enthusiastic students may wish to justify these extensions of the original howlers. Students who at this point have a further desire to seek out additional fractions that permit this strange cancellation should be shown the following fractions. They should verify the legitimacy of this strange cancellation and then set out to discover more such fractions.

$$\frac{3\cancel{3}2}{8\cancel{3}0} = \frac{32}{80} = \frac{2}{5}$$

$$\frac{3\cancel{8}5}{8\cancel{8}0} = \frac{35}{80} = \frac{7}{16}$$

$$\frac{1\cancel{3}8}{\cancel{3}45} = \frac{18}{45} = \frac{2}{5}$$

$$\frac{2\cancel{7}5}{7\cancel{7}0} = \frac{25}{70} = \frac{5}{14}$$

$$\frac{1\cancel{6}\cancel{3}}{\cancel{3}2\cancel{6}} = \frac{1}{2}$$

Aside from providing an algebraic application, which can be used to introduce a number of important topics in a motivational way, this topic can also provide some recreational activities. Here are some more of these "howlers."

$$\frac{48\,4}{8\,47} = \frac{4}{7} \qquad \frac{5\,45}{65\,4} = \frac{5}{6} \qquad \frac{4\,24}{7\,4\,2} = \frac{4}{7} \qquad \frac{24\,0}{0\,96} = \frac{24}{96} = \frac{1}{4}$$

$$\frac{48\,4\,8\,4}{8\,4\,8\,47} = \frac{4}{7} \qquad \frac{5\,4\,5\,45}{65\,4\,5\,4} = \frac{5}{6} \qquad \frac{4\,2\,4\,24}{74\,2\,4\,2} = \frac{4}{7}$$

$$\frac{3\,2\,43}{43\,2\,4} = \frac{3}{4} \qquad \frac{6\,4\,86}{86\,4\,8} = \frac{6}{8} = \frac{3}{4}$$

$$\frac{147\,1\,4}{7\,1\,468} = \frac{14}{68} = \frac{7}{34} \qquad \frac{8\,7\,8\,0\,48}{98\,7\,8\,0\,4} = \frac{8}{9}$$

$$\frac{14\,2\,8\,5\,7\,1}{4\,2\,8\,5\,7\,1\,3} = \frac{1}{3} \qquad \frac{28\,5\,7\,1\,4\,2}{8\,5\,7\,1\,4\,26} = \frac{2}{6} = \frac{1}{3} \qquad \frac{34\,6\,1\,5\,3\,8}{4\,6\,1\,5\,3\,84} = \frac{3}{4}$$

$$\frac{7\,6\,7\,1\,2\,3\,2\,87}{87\,6\,7\,1\,2\,3\,2\,8} = \frac{7}{8} \qquad \frac{3\,2\,4\,3\,2\,4\,3\,2\,43}{43\,2\,4\,3\,2\,4\,3\,2\,4} = \frac{3}{4}$$

$$\frac{1\,0\,2\,5\,6\,41}{4\,1\,0\,2\,5\,6\,4} = \frac{1}{4} \qquad \frac{3\,2\,4\,3\,2\,43}{43\,2\,4\,3\,2\,4} = \frac{3}{4} \qquad \frac{4\,5\,7\,1\,4\,2\,8}{5\,7\,1\,4\,2\,85} = \frac{4}{5}$$

$$\frac{48\,4\,8\,4\,8\,4}{8\,4\,8\,4\,8\,47} = \frac{4}{7} \qquad \frac{59\,5\,2\,3\,8\,0}{9\,5\,2\,3\,8\,08} = \frac{5}{8} \qquad \frac{4\,2\,8\,5\,7\,14}{64\,2\,8\,5\,7\,1} = \frac{4}{6} = \frac{2}{3}$$

$$\frac{5\,4\,5\,4\,5\,45}{65\,4\,5\,4\,5\,4} = \frac{5}{6} \qquad \frac{69\,2\,3\,0\,7\,6}{9\,2\,3\,0\,7\,68} = \frac{6}{8} = \frac{3}{4} \qquad \frac{4\,2\,4\,2\,4\,24}{74\,2\,4\,2\,4\,2} = \frac{4}{7}$$

$$\frac{5\,3\,8\,4\,6\,15}{75\,3\,8\,4\,6\,1} = \frac{5}{7} \qquad \frac{2\,0\,5\,1\,2\,82}{82\,0\,5\,1\,2\,8} = \frac{2}{8} = \frac{1}{4} \qquad \frac{3\,1\,1\,6\,8\,83}{83\,1\,1\,6\,8\,8} = \frac{3}{8}$$

$$\frac{6\,4\,8\,6\,4\,86}{86\,4\,8\,6\,4\,8} = \frac{6}{8} = \frac{3}{4} \qquad \frac{48\,4\,8\,4\,8\,4\,8\,4}{8\,4\,8\,4\,8\,4\,8\,47} = \frac{4}{7}$$

This unit provides a motivating application of elementary algebra to investigate an algebraic situation. It is a good use of "literal equations."

2.10 The Unusual Number 9

Students will be fascinated to learn that the first occurrence in Western Europe of the Hindu–Arabic numerals we use today was in 1202 in the book, *Liber abaci*, by Leonardo of Pisa (otherwise known as Fibonacci). This merchant traveled extensively throughout the Middle East and in the first chapter states that

> these are the nine figures of the Indians 9, 8, 7, 6, 5, 4, 3, 2, 1. With these nine figures, and with the symbol, 0, which in Arabic is called zephirum, any number can be written, as will be demonstrated below.

With this book, the use of these numerals was first publicized in Europe. Before that, Roman numerals were used. They were, certainly, much more cumbersome. Take a moment to have students ponder how they would do their calculations if all they had at their disposal were the Roman numerals.

Fibonacci, fascinated by the arithmetic calculations used in the Islamic world, first introduced the system of "casting out nines"* as a check for arithmetic in this book. Even today, it still comes in useful. However, the nice thing about it is that it again demonstrates a hidden magic in ordinary arithmetic.

Before we discuss this arithmetic-checking procedure, we will consider how the remainder of a division by 9 compares to removing nines from the digit sum of the number. Let us find the remainder when 8,768 is divided by 9. The quotient is 974 with a remainder of 2.

This remainder can also be obtained by "casting out nines" from the digit sum of the number 8,768: $8 + 7 + 6 + 8 = 29$, again casting out nines: $2 + 9 = 11$, and again: $1 + 1 = 2$, which was the remainder from before.

Consider the product $734 \cdot 879 = 645,186$. We can check this by division, but that would be somewhat lengthy. We can see if this could be correct by

---

* "Casting out nines" means taking bundles of nines away from the sum, or subtracting a specific number of nines from this sum.

"casting out nines." Take each factor and the product and add the digits, and then add the digits if the sum is not already a single digit number. Continue this until a single digit number is reached:

For 734: $7 + 3 + 4 = 14$;   then $1 + 4 = 5$
For 879: $8 + 7 + 9 = 24$;   then $2 + 4 = 6$
For 645,186: $6 + 4 + 5 + 1 + 8 + 6 = 30$

Since $5 \cdot 6 = 30$, which yields 3 (casting out nines: $3 + 0 = 3$), is the same as for the product, the answer could be correct.

For practice, have students do another casting-out-nines "check" for the following multiplication:

$$56,589 \cdot 983,678 = 55,665,354,342$$

For 56,589: $5 + 6 + 5 + 8 + 9 = 33$ $3 + 3 = 6$
For 983,678: $9 + 8 + 3 + 6 + 7 + 8 = 41$ $4 + 1 = 5$
For 55,665,354,342: $5 + 5 + 6 + 6 + 5 + 3$
                    $\quad + 5 + 4 + 3 + 4 + 2 = 48$ $4 + 8 = 12$
                    $1 + 2 = 3$

To check for *possibly* having the correct product: $6 \cdot 5 = 30$ or $3 + 0 = 3$, which matches the 3 resulting from the product digits.

The same scheme can be used to check the likelihood of a correct sum or quotient, simply by taking the sum (or quotient) and casting out nines, taking the sum (or quotient) of these "remainders" and comparing it with the remainder of the sum (or quotient). They should be equal if the answer is to be correct.

The number 9 has another unusual feature, which enables us to use a surprising multiplication algorithm. Although it is somewhat complicated, it is nevertheless fascinating to see it work and perhaps try to determine why this happens. This procedure is intended for multiplying a number of two digits or more by 9.

It is best to discuss the procedure with your students in context: Have them consider multiplying 76,354 by 9.

Step 1	Subtract the units digit of the multiplicand from 10	$10 - 4 = \mathbf{6}$
Step 2	Subtract each of the remaining digits (beginning with the tens digit) from 9 and add this result to the previous digit in the multiplicand (for any two-digit sums carry the tens digit to the next sum)	$9 - 5 = 4,\quad 4 + 4 = \mathbf{8}$ $9 - 3 = 6,\quad 6 + 5 = 11, \mathbf{1}$ $9 - 6 = 3,\quad 3 + 3 = 6,\quad 6 + 1 = \mathbf{7}$ $9 - 7 = 2,\quad 2 + 6 = \mathbf{8}$
Step 3	Subtract 1 from the leftmost digit of the multiplicand	$7 - 1 = \mathbf{6}$
Step 4	List the results in reverse order to get the desired product	**687,186**

Although it is a bit cumbersome, especially when compared to the calculator, this algorithm provides some insight into number theory. But above all, it's cute!

2.11 Successive Percentages

Percentage problems have long been the nemesis of most students. Problems get particularly unpleasant when multiple percentages need to be processed in the same problem. This unit can turn this one-time nemesis into a delightfully simple arithmetic algorithm that affords lots of useful applications. This little-known scheme will enchant your students. We will begin by considering the following problem:

> **Wanting to buy a coat, Lisa is faced with a dilemma. Two competing stores next to each other carry the same brand coat with the same list price, but with two different discount offers. Store A offers a 10% discount year round on all its goods, but on this particular day offers an additional 20% on top of its already discounted price. Store B simply offers a discount of 30% on that day in order to stay competitive. How many percentage points difference is there between the two options open to Lisa?**

At first glance, students will assume there is no difference in price, since $10 + 20 = 30$, yielding the same discount in both cases. The clever student will see that this is not correct, since in store A only 10% is calculated on the original list price, with the 20% calculated on the lower price, while at store B, the entire 30% is calculated on the original price. Now, the question to be answered is, what percentage difference is there between the discount in store A and store B?

One expected procedure will have the student assume the cost of the coat to be $100, calculate the 10% discount, yielding a $90 price, and an additional 20% of the $90 price (or $18) will bring the price down to $72. In store B, the 30% discount on $100 would bring the price down to $70, giving a discount difference of $2, which in this case is 2%. This procedure, although correct and not too difficult, is a bit cumbersome and does not always allow a full insight into the situation.

An interesting and quite unusual procedure* is provided for entertainment and fresh insight into this problem situation.

---

* It is provided without justification of its validity so as not to detract from the solution of the problem. However, for further discussion of this procedure, the reader is referred to A. S. Posamentier

Here is a mechanical method for obtaining a single percentage discount (or increase) equivalent to two (or more) successive discounts (or increases).

1. Change each of the percentages involved into decimal form: .20 and .10.
2. Subtract each of these decimals from 1.00: .80 and .90 (for an increase, add to 1.00).
3. Multiply these differences: $(.80)(.90) = .72$.
4. Subtract this number (i.e., .72) from 1.00: $1.00 - .72 = .28$, which represents the combined *discount*.
   (If the result in step 3 is greater than 1.00, subtract 1.00 from it to obtain the percentage of *increase*.)
   When we convert .28 back to percentage form, we obtain 28%, the equivalent of successive discounts of 20% and 10%.

This combined percentage of 28% differs from 30% by 2%.

This procedure can also be used to combine more than two successive discounts following the same approach. In addition, successive increases, combined or not combined with a discount, can also be accommodated in this procedure by adding the decimal equivalent of the increase to 1.00, where the discount was subtracted from 1.00 and then continue in the same way. If the end result comes out greater than 1.00, then this reflects an overall increase rather than the discount as found in the above problem.

This procedure not only streamlines a typically cumbersome situation, but also provides some insight into the overall picture. For example, the question "Is it advantageous to the buyer in the above problem to receive a 20% discount and then a 10% discount, or the reverse, a 10% discount and then a 20% discount?" The answer to this question is not immediately intuitively obvious. Yet, since the procedure just presented shows that the calculation is merely multiplication, a commutative operation, we find immediately that there is no difference between the two.

So here you have a delightful algorithm for combining successive discounts or increases or combinations of these. Not only is it useful, but it will enchant your students (and probably your colleagues as well).

and J. Stepelman, *Teaching Secondary School Mathematics: Techniques and Enrichment Units*, 6th ed. (Columbus, OH: Merrill/Prentice Hall, 2002), pp. 272–274.

2.12 Are Averages Averages?

Begin by asking students to explain what a "baseball batting average" is. Most people, especially after trying to explain this concept, will begin to realize that it is not an average in the way they usually define an "average"—the arithmetic mean. It might be good to search the sports section of the local newspaper to find two baseball players who currently have the same batting average but who have achieved their respective averages with a different number of hits. We shall use a hypothetical example here.

Consider two players, David and Lisa, each with a batting average of .667. David achieved his batting average by getting 20 hits for 30 at bats, while Lisa achieved her batting average by getting 2 hits for 3 at bats.

On the next day, both performed equally, getting 1 hit for 2 at bats (for a .500 batting average); one might expect that they then still have the same batting average at the end of the day. Calculating their respective averages: David now has $20 + 1 = 21$ hits for $30 + 2 = 32$ at bats for a $\frac{21}{32} = .656$ batting average. Lisa now has $2 + 1 = 3$ hits for $3 + 2 = 5$ at bats for a $\frac{3}{5} = .600$ batting average. Surprise! They do not have equal batting averages.

Suppose we consider the next day, where Lisa performs considerably better than David does. Lisa gets 2 hits for 3 at bats, while David gets 1 hit for 3 at bats. We shall now calculate their respective averages: David has $21 + 1 = 22$ hits for $32 + 3 = 35$ at bats for a batting average of $\frac{22}{35} = .629$. Lisa has $3 + 2 = 5$ hits for $5 + 3 = 8$ at bats for a batting average of $\frac{5}{8} = .625$.

Amazingly, despite Lisa's superior performance on this day, her batting average, which was the same as David's at the start, is now lower.

There is much to be learned from this "misuse" of the word "average," but more importantly, students will get an appreciation of the notion of varying weights of items being averaged.

2.13 The Rule of 72

Although lately the school curriculum pays less attention to compound-interest problems than in the past, there is a curious little scheme that works well and is somewhat puzzling to verify. It is called the "Rule of 72," and may still generate some interest in the compound-interest formula.

The Rule of 72 states that, roughly speaking, **money will double in $\frac{72}{r}$ years when it is invested at an annual compounded interest rate of $r\%$.** So, for example, if we invest money at an 8% compounded annual interest rate, it will double its value in $\frac{72}{8} = 9$ years. Similarly, if we leave our money in the bank at a compounded rate of 6%, it would take 12 years for this sum to double its value.

The interested teacher might want to better understand why this is so, and how accurate it really is. The following discussion will explain that.

To investigate why or if this really works, we consider the compound-interest formula:

$$A = P\left(1 + \frac{r}{100}\right)^{n}$$

where A is the resulting amount of money and P is the principal invested for n interest periods at $r\%$ annually We need to investigate what happens when $A = 2P$.

The above equation then becomes

$$2 = \left(1 + \frac{r}{100}\right)^{n} \qquad (1)$$

It then follows that

$$n = \frac{\log 2}{\log(1 + \frac{r}{100})} \qquad (2)$$

Let us make a table of values from the above equation with the help of a scientific calculator:

r	n	nr
1	69.66071689	69.66071689
3	23.44977225	70.34931675
5	14.20669908	71.03349541
7	10.24476835	71.71337846
9	8.043231727	72.38908554
11	6.641884618	73.0607308
13	5.671417169	73.72842319
15	4.959484455	74.39226682

If we take the arithmetic mean (the usual average) of the nr values, we get 72.04092314, which is quite close to 72, and so our Rule of 72 seems to be a very close estimate for doubling money at an annual interest rate of r% for n interest periods.

An ambitious teacher or one with a very strong mathematics class might try to determine a "rule" for tripling and quadrupling money, similar to the way we dealt with the doubling of money. The above equation (2) for k-tupling would be

$$n = \frac{\log k}{\log(1 + \frac{r}{100})}$$

which, for $r = 8$, gives us $n = 29.91884022(\log k)$.

Thus, $nr = 239.3507218 \log k$, which, for $k = 3$ (the tripling effect), gives us $nr = 114.1993167$. We could then say that for tripling money we would have a "Rule of 114."

However far this topic is explored, the important issue here is that the common Rule of 72 can be a nice way to interest students and at the same time give them a useful tool.

2.14 Extracting a Square Root

Why would anyone want to find the square root of a number without using a calculator? Surely, no one would do such a thing, except a teacher trying to demonstrate what the square root of a number really is. Introducing the notion of the extraction of a square root through a manual method, which relies on the notion of what a square root is, makes the concept easier to understand. Experience has shown that students will have a much better appreciation of what the square root of a number represents after this discussion than they have before it. It ought to be stressed at the outset that you are in no way implying that this procedure ought to be used in place of a calculator.

This method was first published in 1690 by the English mathematician Joseph Raphson (or Ralphson) in his book, *Analysis Alquationum Universalis*, attributing it to Newton, and therefore the algorithm bears both names, the *Newton–Raphson method.*

It is perhaps best to see the method used in a specific example: Suppose we wish to find $\sqrt{27}$. Obviously, the calculator would be used here. However, you might like to introduce the task by having students guess at what this value might be. Certainly it is between $\sqrt{25}$ and $\sqrt{36}$, or between 5 and 6, but closer to 5.

Suppose we guess at 5.2. If this were the correct square root, then if we were to divide 27 by 5.2, we would get 5.2. But this is not the case here, since $\sqrt{27} \neq 5.2$.

We seek a closer approximation. To do that, we find $\frac{27}{5.2} \approx 5.192$. Since $27 \approx 5.2 \cdot 5.192$, one of the factors (5.2 in this case) must be bigger than $\sqrt{27}$ and the other factor (5.192 in this case) must be less than $\sqrt{27}$. Hence, $\sqrt{27}$ is sandwiched between the two numbers 5.2 and 5.192, that is,

$$5.192 < \sqrt{27} < 5.2$$

so that it is plausible to infer that the average (5.196) is a better approximation for $\sqrt{27}$ than either 5.2 or 5.192.

This process continues, each time with additional decimal places, so that an allowance is made for a closer approximation. That is, $\frac{5.192+5.196}{2} =$ 5.194, then $\frac{27}{5.194} = 5.19831$. This continuous process provides insight into the finding of the square root of a number that is not a perfect square.

As cumbersome as the method may be, it surely gives some insight into what a square root represents.

3 Problems with Surprising Solutions

Perhaps the most time-tested aspect of mathematics instruction is the role of problem solving. Frequently, problem solving is seen as doing the exercises in the textbook. This is a very narrow aspect of the concept of problem solving. There are many strategies that should be consciously used to solve problems, yet what is most enchanting about problem solving is when you are presented with a simple-to-understand problem and the solution is not directly apparent. Moreover, sometimes the solution comes after some tedious work. This is not always terribly rewarding. What is most interest provoking is when a problem is easily stated, quickly understood, and the solution that is ultimately demonstrated is most unusual and not typically anticipated. These "surprise attacks" are what generate excitement among students.

This chapter offers just such problems. Some of them will end up becoming your favorites (even to show your personal friends—just to impress them with your cleverness!) and will leave your students with "their jaws dropped." With each one of the problems presented here, there is a specific message or strategy that ought to be stressed. Be sure to point these out, even if the students are consumed (or overwhelmed) by the cleverness of the solution.

You must keep focused on the intent of the solution. So go to it. Present the problems, let students struggle a bit, and then enlighten them with the solutions provided in the chapter. You will certainly enjoy the students' reaction to the unusual nature of the solutions. Remember, don't let them get discouraged by thinking that they could never come up with such a clever solution. Just tell them that one aspect of problem solving is recalling previously solved problems and trying these strategies again.

3.1 Thoughtful Reasoning

When students are confronted with a problem, they often resort to rather primitive ways of thinking. Sometimes well-trained students will consciously think of analogous problems previously solved to see if there is anything that these previous experiences can bring to the current problem. When primitive methods are used (which can be called the "peasant's way"), a solution is unlikely, and if it emerges it will have taken considerably more time than an elegant solution (which can be called the "poet's way") that may result from thoughtful reasoning.

Just such a case follows. Your students will enjoy it for it will show the weakness in their ways and open the door to correcting them in the future. It is also entertaining!

Given a chessboard and 32 dominos, each the exact size of two of the squares on the chessboard, can you show how 31 of these dominos can cover the chessboard, when a pair of diagonally opposite squares has been removed?

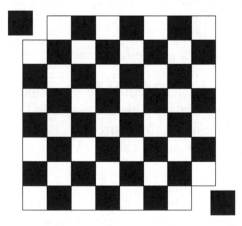

As soon as the question (above) is posed, students get busy trying various arrangements of square covering. This may be done with actual squares or with a graph grid drawn on paper and then shading adjacent squares two at a time. Before long, frustration begins to set in since no one is likely to be successful.

Here the issue is to go back to the question. First of all, the question does not say to do this square covering; it asks if it can be done. Yet, because of the way we have been trained, the question is often misread and interpreted as "do it." A bit of clever insight helps. Ask yourself the question: "When a domino tile is placed on the chessboard, what kind of squares are covered?" A black square and a white square must be covered by each domino placed on the chessboard. Are there an equal number of black and white squares on the truncated chessboard? No! There are two fewer black squares than white squares. Therefore, it is impossible to cover the truncated chessboard with the 31 domino tiles.

Asking the right questions and inspecting the question asked is an important aspect of being successful in mathematics. This unit shows the beauty of mathematical thinking at a very simple, yet profound, level.

3.2 Surprising Solution

Here is a very simple problem with an even simpler solution. Yet the solution most students will come up with is much more complicated. Why? Because they look at the problem in the psychologically traditional way. After you present the problem (without any warning of a surprise solution), have students work the problem in whatever way they wish. Do not try to force them to look for an elegant solution.

Try the problem yourself (don't look below at the solution) and see whether you fall into the "majority-solvers" group.

> **A single elimination (one loss and the team is eliminated) basketball tournament has 25 teams competing. How many games must be played until there is a single tournament champion?**

Typically, the majority-solvers will begin to simulate the tournament, by taking two groups of 12 teams, playing the first round, and thereby eliminating 12 teams (12 games have now been played). The remaining 13 teams play, say 6 against another 6, leaving 7 teams in the tournament (18 games have been played now). In the next round, of the 7 remaining teams, 3 can be eliminated (21 games have so far been played). The four remaining teams play, leaving 2 teams for the championship game (23 games have now been played). This championship game is the 24th game.

A much simpler way to solve this problem, one that most people do not naturally see, is to focus only on the losers and not on the winners as we have done above. We ask students the key question: "How many losers must there be in the tournament with 25 teams in order for there to be one winner?" The answer is simple: 24 losers. How many games must be played to get 24 losers? Naturally, 24. So there you have the answer, very simply done.

Now most people will ask themselves, "Why didn't I think of that?" The answer is, it was contrary to the type of training and experience we have had. Making youngsters aware of the strategy of looking at the problem from a different point of view may sometimes reap nice benefits, as was the case here. One never knows which strategy will work; just try one and see!

3.3 A Juicy Problem

When students are challenged by a problem, they often set it aside if it involves too much reading, for fear that the concentration required would be too exhausting to make the problem pleasurable. Although this problem does require a fair bit of reading, it is rather easy to explain to a class, and could even be dramatized. Once past the statement of the problem, it is very easy to understand, but quite difficult to solve by conventional means.

This is where the beauty of the problem comes in. The solution—as unexpected as it is—almost makes the problem trivial. That is, the problem and its conventional solution will not get much of an enthusiastic reaction from students, but after having struggled with a solution attempt, the novel approach we will present here will gain you much favor with the class.

So let's state the problem:

We have two 1-gallon bottles. One contains a quart of grape juice and the other, a quart of apple juice. We take a tablespoonful of grape juice and pour it into the apple juice. Then we take a

tablespoon of this new mixture (apple juice and grape juice) and pour it into the bottle of grape juice. Is there more grape juice in the apple juice bottle, or more apple juice in the grape juice bottle?

To solve the problem, we can figure this out in any of the usual ways—often referred to as "mixture problems"—or we can use some clever logical reasoning and look at the problem's solution as follows.

With the first "transport" of juice, there is only grape juice on the tablespoon. On the second "transport" of juice, there is as much apple juice on the spoon as there is grape juice in the "apple juice bottle." This may require students to think a bit, but most should "get it" soon.

The simplest solution to understand and the one that demonstrates a very powerful strategy is that of *using extremes*. We use this kind of reasoning in everyday life when we resort to the option: "Such and such would occur in a worst case scenario . . . ."

Let us now employ this strategy for the above problem. To do this, we will consider the tablespoonful quantity to be a bit larger. Clearly, the outcome of this problem is independent of the quantity transported. So we will use an *extremely* large quantity. We'll let this quantity actually be the *entire* 1 quart. That is, following the instructions given in the problem statement, we will take the entire amount (1 quart of grape juice) and pour it into the apple juice bottle. This mixture is now 50% apple juice and 50% grape juice. We then pour 1 quart of this mixture back into the grape juice bottle. The mixture is now the same in both bottles. Therefore, there is as much apple juice in the grape juice bottle as there is grape juice in the apple juice bottle!

We can consider another form of an extreme case, where the spoon doing the juice transporting has a zero quantity. In this case, the conclusion follows immediately: There is as much grape juice in the apple juice bottle as there is apple juice in the grape juice bottle, that is, zero!

Carefully presented, this solution can be very significant in the way students approach future mathematics problems and even how they may analyze everyday decision making.

3.4 Working Backward

There are many situations where a straightforward approach is by far not the best way to solve a problem. Students are rarely shown problems that can be best solved by working backward. A case in point is when a student is asked to prove a theorem deductively. The appropriate approach would be to work backward (analysis) from what is being asked to prove and then write it up in the forward order (synthesis) for presentation. This would make the geometric proofs that students are required to learn much simpler to do. Unfortunately, this is not often shown to students.

Reasoning in reverse order is also useful in everyday life as well as in mathematics. For example, if you want to see a movie that starts at 8:30 P.M., and you know you have certain things to do before you can be at the movie theater, you would be best off to begin at 8:30 P.M. and calculate backward to determine when to start getting ready to leave for the theater. You may figure that it will take you 30 minutes travel time, 1 hour for dinner, 15 minutes to get dressed, and 45 minutes to finish a task you are involved with. This would mean that you would begin to get ready for the theater at 6 P.M.

In mathematics, there are lots of examples where working backward is a truly rewarding way to lead you to an elegant solution. One of the best examples of this is a problem that may be a bit "off the beaten path," but certainly within reach of a good algebra student.

If the sum of two numbers is 2 and the product of the same two numbers is 3, find the sum of the reciprocals of the two numbers.

The usual reaction to this problem is to set up equations that reflect the situation described verbally. Most students would probably get:

$$x + y = 2 \quad \text{and} \quad xy = 3$$

The usual reaction to solving these equations simultaneously is to solve for y in the first equation to get $y = 2 - x$ and substitute this value for y in the second equation. This will certainly lead to a correct solution, but as you plow along, you will come to realize that this must be the "peasant's way" and not the "poet's way." When x and y are finally obtained, you will find them to be complex numbers and then you will have to find the reciprocals and add them.

Working backward, the clever alternative, requires that you ask the question: "Where will we end up with the solution?" Since the sum of the reciprocals is being sought, we must end up with $\frac{1}{x} + \frac{1}{y}$. Continuing in this spirit, we must ask: "What might this have come from?" One possibility is the sum of these fractions, namely, $\frac{x+y}{xy}$. A clever person might now realize that we have the solution to the problem staring us in the face. Remember the two original equations, $x + y = 2$ and $xy = 3$. They essentially give us the numerator value, 2, and the denominator value, 3. So the answer to the original question (problem) is $\frac{2}{3}$.

Be sure to properly dramatize the savings in time and effort to working backward. This illustration does it as well as any might.

3.5 Logical Thinking

When a problem is posed that at first looks a bit daunting, and then a solution is presented—one easily understood—we often wonder why we didn't think of that simple solution ourselves. It is exactly these problems that have a dramatic effect on the learner. Here is one such problem. You might try to actually simulate with your students the situation described.

> **On a shelf in Barbara's basement, there are three boxes. One con-
> tains only nickels, one contains only dimes, and one contains a
> mixture of nickels and dimes. The three labels, "Nickels," "Dimes,"
> and "Mixed," fell off and were all put back on the wrong boxes.
> Without looking, Barbara can select one coin from one of the mis-
> labeled boxes and then correctly label all three boxes. From which
> box should Barbara select the coin?**

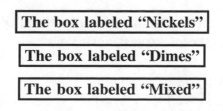

Students may reason that the "symmetry" of the problem situation dictates that whatever we can say about the box mislabeled "Nickels" could just as well have been said about the box mislabeled "Dimes." Thus, if Barbara chooses a coin from either of these boxes, the results would be the same. This eliminates choices A and B. They should, therefore, concentrate their investigations on what happens if we choose from the box mislabeled "Mixed."

Suppose Barbara selects a nickel from the mixed box. Since this box is mislabeled, it cannot be the mixed box and must be, in reality, the nickel box. Since the box marked dimes cannot really be dimes, it must be the mixed box. This leaves the third box to be the dime box.

Stress with your students the importance of the logical reasoning used. Perhaps you can have them recap the argument for the sake of better understanding it.

3.6 It's Just How You Organize the Data

Here is a problem that will draw just a bit on the students' facility with algebra (very elementary!). When the problem is presented, the symmetry makes it look disarmingly simple, but just wait.

Here is the problem:

Find the numerical value of the following expression:

$$\left(1-\frac{1}{4}\right)\left(1-\frac{1}{9}\right)\left(1-\frac{1}{16}\right)\left(1-\frac{1}{25}\right)\cdots\left(1-\frac{1}{225}\right)$$

The usual first attempt by a student faced with this problem is to simplify each of the 15 parentheses expressions to get:

$$\left(\frac{3}{4}\right)\left(\frac{8}{9}\right)\left(\frac{15}{16}\right)\left(\frac{24}{25}\right)\cdots\left(\frac{224}{225}\right)$$

Typically, students try to change each fraction to a decimal (with a calculator) and multiply the results (again with their calculators). This is obviously a very cumbersome calculation.

An alternative method would be to organize the data in a different way. This will permit the students to look at the problem from a different point of view, hoping to see some sort of pattern that will enable them to simplify their work.

$$\left(1^2 - \frac{1}{2^2}\right)\left(1^2 - \frac{1}{3^2}\right)\left(1^2 - \frac{1}{4^2}\right)\left(1^2 - \frac{1}{5^2}\right)\cdots\left(1^2 - \frac{1}{15^2}\right)$$

They can now factor each parenthetical expression as the difference of two perfect squares, which yields

$$\left(1 - \frac{1}{2}\right)\left(1 + \frac{1}{2}\right)\left(1 - \frac{1}{3}\right)\left(1 + \frac{1}{3}\right)\left(1 - \frac{1}{4}\right)\left(1 + \frac{1}{4}\right)\left(1 - \frac{1}{5}\right)$$
$$\times \left(1 + \frac{1}{5}\right)\cdots\left(1 - \frac{1}{15}\right)\left(1 + \frac{1}{15}\right)$$

Now have students do the subtraction or addition within each pair of parentheses to get

$$\left(\frac{1}{2}\right)\left(\frac{3}{2}\right)\left(\frac{2}{3}\right)\left(\frac{4}{3}\right)\left(\frac{3}{4}\right)\left(\frac{5}{4}\right)\left(\frac{4}{5}\right)\left(\frac{6}{5}\right)\cdots\left(\frac{13}{14}\right)\left(\frac{15}{14}\right)\left(\frac{14}{15}\right)\left(\frac{16}{15}\right)$$

A pattern is now evident, and they may "cancel" throughout the expression. As a result, they are left with

$$\left(\frac{1}{2}\right)\left(\frac{16}{15}\right) = \frac{8}{15}$$

Students will probably appreciate the ease with which this seemingly "impossible" problem was solved.

3.7 Focusing on the Right Information

When faced with a problem with various bits of information, the trick is not to be distracted from the necessary information. This point is perhaps best made with the following problem.

To extend the amount of orange juice in a 16-ounce bottle, Alice decides upon the following procedure:

On the *first* day, she will drink only 1 ounce of the orange juice and then fill the bottle with water.

On the *second* day, she will drink 2 ounces of the mixture and then again fill the bottle with water.

On the *third* day, she will drink 3 ounces of the mixture and again fill the bottle with water.

She will continue this procedure for succeeding days until she empties the bottle by drinking 16 ounces of mixture on the 16th day. How many ounces of water will Alice drink altogether?

It is very easy for a student to get bogged down with a problem like this one. Many students will begin to make a table showing the amount of orange juice and water in the bottle on each day and attempt to compute the proportional amounts of each type of liquid Alice drinks on any given day. We could more easily resolve the problem by examining it from another point of view, namely, "How much water does Alice add to the mixture each day?" Don't get bogged down with the quantity of orange juice; this is merely a distractor in this problem situation. Since she eventually empties the bottle (on the 16th day), and it held no water to begin with, she must have consumed all the water that was put into the bottle. So we merely calculate the amount of water Alice added each time.

On the first day, Alice added 1 ounce of water.
On the second day, she added 2 ounces of water.
On the third day, she added 3 ounces of water.
On the 15th day, she added 15 ounces of water. (You should ask your students why no water was added on the 16th day.)

Therefore, the number of ounces of water Alice consumed was

$$1 + 2 + 3 + 4 + 5 + 6 + 7 + 8 + 9 + 10 + 11 + 12 + 13 + 14 + 15$$
$$= 120 \text{ ounces}$$

While this solution is indeed valid, a slightly simpler analogous problem to consider would be to find out how much liquid Alice drank altogether and then simply deduct the amount of orange juice, namely, 16 ounces. Thus,

$$1 + 2 + 3 + 4 + 5 + 6 + 7 + 8 + 9 + 10 + 11 + 12 + 13 + 14 + 15$$
$$+ 16 - 16 = 120$$

Alice consumed 136 ounces of liquid, of which 16 ounces was orange juice and the rest, 120 ounces, must have been water.

3.8 The Pigeonhole Principle

One of the famous (although often neglected in the instructional program) problem-solving techniques is to consider the pigeonhole principle. In its simplest form, the pigeonhole principle states that *if you have $k+1$ objects that must be put into k holes, then there will be at least one hole with 2 or more objects in it.*

Here is one illustration of the pigeonhole principle at work. Present your students with this problem to see how they will approach it.

There are 50 teachers' letterboxes in the school's general office. One day the letter carrier delivers 151 pieces of mail for the teachers. After all the letters have been distributed, one mailbox has more letters than any other mailbox. What is the smallest number of letters it can have?

Students have a tendency to "fumble around" aimlessly with this sort of problem, usually not knowing where to start. Sometimes, guess and test may work here. However, the advisable approach for a problem of this sort is to consider extremes. Naturally, it is possible for one teacher to get all the delivered mail, but this is not *guaranteed*.

To best assess this situation, we shall consider the extreme case, where the mail is as evenly distributed as possible. This would have each teacher receiving three pieces of mail with the exception of one teacher, who would have to receive the 151st piece of mail. Therefore, the least number of letters that the box with the most letters received is 4.

By the pigeonhole principle, there were 50 3-packs of letters for the 50 boxes. The 151st letter had to be placed into one of those 50 boxes. Your students may want to try other problems that use the pigeonhole principle.

3.9 The Flight of the Bumblebee

Problem solving is not only done to solve the problem at hand; it is also provided to present various types of problems and, perhaps more important, various procedures for solution. It is from these types of solutions that students really learn problem solving, since one of the most useful techniques in approaching a problem to be solved is to ask yourself: "Have I ever encountered such a problem before?" With this in mind, a problem with a very useful "lesson" is presented here. Do not let your students be deterred by the relatively lengthy reading required to get through the problem. They will be delighted with the unexpected simplicity of its solution.

Two trains, serving the Chicago to New York route, a distance of 800 miles, start toward each other at the same time (along the same tracks). One train is traveling uniformly at 60 miles per hour, and the other at 40 miles per hour. At the same time, a bumblebee begins to fly from the front of one of the trains, at a speed of 80 miles per hour, toward the oncoming train. After touching the front of this second train, the bumblebee reverses direction and flies toward the first train (still at the same speed of 80 miles per hour). The bumblebee continues this back-and-forth flying until the two trains collide, crushing the bumblebee. How many miles did the bumblebee fly before its demise?

Students will be naturally drawn to find the individual distances that the bumblebee traveled. An immediate reaction by many students is to set up an equation based on the relationship: "rate times time equals distance." However, this back-and-forth path is rather difficult to determine, requiring considerable calculation. Just the notion of having to do this will cause frustration among the students. Do not allow this frustration to set in. Even if they were able to determine each part of the bumblebee's flight, it is still very difficult to solve the problem in this way.

A much more elegant approach would be to solve a simpler analogous problem (one might also say we are looking at the problem from a different point of view). We seek to find the distance the bumblebee traveled. If we knew the time the bumblebee traveled, we could determine the bumblebee's distance because we already know the speed of the bumblebee. Again, have your students realize that having two parts of the equation "rate × time = distance" will provide the third part. So having the time and the speed will yield the distance traveled, albeit in various directions.

The time the bumblebee traveled can be easily calculated, since it traveled the entire time the two trains were traveling toward each other (until they collided). To determine the time, t, the trains traveled, we set up an equation as follows: The distance of the first train is $60t$ and the distance of the second train is $40t$. The total distance the two trains traveled is 800 miles. Therefore, $60t + 40t = 800$, so $t = 8$ hours, which is also the time the bumblebee traveled. We can now find the distance the bumblebee traveled, using the relationship, rate × time = distance, which gives us $(8)(80) = 640$ miles.

It is important to stress to students how to avoid falling into the trap of always trying to do what the problem calls for directly. Sometimes a more circuitous method is much more efficient. Lots can be learned from this solution. It must be emphasized to your class. You see, dramatic solutions are often more useful than traditional solutions, since they give students an opportunity "to think outside of the box."

3.10 Relating Concentric Circles

More important than the problem itself is the solution method that will be used. More about that later (so as not to spoil the surprise awaiting the class).

Consider the following problem:

Two concentric circles are 10 units apart, as shown below. What is the difference between the circumferences of the circles?

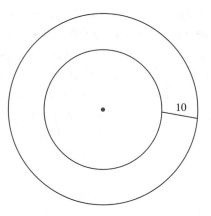

The traditional, straightforward method for solving this problem is to find the diameters of the two circles, find the circumference of each circle, and then find their difference. Since the lengths of the diameters are not given, the problem is a bit more complicated than usual. Let d represent the diameter of the smaller circle. Then $d + 20$ is the diameter of the larger circle. The circumferences of the two circles will then be πd and $\pi(d + 20)$, respectively. Their difference is $\pi(d + 20) - \pi d = 20\pi$.

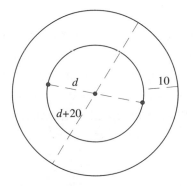

A more elegant, and vastly more dramatic, procedure would be to use an extreme case. To do this, we will let the smaller of the two circles become smaller and smaller until it reaches an "extreme smallness" and becomes a "point." In this case, it would become the center of the larger circle. The distance between the two circles now becomes simply the radius of the larger circle. The difference between the lengths of the circumferences of the two circles at the start now becomes merely the circumference of the larger circle,* or 20π.

Although both procedures yield the same answer, notice how much more work is used for the traditional solution by actually taking the difference of the lengths of the circumferences of the two circles, and how using the idea of considering an extreme situation (without compromising any generality) we reduce the problem to something trivial. Thus, here the beauty of mathematics is manifested in the procedure by which we approach a problem. Clearly, this point needs to be emphasized for the students.

3.11 Don't Overlook the Obvious

Here is a very entertaining problem that often elicits feelings of self-disappointment when the solution is exposed.

It is a problem that is certainly solvable when a student has been shown the Pythagorean theorem. As a matter of fact, that knowledge often gets in the way of an elegant solution. Have the students consider the following problem:

> **The point P is any point on the circle with center O. Perpendicular lines are drawn from P to perpendicular diameters, $\overline{AB}$ and $\overline{CD}$, meeting them at points F and E, respectively. If the diameter of the circle is 8, what is the length of $\overline{EF}$?**

---

* Since the big circle's circumference minus the smaller circle's circumference, which is now 0, is the big circle's circumference.

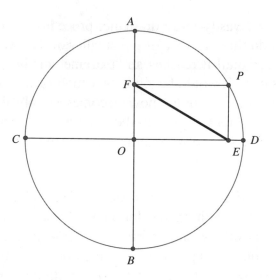

From the training we give students, they would most likely look to apply the Pythagorean theorem and find that there is no "neat" way to use it. Stepping back from the problem and looking at it in a refreshed way will expose the fact that the quadrilateral *PFOE* is a rectangle (it was given to have three right angles). Since the diagonals of a rectangle are equal in length, *FE* must equal *PO*, which is the radius of the circle and equals half the diameter, or 4.

Another way to look at the problem is to take the location of *P* at a more convenient point, say at point *A*. In that case, $\overline{FE}$ would coincide with $\overline{AO}$, which is the radius of the circle.

With either solution, the student is caught off guard. This is not only entertaining but also a good illustration for future use.

3.12 Deceptively Difficult (Easy)

Here is a problem that looks very simple and is not. It has baffled entire high school mathematics departments! Yet once the solution is shown, it becomes quite simple. The result is that you are disappointed in not having seen the solution right from the start. So here it is. Try it without looking at the second diagram. It will give away the solution. You might have students try this one at home so that they have ample time to ponder the solution.

> **In the figure shown below, point E lies on $\overline{AB}$ and point C lies on $\overline{FG}$. The area of parallelogram $ABCD = 20$ square units. Find the area of parallelogram $EFGD$.**

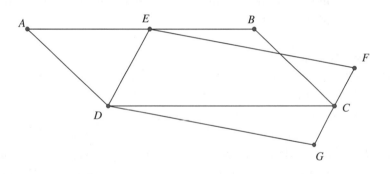

Although the solution is not one that would occur to many students at first thought, the problem can be readily solved using only the tools found in a high school geometry course. Begin by drawing $\overline{EC}$ as in the figure below.

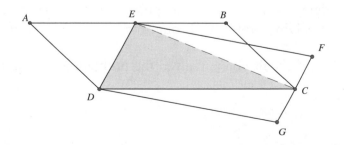

Since triangle *EDC* and parallelogram *ABCD* share a common base ($\overline{DC}$) and a common altitude (a perpendicular from *E* to $\overline{DC}$), the area of triangle *EDC* is equal to one-half the area of parallelogram *ABCD*.

Similarly, since triangle *EDC* and parallelogram *EFGD* share the same base ($\overline{ED}$) and the same altitude to that base (a perpendicular from *C* to $\overline{ED}$), the area of triangle *EDC* equals one-half the area of parallelogram *EFGD*.

Now, since the area of parallelogram *ABCD* and the area of parallelogram *EFGD* are both equal to twice the area of triangle *EDC*, the areas of the two parallelograms must be equal. Thus, the area of parallelogram *EFGD* equals 20 square units.

Although the solution method that we have just shown is not often used, it is effective and efficient.

Nevertheless, this problem can be solved quite elegantly by solving a simpler analogous problem (without loss of generality). Recall that the original given conditions were that the two parallelograms had to have a common vertex (*D*), and a vertex of one had to be on the side of the other as shown with points *E* and *C*. Now, let us suppose that *C* coincided with *G*, and *E* coincided with *A*. This satisfies the given condition of the original problem and makes the two parallelograms coincide. Thus, the area of parallelogram $EFGD = 20$ square units.

We could also look at this last solution as one of using extremes. That is, we might consider point *E* on $\overline{AB}$, yet placed at an extreme, such as on point *A*. Similarly, we could place *C* on *G* and satisfy all the conditions of the original problem. Thus, the problem is trivial, in that the two parallelograms coincide. This point is one of the more neglected techniques for solving problems. It ought to be emphasized now.

Remember how difficult you perceived the problem at the start?

3.13 The Worst Case Scenario

Reasoning with extremes is a particularly useful strategy to solve some problems. It can also be seen as a "worst case scenario" strategy. The best way to appreciate this kind of thinking is through example. So let's begin to appreciate some really nice reasoning strategies.

> **In a drawer, there are 8 blue socks, 6 green socks, and 12 black socks. What is the minimum number of socks Henry must take from the drawer, without looking, to be certain that he has two socks of the same color?**

The phrase "... *certain* ... two socks of the same color" is the key to the problem. The problem does not specify which color, so any of the three would be correct. To solve this problem, have your students reason from a "worst case scenario." Henry picks one blue sock, one green sock, and then one black sock. He now has one of each color, but no matching pair. (True, he might have picked a pair on his first two selections, but the problem calls for "certain.") Notice that as soon as he picks the fourth sock, he must have a pair of the same color.

Consider a second problem:

> **In a drawer, there are 8 blue socks, 6 green socks, and 12 black socks. What is the minimum number of socks that Evelyn must take from the drawer, without looking, to be certain that she has two black socks?**

Although this problem appears to be similar to the previous one, there is one important difference. In this problem, a specific color has been specified. Thus, it is a pair of black socks that we must guarantee being selected. Again, let's use deductive reasoning and construct the "worst case scenario." Suppose Evelyn first picks all of the blue socks (8). Next she picks all of the green socks (6). Still not one black sock has been chosen. She now has 14 socks in all, but none of them is black. However, the next two socks she picks must be black, since that is the only color remaining. To be certain of picking two black socks, Evelyn must select $8 + 6 + 2 = 16$ socks in all. Have students create similar problems and present solutions.

4 Algebraic Entertainments

It is not easy to imagine algebra as a form of entertainment. Students often see algebra as a series of rules to follow—a language of mathematics that has to be learned. Well, in this chapter algebra is used to make some sense of mathematical phenomena, for example, in the behavior of numbers. Arithmetic shortcuts are explored, some unusual number relationships are explained, and some beautiful patterns in mathematics are exploited. All of this makes for a rather refreshing use of algebra, which usually manifests itself in the form of tedious exercises that often do not impress students as being particularly useful. When algebra is used in the school setting, it is used to solve rather routine problems. Here we use algebra to explore other branches of mathematics. For example, the unit on Pythagorean triples gives some very deep insight into these popular triples.

Show your students how algebra can be used to shed new light on and a deeper appreciation for mathematical relationships. It will entertain them while demonstrating the beauty of algebraic processes.

4.1 Using Algebra to Establish Arithmetic Shortcuts

Suppose you needed to calculate $36^2 - 35^2$. This is rather simple to do with a calculator. But suppose that calculators were not readily available. Ask your students how they would get the answer in a simple way.

We could **employ factoring the difference of two squares**: $x^2 - y^2 = (x - y)(x + y)$. That would give us

$$36^2 - 35^2 = (36 - 35)(36 + 35) = (1)(71) = 71$$

Your students will be quite amazed at how this common form of factoring has reduced this multiplication problem to a trivial situation.

The **distributive property** is always useful, as for multiplying $8 \cdot 67$. Replacing 67 with $(70 - 3)$ allows us to rewrite the multiplication as $8(70 - 3) = 8(70) - 8(3) = 560 - 24 = 536$.

Or to multiply $36 \cdot 14$, we can rewrite this as $36(10 + 4) = 36(10) + 36(4) = 360 + 144 = 504$. In the absence of a calculator, this is a much more efficient way to look at multiplication.

Multiplying two numbers with a difference of 4 can also be simply done by first inspecting the situation in general terms (i.e., algebraically):

The two numbers can be $(x + 2)$ and $(x - 2)$. These have a difference of 4. Their product is $(x + 2)(x - 2) = x^2 - 4$. Thus, we must find the average of the two numbers, x, and square it and subtract 4.

For example, to use this notion to multiply 67 by 71, we find the average, 69. Then square 69 to get 4,761 and subtract 4 to get 4,757. It may not always be easier to do the multiplication, but it will give the students a sense of "usefulness" of some of the algebra they know.

Multiplying two consecutive numbers uses the property $x(x + 1) = x^2 + x$. This applied to $23 \cdot 24 = 23^2 + 23 = 529 + 23 = 552$ provides a refreshing alternative to the usual multiplication algorithm. Again, it must be stressed that this is not a replacement for the calculator—something students would clearly not accept.

By this time, students might be motivated to discover or establish their own shortcut algorithms. It ought to be done for fun—though not a calculator replacement!

4.2 The Mysterious Number 22

At first, this unit will enchant your students and then (if properly presented) have them wonder why the result is what it is. This is a wonderful opportunity to show your students the usefulness of algebra, for it will be through algebra that their curiosity will be quenched.

Have the students work individually with the following oral instructions:

> **Select any three-digit number with all digits different from one another. Write all possible two-digit numbers that can be formed from the three-digits selected earlier. Then divide their sum by the sum of the digits in the original three-digit number.**

Students should *all* get the same answer, 22. There ought to be a big resulting "Wow!"

For example, consider the three-digit number 365. Take the sum of all the possible two-digit numbers that can be formed from these three digits: $36 + 35 + 63 + 53 + 65 + 56 = 308$. The sum of the digits of the original number is $3 + 6 + 5 = 14$. Then $\frac{308}{14} = 22$.

To analyze this unusual result, we will begin with a general representation of the number: $100x + 10y + z$.

We now take the sum of all the two-digit numbers taken from the three digits:

$$(10x+y)+(10y+x)+(10x+z)+(10z+x)+(10y+z)+(10z+y)$$
$$=10(2x+2y+2z)+(2x+2y+2z)$$
$$=11(2x+2y+2z)$$
$$=22(x+y+z)$$

which, when divided by the sum of the digits, $(x+y+z)$, is 22.

These illustrations show the value of algebra in explaining simple arithmetic phenomena.

4.3 Justifying an Oddity

Here is a fun activity that can be presented in a number of different ways. The best suited method should be selected by the classroom teacher. The justification uses simple algebra, but the fun is in the oddity. Have your students consider this very unusual relationship.

Any two-digit number ending in 9 can be expressed as the sum of the product of the digits and the sum of the digits.

More simply stated:

Any two-digit number ending in 9
$$= [\text{product of digits}] + [\text{sum of digits}]$$

One of the real advantages of algebra is the facility with which, through its use, we can justify many mathematical applications. Why is it possible to represent a number ending in a 9 in the following way?

$$9 = (0 \cdot 9) + (0 + 9)$$
$$19 = (1 \cdot 9) + (1 + 9)$$
$$29 = (2 \cdot 9) + (2 + 9)$$
$$39 = (3 \cdot 9) + (3 + 9)$$

$$49 = (4 \cdot 9) + (4 + 9)$$
$$59 = (5 \cdot 9) + (5 + 9)$$
$$69 = (6 \cdot 9) + (6 + 9)$$
$$79 = (7 \cdot 9) + (7 + 9)$$
$$89 = (8 \cdot 9) + (8 + 9)$$
$$99 = (9 \cdot 9) + (9 + 9)$$

Students will certainly be turned on by this neat pattern of calculation. You must be careful not to allow this pattern to be an end in itself, but rather a means to an end, namely, a consideration of why this actually works.

Let's use algebra to clear up this very strange result, established above by example. Point out to students that we will be using algebra to help us understand this mathematical quirk.

We typically represent a two-digit number as $10t + u$, where t represents the tens digit and u represents the units digit. Then the sum of the digits is $t + u$ and the product of the digits is tu.

The number meeting the above conditions $= 10t + u$
$$= (tu) + (t + u)$$
$$10t = tu + t$$
$$9t = tu$$
$$u = 9 \qquad (\text{for } t \neq 0^*)$$

This discussion should evoke a curiosity among students about numbers with more than two digits. For example:

$$109 = (10 \cdot 9) + (10 + 9)$$
$$119 = (11 \cdot 9) + (11 + 9)$$
$$129 = (12 \cdot 9) + (12 + 9)$$

Here the digits to the left of the 9 are considered as a number and treated just as we treated the tens digit above. The results are the same.

This can be extended to any number of digits as long as the units digit is a 9.

---

* In this case, the rule also holds if $t = 0$.

4.4 Using Algebra for Number Theory

There are lots of unusual number patterns and relationships. Some cannot be proved (as yet!), such as the famous Goldbach conjecture,* which states that *every even number greater than 2 can be expressed as the sum of two prime numbers.* He also asserted that *every odd number greater than 5 can be expressed as the sum of three primes.*

Have students experiment with a calculator and discover the following conjecture on their own:

> **One plus the sum of the squares of any three consecutive odd numbers is always divisible by 12.**

The beauty and the instructional benefit of this are manifested in the simplicity of the procedure used to prove this statement. First, establish a way to represent an odd and an even number. For any integer n, $2n$ will always be *even* and $2n + 1$ must then be *odd*.

We begin by letting $2n + 1$ be the middle number of the three consecutive odd numbers under consideration. Then $[2n + 1] - 2 = 2n - 1$ is the next smaller odd number and $[2n + 1] + 2 = 2n + 3$ is the next larger odd number. We are now ready to represent the relationship we are seeking to prove.

$$(2n - 1)^2 + (2n + 1)^2 + (2n + 3)^2 + 1 = 12n^2 + 12n + 12$$
$$= 12(n^2 + n + 1) = 12M$$

where M represents some integer.**

We can then conclude that this sum of squares plus 1 is always divisible by 12. This should be merely a springboard to other similar algebraic investigations into number theory.

---

* Named for Christian Goldbach (1690–1764) and transmitted in a letter to the famous mathematician Leonhard Euler in 1742.

** Since n is an integer, n^2 is also an integer, so the sum $n^2 + n + 1$ must also be an integer. Represent that integer as M.

4.5 Finding Patterns Among Figurate Numbers

We should recall that figurate numbers are those that can be represented by dots in polygonal fashion, as shown below. There are lots of very surprising relationships that occur with these numbers. We shall present just a few of these here, with the hope that your students will want to explore further and find some that they can claim as "their own."

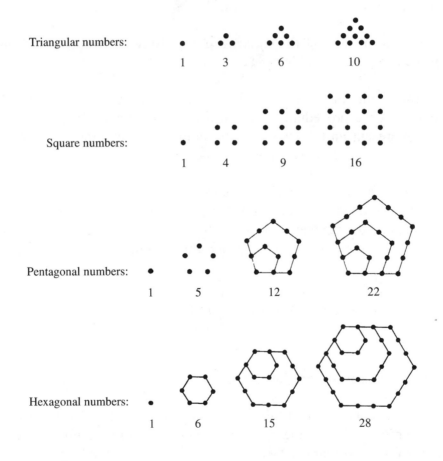

Consider the following table:

	Triangular numbers	Square numbers	Pentagonal numbers	Hexagonal numbers
1	1	1	1	1
2	3	4	5	6
3	6	9	12	15
4	10	16	22	28
5	15	25	35	45
6	21	36	51	66
7	28	49	70	91
8	36	64	92	120
9	45	81	117	153
10	55	100	145	190
11	66	121	176	231
12	78	144	210	276
13	91	169	247	325
14	105	196	287	378
15	120	225	330	435
16	136	256	376	496
17	153	289	425	561
18	171	324	477	630
19	190	361	532	703
20	210	400	590	780
n	$\dfrac{n(n+1)^*}{2}$	$\dfrac{n(2n-0)}{2} = n^2$	$\dfrac{n(3n-1)}{2}$	$\dfrac{n(4n-2)}{2}$

Based on the pattern developing across the nth row, have your students determine what the general forms of the heptagonal, octagonal, decagonal, etc., numbers are.

They are

$$\frac{n(5n-3)}{2}, \quad \frac{n(6n-4)}{2}, \quad \frac{n(7n-5)}{2}, \ldots$$

---

* This comes from $\dfrac{n(1n-(-1))}{2} = \dfrac{n(n+1)}{2}$.

In Unit 1.17, we introduced *oblong numbers*, which are the product of two consecutive natural numbers in the form $n(n + 1)$,

$$1 \cdot 2 = 2$$
$$2 \cdot 3 = 6$$
$$3 \cdot 4 = 12$$
$$4 \cdot 5 = 20$$
$$5 \cdot 6 = 30$$
$$\vdots$$

You now have the option of having your students try to justify the following relationships by using algebra or by convincing themselves through examples that they are, in fact, true. Remember, only a general proof will show they hold for all cases.

An oblong number can be expressed as the sum of consecutive even integers, beginning with 2:

$$2 + 4 + 6 + 8 = 20$$

An oblong number is twice a triangular number:

$$15 \cdot 2 = 30$$

The sum of two consecutive squares and the square of the oblong between them is a square*:

$$9 + 16 + 12^2 = 169 = 13^2$$

---

* This is a tricky one so it is provided for you here. Represent the statement algebraically as $n^2 + (n + 1)^2 + [n(n + 1)]^2$. Expanding and collecting like terms gives us

$$n^2 + n^2 + 2n + 1 + (n^2 + n)^2 = 2n^2 + 2n + 1 + n^4 + 2n^3 + n^2$$
$$= n^4 + 2n^3 + 3n^2 + 2n + 1 = (n^2 + n + 1)^2$$

Obviously, we have a square!

The sum of two consecutive oblong numbers and twice the square between them is a square:

$$12 + 20 + 2 \cdot 16 = 64 = 8^2$$

The sum of an oblong number and the next square is a triangular number:

$$20 + 25 = 45$$

The sum of a square number and the next oblong number is a triangular number:

$$25 + 30 = 55$$

The sum of a number and the square of that number is an oblong number:

$$9 + 81 = 90$$

Here are some relationships to have your students try to establish. They might try to convince themselves that they are true using some specific examples, and then do them algebraically.

- Every odd square number is the sum of eight times a triangular number and 1.
- Every pentagonal number is the sum of three triangular numbers.
- Hexagonal numbers are equal to the odd-numbered triangular numbers.

Students ought to be encouraged to find other patterns and then prove that they are true—algebraically.

4.6 Using a Pattern to Find the Sum of a Series

Faced with summing a series, most students would just plow right into the problem, using whatever means they learned to sum series. If this did not look promising, many would just begin to add the terms. Very inelegant!

Let's look at a situation that lends itself to a few nifty alternatives. Consider the problem of finding the sum of the following series:

$$\frac{1}{1\cdot 2}+\frac{1}{2\cdot 3}+\frac{1}{3\cdot 4}+\cdots+\frac{1}{49\cdot 50}$$

One way to begin is to see if there is any visible pattern.

$$\frac{1}{1\cdot 2}=\frac{1}{2}$$

$$\frac{1}{1\cdot 2}+\frac{1}{2\cdot 3}=\frac{2}{3}$$

$$\frac{1}{1\cdot 2}+\frac{1}{2\cdot 3}+\frac{1}{3\cdot 4}=\frac{3}{4}$$

$$\frac{1}{1\cdot 2}+\frac{1}{2\cdot 3}+\frac{1}{3\cdot 4}+\frac{1}{4\cdot 5}=\frac{4}{5}$$

From this pattern, we guess the following pattern:

$$\frac{1}{1\cdot 2}+\frac{1}{2\cdot 3}+\frac{1}{3\cdot 4}+\frac{1}{4\cdot 5}+\cdots+\frac{1}{49\cdot 50}=\frac{49}{50}$$

Another pattern for this series can be obtained by representing each fraction in the series as a difference in the following way:

$$\frac{1}{1\cdot 2}=\frac{1}{1}-\frac{1}{2}$$

$$\frac{1}{2\cdot 3}=\frac{1}{2}-\frac{1}{3}$$

$$\frac{1}{3 \cdot 4} = \frac{1}{3} - \frac{1}{4}$$

$$\vdots$$

$$\frac{1}{49 \cdot 50} = \frac{1}{49} - \frac{1}{50}$$

Adding these equations, the left-hand side gives us our sought-after sum, and on the right-hand side almost all the fractions drop out, leaving $\frac{1}{1} - \frac{1}{50} = \frac{49}{50}$.

These very surprising illustrations of useful patterns will get a reaction from your students, "Oh, I would never be able to do this on my own," but this should be an unacceptable response, for "practice makes perfect"!

4.7 Geometric View of Algebra

There are times when the rudiments of algebra can be made concrete by showing that they also "make sense" from a geometric point of view. More important, it is fun to show the algebraic identities geometrically. Students will also want to try some for themselves after you have shown them a few of these.

The concept that an algebraic identity can be demonstrated geometrically by using areas to show, for example, $(a + b)^2 = a^2 + 2ab + b^2$.

To begin, have students draw a square of side length $(a + b)$. The square should then be partitioned into various squares and rectangles, as shown in Figure 4.1. The lengths of the various sides are appropriately labeled.

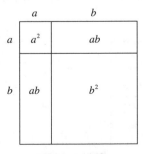

Figure 4.1

Students can easily determine the area of each region. Since the area of the large square equals the sum of the areas of the four quadrilaterals into which it was partitioned, students should get

$$(a+b)^2 = a^2 + ab + ab + b^2 = a^2 + 2ab + b^2$$

A more rigorous proof can be found in Euclid's *Elements*, Proposition 4, Book 11.

Next, illustrate geometrically the identity $a(b+c) = ab + ac$. To begin, have students draw a rectangle whose adjacent sides are of lengths a and $(b+c)$. The rectangle should then be partitioned into smaller rectangles, as shown in Figure 4.2. The lengths of these sides are also labeled.

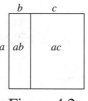

Figure 4.2

Students can easily determine the area of each region. Elicit from students that since the area of the large rectangle equals the sum of the areas of the two quadrilaterals into which it was partitioned, the diagram illustrates $a(b+c) = ab + ac$.

Have students consider the identity $(a+b)(c+d) = ac + ad + bc + bd$.

Guide students to draw the appropriate rectangle with side lengths $(a+b)$ and $(c+d)$. The rectangle should be partitioned into smaller rectangles, as shown in Figure 4.3. The lengths of sides and areas of regions have been

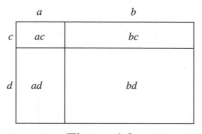

Figure 4.3

labeled. As in the other cases, the area of the large rectangle equals the sum of the areas of the four quadrilaterals into which it was partitioned.

The diagram (Figure 4.3) illustrates the identity $(a + b)(c + d) = ac + ad + bc + bd$.

Explain to students that the method of application of areas can be used to prove most algebraic identities. The difficulty will lie in their choice of dimensions for the quadrilateral and the partitions made.

After students feel comfortable using areas to represent algebraic identities, have them consider the Pythagorean relationship, $a^2 + b^2 = c^2$. Although this is not an identity, the application of areas is still appropriate. Have students draw a square of side length $(a + b)$. Show students how to partition this square into four congruent triangles and a square, as shown in Figure 4.4. The lengths of the sides have been labeled.

The diagram (Figure 4.4) illustrates:

1. Area $DEFG = 4(\text{Area} \triangle GNM) + \text{Area } KLMN$.
2. Therefore, $(a + b)^2 = 4(\frac{1}{2}ab) + c^2$.
3. If we now substitute the identity for $(a+b)^2$, which was proved above, we obtain $a^2 + 2ab + b^2 = 2ab + c^2$.

Then clearly $a^2 + b^2 = c^2$, which is, of course, the Pythagorean theorem.

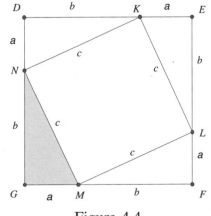

Figure 4.4

4.8 Some Algebra of the Golden Section

When we talk about the beauty of mathematics, we tend to think of the most beautiful rectangle. This rectangle, often called the Golden Rectangle, has been shown by psychologists to be the most esthetically pleasing rectangle. We treat it in Unit 5.11. Now we will look at this Golden Section from the algebraic point of view.

Begin by having students recall the Golden Ratio:

$$\frac{1-x}{x} = \frac{x}{1}$$

This gives us

$$x^2 + x - 1 = 0 \qquad \text{and} \qquad x = \frac{\sqrt{5}-1}{2}, \qquad \text{for positive } x.$$

We let

$$\frac{\sqrt{5}-1}{2} = \frac{1}{\phi}$$

Not only does $\phi \cdot \frac{1}{\phi} = 1$ (obviously!), but $\phi - \frac{1}{\phi} = 1$.

This is the only number for which this is true.

Your students may want to verify this.*

---

* Here is the result derived.
Since

$$\frac{1}{\phi} = \frac{\sqrt{5}-1}{2}$$

then

$$\phi = \frac{2}{\sqrt{5}-1} \cdot \frac{\sqrt{5}+1}{\sqrt{5}+1} = \frac{\sqrt{5}+1}{2}$$

and

$$\phi - \frac{1}{\phi} = \frac{\sqrt{5}+1}{2} - \frac{\sqrt{5}-1}{2} = 1$$

By the way, students may want to know what value ϕ has. They can easily determine it with the help of a calculator:

$$\phi = 1.6180339887498948482045868343656381177203091798057 6\ldots$$

and

$$\frac{1}{\phi} = 0.6180339887498948482045868343656381177203091798057 6\ldots$$

There are lots of other interesting features of ϕ. Your students ought to be guided to develop some after you give them the proper hints. They might want to show that this infinite continued fraction has the value ϕ.

$$\phi = 1 + \cfrac{1}{1 + \cfrac{1}{1 + \cfrac{1}{1 + \cfrac{1}{1 + \cfrac{1}{1 + \cfrac{1}{1 + \cdots}}}}}}$$

To do this, students ought to realize that nothing is lost by truncating the continued fraction at the first numerator. This will give them the following:

$$\phi = 1 + \frac{1}{\phi}$$

which yields the Golden Ratio.

Another curious relationship is

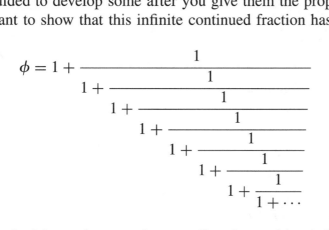

$$\phi = \sqrt{1 + \sqrt{1 + \sqrt{1 + \sqrt{1 + \sqrt{1 + \sqrt{1 + \sqrt{1 + \sqrt{1 + \cdots}}}}}}}}$$

Each of these is easily verifiable and can be done with a similar technique. We shall do the second one here and leave the first one to be justified by your students.

$$x = \sqrt{1 + \sqrt{1 + \sqrt{1 + \sqrt{1 + \sqrt{1 + \sqrt{1 + \sqrt{1 + \sqrt{1 + \cdots}}}}}}}}$$

$$x^2 = 1 + \sqrt{1 + \sqrt{1 + \sqrt{1 + \sqrt{1 + \sqrt{1 + \sqrt{1 + \sqrt{1 + \cdots}}}}}}}$$

$$x^2 = 1 + x$$

$$x = \phi \qquad \text{from the definition of } \phi$$

It is fascinating to observe what happens when we find the powers of ϕ.

$$\phi^2 = \left(\frac{\sqrt{5} + 1}{2} \right)^2 = \frac{\sqrt{5} + 3}{2} = \frac{\sqrt{5} + 1}{2} + 1 = \phi + 1$$

$$\phi^3 = \phi \cdot \phi^2 = \phi(\phi + 1) = \phi^2 + \phi$$
$$= (\phi + 1) + \phi = 2\phi + 1$$

$$\phi^4 = \phi^2 \cdot \phi^2 = (\phi + 1)(\phi + 1) = \phi^2 + 2\phi + 1$$
$$= (\phi + 1) + 2\phi + 1 = 3\phi + 2$$

$$\phi^5 = \phi^3 \cdot \phi^2 = (2\phi + 1)(\phi + 1) = 2\phi^2 + 3\phi + 1$$
$$= 2(\phi + 1) + 3\phi + 1 = 5\phi + 3$$

$$\phi^6 = \phi^3 \cdot \phi^3 = (2\phi + 1)(2\phi + 1) = 4\phi^2 + 4\phi + 1$$
$$= 4(\phi + 1) + 4\phi + 1 = 8\phi + 5$$

$$\phi^7 = \phi^4 \cdot \phi^3 = (3\phi + 2)(2\phi + 1) = 6\phi^2 + 7\phi + 2$$
$$= 6(\phi + 1) + 7\phi + 2 = 13\phi + 8$$

$$\vdots$$

A summary chart reveals a pattern among the coefficients of ϕ:

$$\phi^2 = \phi + 1$$
$$\phi^3 = 2\phi + 1$$
$$\phi^4 = 3\phi + 2$$
$$\phi^5 = 5\phi + 3$$
$$\phi^6 = 8\phi + 5$$
$$\phi^7 = 13\phi + 8$$

These are the Fibonacci numbers (see Unit 1.18).

By this time, your students are probably thinking that there is no end to the connections that one can draw to the Golden Section. Indeed, they are correct!

4.9 When Algebra Is Not Helpful

There are lots of examples to exhibit the power of algebra. However, there are times when an algebraic solution to a problem is not an advantage. This approach may seem strange to students, but as this unit will show you, the point is to be made. Consider the challenge:

 Find four consecutive numbers whose product is 120.

Give your students a bit of time to begin to tackle this question. Most will probably write an algebraic equation to depict the situation. It may look like this:

$$x(x + 1)(x + 2)(x + 3) = 120$$

Ridding the parentheses here leaves us with a fourth-degree equation (a quartic equation) in one variable. Rather than to try to solve this quartic equation, a nonalgebraic solution might be preferable. Simply guess intelligently and check to get the solution: $2 \cdot 3 \cdot 4 \cdot 5 = 120$. The students should see from this demonstration that although algebra is very useful to introduce or explain some arithmetic relationships, it is not always the best method.

4.10 Rationalizing a Denominator

Students often find the exercise of rationalizing a denominator as merely an exercise without much purpose, although it is clearly easier to divide by an integer than an irrational number. Naturally, they are given applications that show a need for this technique, but somehow these applications usually do not convince students of the usefulness of the procedure. There are applications (albeit, somewhat dramatic) that drive home the usefulness argument quite nicely.

Consider the following series for which we are asked to find the sum:

$$\frac{1}{\sqrt{1}+\sqrt{2}} + \frac{1}{\sqrt{2}+\sqrt{3}} + \frac{1}{\sqrt{3}+\sqrt{4}}$$
$$+ \cdots + \frac{1}{\sqrt{2001}+\sqrt{2002}} + \frac{1}{\sqrt{2002}+\sqrt{2003}}$$

Students are taught that they cannot do much with a fraction where the denominator is irrational and so must seek to change it to an equivalent fraction with a rational denominator. To do this, they know to multiply the fraction by 1 so as not to change its value. Yet, the form that 1 should take on is the conjugate of the current denominator in both the numerator and the denominator.

The general term of this series may be written as $\frac{1}{\sqrt{k}+\sqrt{k+1}}$.

We shall now rationalize the denominator of this fraction by multiplying it by 1 in the form of $\frac{\sqrt{k}-\sqrt{k+1}}{\sqrt{k}-\sqrt{k+1}}$ to get

$$\frac{1}{\sqrt{k}+\sqrt{k+1}} \cdot \frac{\sqrt{k}-\sqrt{k+1}}{\sqrt{k}-\sqrt{k+1}} = \frac{\sqrt{k}-\sqrt{k+1}}{-1}$$

That is, we have found

$$\frac{1}{\sqrt{k}+\sqrt{k+1}} = \sqrt{k+1} - \sqrt{k}$$

We can then rewrite the series as

$$(\sqrt{2}-\sqrt{1}) + (\sqrt{3}-\sqrt{2}) + (\sqrt{4}-\sqrt{3})$$
$$+ \cdots + (\sqrt{2002}-\sqrt{2001}) + (\sqrt{2003}-\sqrt{2002})$$

which then becomes simply

$$\sqrt{2003} - 1 \approx 44.754888 - 1 = 43.754888$$

Students can readily see how rationalizing the denominator is not just an exercise without purpose. It is useful, and here we have had a prime example.

4.11 Pythagorean Triples

When the Pythagorean theorem is mentioned, one immediately recalls the famous relationship: $a^2 + b^2 = c^2$. Then while presenting the Pythagorean theorem, teachers often suggest that students recognize (and memorize) certain common ordered triples that can represent the lengths of the sides of a right triangle. Some of these ordered sets of three numbers, known as Pythagorean triples, are $(3, 4, 5)$, $(5, 12, 13)$, $(8, 15, 17)$, and $(7, 24, 25)$. The student is asked to discover these Pythagorean triples as they come up in selected exercises. How can one generate more triples without a guess-and-test method? This question, often asked by students, will be answered here and, in the process, will show some really nice mathematics, all too often not presented to students. This is an unfortunate neglect that ought to be rectified.

Ask your students to supply the number(s) that will make each a Pythagorean triple:

1. $(3, 4, \_\_)$
2. $(7, \_\_, 25)$
3. $(11, \_\_, \_\_)$

The first two triples can be easily determined using the Pythagorean theorem. However, this method will not work with the third triple. At this point, your students will be quite receptive to learning about a method to discover the missing triple. So, with properly motivated students as your audience, you can embark on the adventure of developing a method for establishing Pythagorean triples.

However, before beginning to develop formulas, we must consider a few simple "lemmas" (these are "helper" theorems).

Lemma 1 *When the square of an odd number is divided by* 8, *the remainder is* 1.

Proof   We can represent an odd number by $2k + 1$, where k is an integer. The square of this number is

$$(2k + 1)^2 = 4k^2 + 4k + 1 = 4k(k + 1) + 1$$

Since k and $k + 1$ are consecutive, one of them must be even. Therefore, $4k(k + 1)$ must be divisible by 8. Thus, $(2k + 1)^2$, when divided by 8, leaves a remainder of 1.

The next lemmas follow directly.

Lemma 2 *When the sum of two odd square numbers is divided by* 8, *the remainder is* 2.

Lemma 3 *The sum of two odd square numbers cannot be a square number.*

Proof   Since the sum of two odd square numbers, when divided by 8, leaves a remainder of 2, the sum is even, but not divisible by 4. It therefore cannot be a square number.

We are now ready to begin our development of formulas for Pythagorean triples. Let us assume that (a, b, c) is a primitive Pythagorean triple. This implies that a and b are relatively prime.* Therefore, they cannot both be even. Can they both be odd?

If a and b are both odd, then, by Lemma 3, $a^2 + b^2 \neq c^2$. This contradicts our assumption that (a, b, c) is a Pythagorean triple; therefore, a and b cannot both be odd. Therefore, one must be odd and one even.

---

* *Relatively prime* means that they do not have any common factors aside from 1.

Let us suppose that a is odd and b is even. This implies that c is also odd. We can rewrite $a^2 + b^2 = c^2$ as

$$b^2 = c^2 - a^2$$
$$b^2 = (c + a)(c - a)$$

Since the sum and the difference of two odd numbers are even, $c + a = 2p$ and $c - a = 2q$ (p and q are natural numbers).

By solving for a and c, we get

$$c = p + q \qquad \text{and} \qquad a = p - q$$

We can now show that p and q must be relatively prime. Suppose p and q were not relatively prime; say $g > 1$ was a common factor. Then g would also be a common factor of a and c. Similarly, g would also be a common factor of $c + a$ and $c - a$. This would make g^2 a factor of b^2, since $b^2 = (c + a)(c - a)$. It follows that g would then have to be a factor of b. Now if g is a factor of b and also a common factor of a and c, then a, b, and c are not relatively prime. This contradicts our assumption that (a, b, c) is a *primitive* Pythagorean triple. Thus, p and q must be relatively prime.

Since b is even, we may represent b as

$$b = 2r$$

But

$$b^2 = (c + a)(c - a)$$

Therefore,

$$b^2 = (2p)(2q) = 4r^2 \qquad \text{or} \qquad pq = r^2$$

If the product of two relatively prime natural numbers (p and q) is the square of a natural number (r), then each of them must be the square of a natural number.

Therefore, we let $p = m^2$ and $q = n^2$, where m and n are natural numbers. Since they are factors of relatively prime numbers (p and q), they (m and n) are also relatively prime.

Since $a = p - q$ and $c = p + q$, it follows that $a = m^2 - n^2$ and $c = m^2 + n^2$.

Also, since $b = 2r$ and $b^2 = 4r^2 = 4pq = 4m^2n^2$, $b = 2mn$.

To summarize, we now have formulas for generating Pythagorean triples:

$$a = m^2 - n^2 \qquad b = 2mn \qquad c = m^2 + n^2$$

The numbers m and n cannot both be even, since they are relatively prime. They cannot both be odd, for this would make $c = m^2 + n^2$ an even number, which we established earlier as impossible. Since this indicates that one must be even and the other odd, $b = 2mn$ must be divisible by 4. Therefore, no Pythagorean triple can be composed of three prime numbers. This does *not* mean that the other members of the Pythagorean triple may not be prime.

Let us reverse the process for a moment. Consider relatively prime numbers m and n (where $m > n$), where one is even and the other odd.

We will now show that (a, b, c) is a primitive Pythagorean triple where $a = m^2 - n^2$, $b = 2mn$, and $c = m^2 + n^2$. It is simple to verify algebraically that $(m^2 - n^2)^2 + (2mn)^2 = (m^2 + n^2)^2$, thereby making it a Pythagorean triple. What remains is to prove that (a, b, c) is a *primitive* Pythagorean triple.

Suppose a and b have a common factor $h > 1$. Since a is odd, h must also be odd. Because $a^2 + b^2 = c^2$, h would also be a factor of c. We also have h a factor of $m^2 - n^2$ and $m^2 + n^2$ as well as of their sum, $2m^2$, and their difference, $2n^2$.

Since h is odd, it is a common factor of m^2 and n^2. However, m and n (and as a result, m^2 and n^2) are relatively prime. Therefore, h cannot be a common factor of m and n. This contradiction establishes that a and b are relatively prime.

Having finally established a method for generating primitive Pythagorean triples, students should be eager to put it to use. The table below gives some of the smaller primitive Pythagorean triples.

Pythagorean Triples

m	n	a	b	c
2	1	3	4	5
3	2	5	12	13
4	1	15	8	17
4	3	7	24	25
5	2	21	20	29
5	4	9	40	41
6	1	35	12	37
6	5	11	60	61
7	2	45	28	53
7	4	33	56	65
7	6	13	84	85

A fast inspection of the above table indicates that certain primitive Pythagorean triples (a, b, c) have $c = b + 1$. Have students discover the relationship between m and n for these triples.

They should notice that for these triples $m = n + 1$. To prove this will be true for other primitive Pythagorean triples (not in the table), let $m = n + 1$ and generate the Pythagorean triples.

$$a = m^2 - n^2 = (n + 1)^2 - n^2 = 2n + 1$$
$$b = 2mn = 2n(n + 1) = 2n^2 + 2n$$
$$c = m^2 + n^2 = (n + 1)^2 + n^2 = 2n^2 + 2n + 1$$

Clearly, $c = b + 1$, which was to be shown!

A natural question to ask your students is to find all primitive Pythagorean triples that are consecutive natural numbers. In a method similar to that used above, they ought to find that the only triple satisfying that condition is $(3, 4, 5)$.

Students should have a far better appreciation for Pythagorean triples and elementary number theory after completing this unit. Other investigations that students may wish to explore are presented below.

1. Find six primitive Pythagorean triples that are not included in the table.
2. Prove that every primitive Pythagorean triple has one member that is divisible by 3.
3. Prove that every primitive Pythagorean triple has one member that is divisible by 5.
4. Prove that for every primitive Pythagorean triple the product of its members is a multiple of 60.
5. Find a Pythagorean triple (a, b, c), where $b^2 = a + 2$.

5 Geometric Wonders

This chapter is larger than the others since the visual effect of geometry lends itself to entertaining students at various levels. Most of the units can be used by students at the pre-geometry-course level. Those that appear to require some level of geometric sophistication can also be treated in a more elementary fashion. Once you become familiar with the scope of this chapter, you will be in a better position to select and modify appropriate units for your class.

There are a number of units that demonstrate the beautiful concept of an invariant in geometry. What that means is that, in some situations, critical aspects of a figure remain constant even when other parts are changed. These invariants can be nicely demonstrated on the computer with the help of the Geometer's Sketchpad program. For example, the perpendiculars drawn to the three sides of a triangle from any point on its circumcircle intersect the sides in three collinear points (Simson's invariant). These points will always be on a straight line. This invariant is just one of several shown in this chapter.

There are several very entertaining proofs of the Pythagorean theorem, one by paper folding, one extraordinarily simple, and one done by a former U.S. president. There are units that will require the students to do some activities, "moving" along a figure, paper folding, and exposing some extraordinary properties/phenomena.

The chapter is full of unusual geometric properties, all pointing to the beauty of the subject matter. It is for you to present the material in the most interesting way possible. This will, of course, depend in large measure on your personality and your taste for the delights of the geometric menu offered here.

5.1 Angle Sum of a Triangle

Students are often "told" that the sum of (the measures of) the angles of a triangle is 180°. This by no means ensures that they know what that really means and consequently it doesn't etch a lasting mark in their memory. This basis for Euclidean geometry ought to be genuinely understood by all. Most people know that when they make one complete revolution, that represents 360°. There is nothing sacrosanct about this measure, other than it is generally accepted and so used.

So now how does the angle sum of a triangle relate to this? The simplest and perhaps the most convincing way to demonstrate this angle sum is to tear the three vertices from a paper triangle and place them together to form a straight line. This straight line represents one-half of a complete revolution, hence, the 180°.

It is perhaps more elegant to use a folding procedure. Students should be told to cut a conveniently large scalene triangle from a piece of paper. They should then fold one vertex so that it touches the opposite side and so that the crease is parallel to that side. (See Figure 5.1).

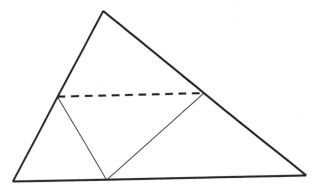

Figure 5.1

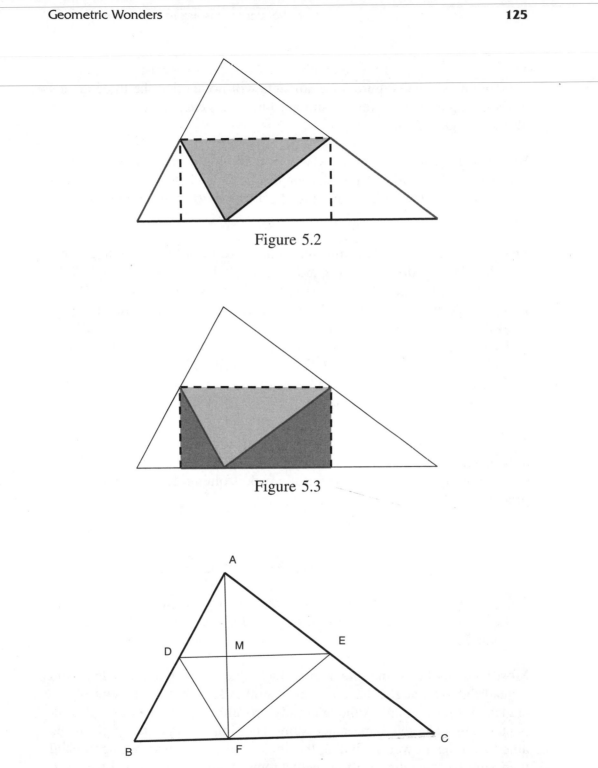

Figure 5.2

Figure 5.3

Figure 5.4

They should then fold the remaining two vertices to meet the first vertex at a common point (Figure 5.2). Students will notice that the three angles of the triangle together form a straight line, and hence have an angle sum of 180° (Figure 5.3).

However, it is also nice to show why this folding procedure has the vertices meet at a point on the side of the triangle. Establishing this phenomenon is tantamount to proving the theorem of the angle sum of a triangle.

The proof of this theorem follows directly from the paper-folding exercise. By folding the top vertex along a parallel crease (i.e., $\overline{DE} \parallel \overline{BC}$), $\overline{AF} \perp \overline{ED}$ at M. Since $\overline{MF} \cong \overline{AM}$, or M is the midpoint of $\overline{AF}$, D and E are midpoints of $\overline{AB}$ and $\overline{AC}$, respectively, since a line parallel to one side of a triangle (either $\triangle BAF$ or $\triangle CAF$) and bisecting a second side ($\overline{AF}$) of the triangle also bisects the third side. It is then easy to show that since $\overline{AD} \cong \overline{DF}$, $\overline{DB} \cong \overline{DF}$ and similarly $\overline{EF} \cong \overline{EC}$, so that the folding over of vertices B and C would fit at F, forming a straight line along $\overleftrightarrow{BFC}$ (Figure 5.4, p. 125).

The most important part of this unit is to convince your students that a paper-folding exercise can be quite valid in demonstrating a property. Mention the difference between a paper-folding demonstration and a proof.

5.2 Pentagram Angles

The pentagram is one of the favorite figures in geometry. It contains the Golden Ratio, when it is a regular pentagram, and in that shape it adorns our flag 50 times!

Most students know that the sum of the angles of a triangle is 180° and a quadrilateral's angles have a sum of 360°. But what is the sum of the angles of a pentagram? Although easily provable, we shall assume that all pentagrams have the same angle sum. This implies that we ought to be able to get the answer by finding the angle sum of a regular pentagram and then simply generalize it to all pentagrams. Students ought to be able to "stumble" on this angle sum once they have been able to find the measure of one vertex angle, not very difficult since the angles are all congruent and there is lovely symmetry throughout.

However, suppose we didn't make this connection and were simply trying to get the angle sum of an "ugly" pentagram, such as the one below.

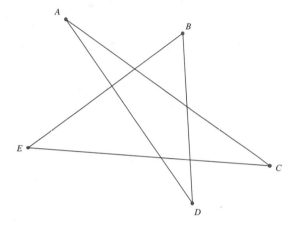

We could determine this by placing a pencil on $\overline{AC}$ in the direction pointing at A and rotating it through $\angle A$, so that it is now on $\overline{AD}$ pointing at A. Then rotate it through $\angle D$ so that it is now on $\overline{BD}$ pointing at B. Then rotate it through $\angle B$ so that it is now on $\overline{BE}$ pointing at B. Then rotate it through $\angle E$ so that it is now on $\overline{EC}$ pointing at C. Lastly, rotate it through $\angle C$ so that it is now on $\overline{AC}$ pointing at C, which is the opposite direction of its starting position. Therefore, the pencil reversed its direction, which is the same thing as a rotation of 180°, implying that the angle sum of the pentagram (through which the pencil was rotated, angle by angle) is 180°.

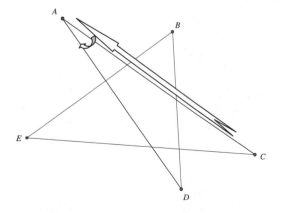

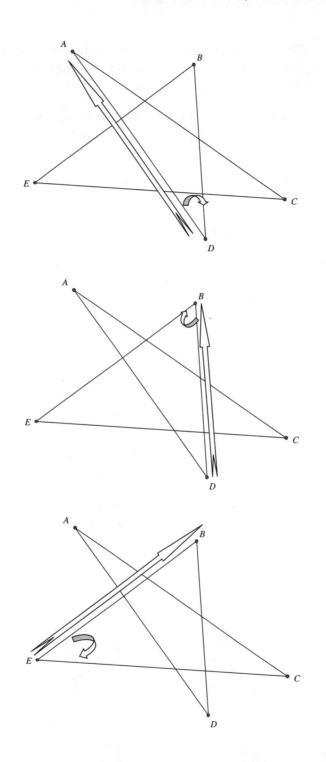

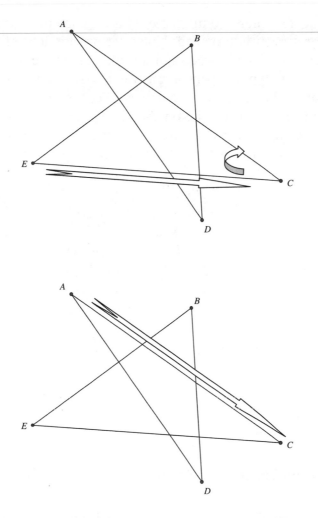

Again, notice how, through the sequence of angle moves, the pencil's direction changed by 180°.

For those who feel more comfortable with a geometric "proof," the following demonstration is provided. Note that we are accepting the notion that the angle sum of the "corners" of a pentagram is the same for all pentagrams. Since the type of pentagram was not specified, we can assume the pentagram to be regular, or that it is one, which is inscribable in a circle (i.e., all of its vertices lie on the circle). In either case, we notice that each of the angles is now an inscribed angle of the circle, and so has half the measure of the intercepted arc (see below).

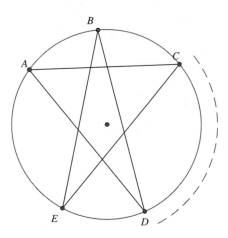

Consequently, we obtain the following:

$$m\angle A = \frac{1}{2}\ m\overset{\frown}{CD}$$ (this reads "the measure of angle A
equals one-half the measure of arc CD")

$$m\angle B = \frac{1}{2}\ m\overset{\frown}{ED}$$

$$m\angle C = \frac{1}{2}\ m\overset{\frown}{AE}$$

$$m\angle D = \frac{1}{2}\ m\overset{\frown}{AB}$$

$$m\angle E = \frac{1}{2}\ m\overset{\frown}{BC}$$

If we add these equalities, we obtain

$$m\angle A + m\angle B + m\angle C + m\angle D + m\angle E$$
$$= \frac{1}{2}m(\overset{\frown}{CD} + \overset{\frown}{ED} + \overset{\frown}{AE} + \overset{\frown}{AB} + \overset{\frown}{BC})$$
$$= \frac{1}{2} \cdot 360° = 180°$$

That is, the sum (of the measures) of the angles of a pentagram is one-half the degree measure of a circle, or 180°. Again, note that there was no loss of generality by allowing the nonspecified pentagram to assume a more useful configuration.

5.3 Some Mind-Bogglers on π

From early exposure to mathematics, students become familiar with π. As the most popular formulas in elementary mathematics (and those that seem to stick with us long after we really know what they mean) are $2\pi r$ and πr^2, many students begin to lose sight of what π means and may need some reminding. The best way to accomplish this is to show them something a bit dramatic. Perhaps starting with the following "experiment" would do the trick.

Take a tall and narrow cylindrical drinking glass. Ask a student if the circumference is greater than or less than the height. The glass should be chosen so that it would "appear" to have a longer height than its circumference. (The typical tall narrow drinking glass fits this requirement.) Now ask the student how he/she might test his/her conjecture (aside from using a piece of string). Recall for him/her that the formula for the circumference of a circle is $C = \pi d$ (π times the diameter). He/she may recall that $\pi = 3.14$ is the usual approximation, but we'll be even more crude and use $\pi = 3$. Thus, the circumference will be 3 times the diameter, which can be easily "measured" with a stick or a pencil and then marked off 3 times along the height of the glass. Usually, you will find that the circumference is longer than the tall glass, even though it does not "appear" to be so. This little optical trick is useful to demonstrate the value of π.

Now for a real "mindblower"! To appreciate the next revelation on π, you need to know that virtually all the books on the history of mathematics state that in its earliest manifestation in history, namely the Bible (Old Testament), its value is given as 3. Yet recent "detective work" shows otherwise.*

Students always relish the notion that a hidden code can reveal long lost secrets. Such is the case with the common interpretation of the value of π in the Bible. There are two places in the Bible where the same sentence appears, identical in every way except for one word, spelled differently in the two citations. The description of a pool or fountain in King Solomon's temple is referred to in the passages that may be found in 1 Kings 7:23 and 2 Chronicles 4:2 and that read as follows:

> And he made the molten sea of ten cubits from brim to brim, round in compass, and the height thereof was five cubits; and *a line* of thirty cubits did compass it round about.

The circular structure described here is said to have a circumference of 30 cubits and a diameter of 10 cubits. (A cubit is the length of a person's fingertip to his elbow.) From this, we notice that the Bible has $\pi = \frac{30}{10} = 3$.

This is obviously a very primitive approximation of π. A late-18th-century rabbi, Elijah of Vilna (Poland), one of the great modern biblical scholars, who earned the title "Gaon of Vilna" (meaning brilliance of Vilna), came up with a remarkable discovery, one that could make most history of mathematics books faulty if they say that the Bible approximated the value of π as 3. Elijah of Vilna noticed that the Hebrew word for "line measure" was written differently in each of the two biblical passages mentioned above.

In 1 Kings 7:23, it was written as קוה, whereas in 2 Chronicles 4:2 it was written as קו. Elijah applied the biblical analysis technique (still used today) called *gematria*, where the Hebrew letters are given their appropriate numerical values according to their sequence in the Hebrew alphabet, to the two spellings of the word for "line measure" and found the following.

---

* Alfred S. Posamentier and Noam Gordon, "An Astounding Revelation on the History of π," *Mathematics Teacher*, Vol. 77, No. 1, Jan. 1984, p. 52.

The letter values are ק = 100, ו = 6, and ה = 5. Therefore, the spelling for "line measure" in 1 Kings 7:23 is קוה = 5 + 6 + 100 = 111, while in 2 Chronicles 4:2 the spelling קו = 6 + 100 = 106. He then took the ratio of these two values: $\frac{111}{106}$ = 1.0472 (to four decimal places), which he considered the necessary correction factor, for when it is multiplied by 3, which is believed to be the value of π stated in the Bible, one gets 3.1416, which is π correct to four decimal places! "Wow!" is a usual reaction. Such accuracy is quite astonishing for ancient times. To support this notion, have students take string to measure the circumference and diameter of several circular objects and find their quotient. They will most likely not get near this four-place accuracy. Moreover, to really push the point of the high degree of accuracy of four decimal places, chances are if you took the average of all the students' π measurements, you still probably wouldn't get to four-place accuracy.

5.4 The Ever-Present Parallelogram

Have each of your students draw an ugly (i.e., any shaped) quadrilateral. Then have them (very carefully) locate the midpoints of the four sides of the quadrilateral. Now have them join these points consecutively. Everyone's drawing should have resulted in a parallelogram. Wow! How did this happen? Everyone began (most likely) with a different-shaped quadrilateral. Yet everyone ended up with a parallelogram.

Here are a few possible results:

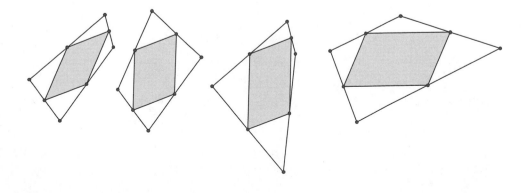

A question that ought to be asked at this point is how might the original quadrilateral have been shaped for the parallelogram to be a rectangle, rhombus, or square?

Either through guess and check or by an analysis of the situation, students should discover the following: When the diagonals of the original quadrilateral are perpendicular, the parallelogram is a **rectangle**.

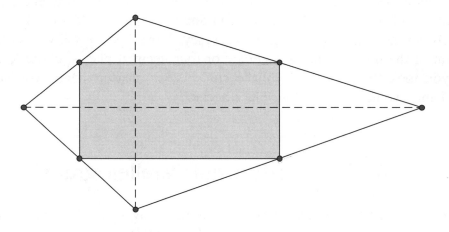

When the diagonals of the original quadrilateral are congruent, then the parallelogram is a **rhombus**.

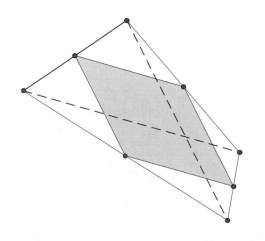

When the diagonals of the original quadrilateral are congruent and perpendicular, then the parallelogram is a **square**.

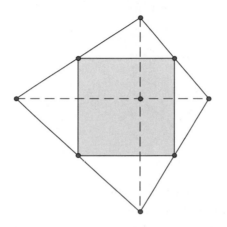

For the teacher who wishes to demonstrate this for the class, the Geometer's Sketchpad software is highly recommended. For the teacher who wishes to prove that all of the above is "really true," a short proof outline is provided, one that should be within easy reach for a high school geometry student.

Proof Outline   The proof is based on a simple theorem that states that a line segment joining the midpoints of two sides of a triangle is parallel to and half the length of the third side of the triangle. This is precisely what happens here.

In $\triangle ADB$, the midpoints of sides $\overline{AD}$ and $\overline{AB}$ are F and G, respectively.

Therefore, $\overline{FG} \parallel \overline{DB}$ and $FG = \frac{1}{2}BD$, and $\overline{EH} \parallel \overline{DB}$ and $EH = \frac{1}{2}BD$.

Therefore, $\overline{FG} \parallel \overline{EH}$ and $FG = EH$. This establishes that $FGHE$ is a **parallelogram** (see p. 136).

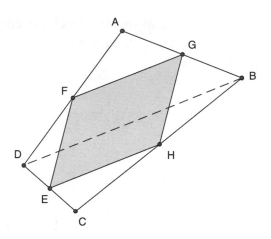

Furthermore, if the diagonals, $\overline{DB}$ and $\overline{AC}$, are congruent (as above), then the sides of the parallelogram must also be congruent, since they are each one-half the length of the diagonals of the original quadrilateral. This results in a rhombus.

Similarly, if the diagonals of the original quadrilateral are perpendicular and congruent, then since the sides of the parallelogram are, in pairs, parallel to the diagonals and half their length, the adjacent sides of the parallelogram must be perpendicular and congruent to each other, making it a square.

5.5 Comparing Areas and Perimeters

Comparing areas and perimeters is a very tricky thing. A given perimeter can yield many different areas. You might use a string and form different-shaped rectangles with it. This would allow you to show your students how a fixed perimeter can generate a variety of different areas. Let's take, for example, rectangles of perimeter 20. As seen below, they may have very different areas.

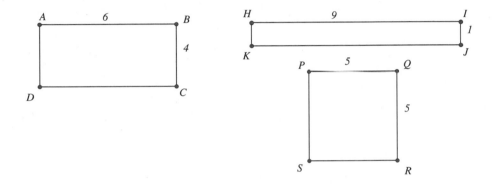

With a perimeter of 20, the area of rectangle *ABCD* is 24.
With a perimeter of 20, the area of rectangle *HIJK* is 9.
With a perimeter of 20, the area of rectangle *PQRS* is 25.

It can be shown that the maximum area of a rectangle with a fixed perimeter is the one with equal length and width, that is, a square.

It is interesting to compare areas of similar figures. We will consider circles.

Suppose you have four equal pieces of string. With the **first piece of string,** one circle is formed. The **second piece of string** is cut into two equal parts and two congruent circles are formed. The **third piece of string** is cut into three equal pieces and three congruent circles are formed. In a similar way, four congruent circles are formed from the **fourth piece of string.** Note that the sum of the circumferences of each group of congruent circles is the same (see p. 138 for illustration).

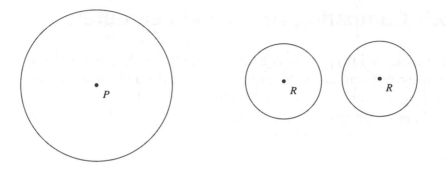

Circle	Diameter	Each circle's circumference	Sum of the circles' circumferences	Each circle's area	Sum of the circles' areas	Percentage of area of circle P represented by the sum of the areas of the smaller circles
P	12	12π	12π	36π	36π	100
R	6	6π	12π	9π	18π	50
Q	4	4π	12π	4π	12π	$33\frac{1}{3}$
S	3	3π	12π	2.25π	9π	25

An inspection of the above chart shows that the sum of the circumferences for each group of circles is the same yet the sum of the areas is quite different. The more circles we formed with the same total length of string, the smaller the total area of the circles. Just what you would *not* expect to happen!

That is, when two equal circles were formed, the total area of the two circles was one-half that of the large circle. Similarly, when four equal circles were formed, the total area of the four circles was one-fourth of the area of the large circle.

This seems to go against one's intuition. Yet if we consider a more extreme case, with say 100 smaller equal circles, we would see that the area of each circle becomes extremely small and the *sum* of the areas of these 100 circles is one-hundredth of the area of the larger circle.

Have students explain this rather disconcerting concept. It ought to give them an interesting perspective on comparison of areas.

5.6 How Eratosthenes Measured the Earth

Measuring the earth today is not terribly difficult, but thousands of years ago this was no mean feat. Remember, the word "geometry" is derived from "earth measurement." Therefore, it is appropriate to consider this issue in one of its earliest forms. One of these measurements of the circumference of the earth was made by the Greek mathematician, Eratosthenes, about 230 B.C. His measurement was remarkably accurate, having less than a 2% error. To make this measurement, Eratosthenes used the relationship of alternate-interior angles of parallel lines.

As librarian of Alexandria, Eratosthenes had access to records of calendar events. He discovered that at noon on a certain day of the year, in a town on the Nile called Syene (now called Aswan), the sun was directly overhead. As a result, the bottom of a deep well was entirely lit and a vertical pole, being parallel to the rays hitting it, cast no shadow.

At the same time, however, a vertical pole in the city of Alexandria did cast a shadow. When that day arrived again, Eratosthenes measured the angle ($\angle 1$ in the figure on page 140) formed by such a pole and the ray of light from the sun going past the top of the pole to the far end of the shadow. He found it to be about $7°12'$, or $\frac{1}{50}$ of 360°.

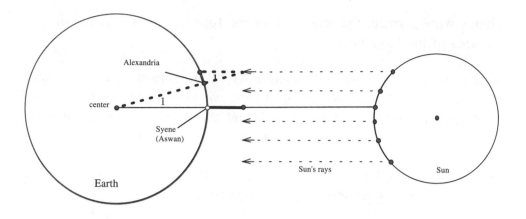

Assuming the rays of the sun to be parallel, he knew that the angle at the center of the earth must be congruent to $\angle 1$, and hence must also measure approximately $\frac{1}{50}$ of 360°. Since Syene and Alexandria were almost on the same meridian, Syene must be located on the radius of the circle, which was parallel to the rays of the sun. Eratosthenes thus deduced that the distance between Syene and Alexandria was $\frac{1}{50}$ of the circumference of the earth. The distance from Syene to Alexandria was believed to be about 5,000 Greek *stadia*. A *stadium* was a unit of measurement equal to the length of an Olympic or Egyptian stadium. Therefore, Eratosthenes concluded that the circumference of the earth was about 250,000 Greek stadia, or about 24,660 miles. This is very close to modern calculations. So how's that for some *real* geometry! Your students should be able to appreciate this ancient use of geometry.

5.7 Surprising Rope Around the Earth

This unit will show your students that their intuition cannot always be trusted. This unit will surprise (or even shock) them. As always, take time to understand the situation and then try to grapple with it. Only then will the conclusion have its dramatic effect.

Consider the globe of the earth with a rope wrapped tightly around the equator. The rope will be about 24,900 miles long. We now lengthen the rope by exactly 1 yard. We position this (now loose) rope around the equator so that it is uniformly spaced off the globe. Will a mouse fit under the rope?

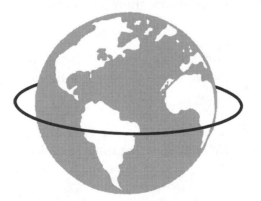

The traditional way to determine the distance between the circumferences is to find the difference between the radii. Let R be the length of the radius of the circle formed by the rope (circumference $C + 1$) and r the length of the radius of the circle formed by the earth (circumference C).

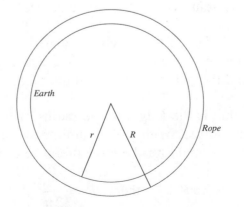

The familiar circumference formulas give us

$$C = 2\pi r \qquad \text{or} \qquad r = \frac{C}{2\pi}$$

and

$$C + 1 = 2\pi R \qquad \text{or} \qquad R = \frac{C + 1}{2\pi}$$

We need to find the difference of the radii, which is

$$R - r = \frac{C + 1}{2\pi} - \frac{C}{2\pi} = \frac{1}{2\pi} \approx 0.159 \text{ yards} \approx 5.7 \text{ inches}$$

Wow! There is a space of **more than $5\frac{1}{2}$ inches** for a mouse to crawl under.

Your students must really appreciate this astonishing result. Imagine, by lengthening the 24,900-mile rope by 1 yard, it lifted off the equator about $5\frac{1}{2}$ inches!

Now for an even more elegant solution. This unit lends itself to a very powerful problem-solving strategy that may be called *considering extreme cases*.

Have students consider the original problem mentioned above. They should realize that the solution was independent of the circumference of the earth, since the end result did not include the circumference in the calculation. It only required calculating $\frac{1}{2\pi}$.

Here is a really nifty solution using an extreme case.

Suppose the inner circle (on the previous page) is very small, so small that it has a zero-length radius (that means it is actually just a point). We were required to find the difference between the radii, $R - r = R - 0 = R$.

So all we need to find is the length of the radius of the larger circle and our problem will be solved. With the circumference of the smaller circle now 0, we apply the formula for the circumference of the larger circle:

$$C + 1 = 0 + 1 = 2\pi R, \qquad \text{then} \qquad R = \frac{1}{2\pi}$$

This unit has two lovely little treasures. First, it reveals an astonishing result, clearly not to be anticipated at the start, and, second, it provides your students with a nice problem-solving strategy that can serve as a useful model for future use.

5.8 Lunes and Triangles

Begin by reminding students that a lune is a crescent-shaped figure (such as that in which the moon often appears) formed by two circular arcs. You ought to take a moment to point out to the students that the area of a circle is not typically commensurate with the areas of rectilinear figures. A case in point is one of the so-called "Three Famous Problems of Antiquity," namely, squaring the circle. That means we have now proved it impossible to construct a square (with unmarked straightedge and compasses) equal in area to a given circle. However, we shall provide you with a delightfully simple example where a circular area is equal to the area of a triangle.

Let's first recall the Pythagorean theorem. It stated the following:

> **The sum of the squares *of* the legs of a right triangle is equal to the square *of* the hypotenuse.**

This can be stated a bit differently with the same effect.

> **The sum of the squares *on* the legs of a right triangle is equal to the square *on* the hypotenuse.**

We can take this a step further.

> **The sum of *the areas of* the squares on the legs of a right triangle is equal to *the area of* the square on the hypotenuse.**

As a matter of fact, we can easily show that the square can be replaced by any similar figures drawn on the sides of a right triangle:

> **The sum of *the areas of* the *similar polygons* on the legs of a right triangle is equal to *the area of* the *similar polygon* on the hypotenuse.**

This can then be restated for the specific case of semicircles (which are, of course, similar) to read:

> **The sum of _the areas of_ the semicircles on the legs of a right triangle is equal to _the area of_ the semicircle on the hypotenuse.**

Thus, for the figure below, we can say that the areas of the semicircles relate as follows:

$$\text{Area } P = \text{Area } Q + \text{Area } R$$

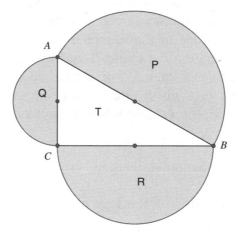

Suppose we now flip semicircle P over the rest of the figure (using $\overline{AB}$ as its axis). We would get a figure as shown below.

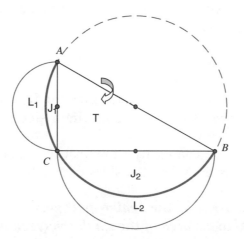

Let us now focus on the lunes formed by the two semicircles. We mark them L_1 and L_2.

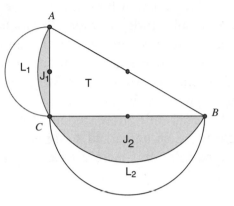

Earlier we established that

$$\text{Area } P = \text{Area } Q + \text{Area } R$$

In the figure above, that same relationship can be written as follows:

$$\text{Area } J_1 + \text{Area } J_2 + \text{Area } T = \text{Area } L_1 + \text{Area } J_1 + \text{Area } L_2 + \text{Area } J_2$$

If we subtract Area J_1 + Area J_2 from both sides, we get the astonishing result:

$$\text{Area } T = \text{Area } L_1 + \text{Area } L_2$$

That is, we have a rectilinear figure (the triangle) equal to some nonrectilinear figures (the lunes).

5.9 The Ever-Present Equilateral Triangle

One of the most astonishing relationships in Euclidean geometry is a theorem first published by Frank Morley (writer Christopher Morley's father). In 1904, he discussed it with his colleagues at Cambridge University, yet didn't publish it until 1924, while he was in Japan. To really appreciate the beauty of this theorem, you would be best off examining it with the Geometer's Sketchpad program. We will do the best we can to appreciate it here on these pages. Don't allow students to get confused with the trisection of an angle using an unmarked straightedge and a pair of compasses (which is impossible) and merely trisecting an angle with other tools.

The theorem states the following:

The adjacent angle trisectors of any triangle intersect at three points determining an equilateral triangle.

Let us look at the following figure.

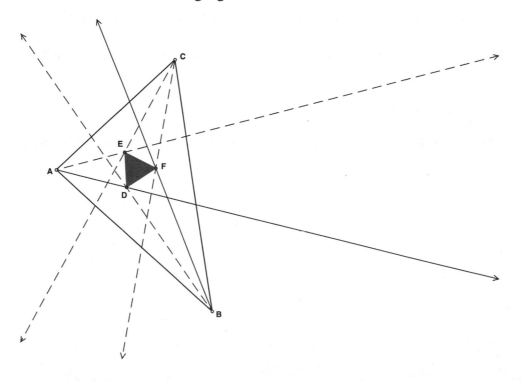

Notice how the points D, E, and F are the intersection points of the adjacent trisectors of the angles of $\triangle ABC$, and $\triangle DEF$ is an equilateral triangle. Wow! This equilateral triangle evolved by beginning with *any shaped* triangle. Drawing on the Geometer's Sketchpad allows you to change the shape of the original $\triangle ABC$ and observe that each time $\triangle DEF$ remains equilateral, although of different size.

The following figures demonstrate a few variations that you can create on the Geometer's Sketchpad to witness this amazing relationship. This is truly one of the most dramatic (i.e., surprising) relationships in geometry and should be presented that way. Be cautioned, the proof is one of the most difficult in Euclidean geometry.*

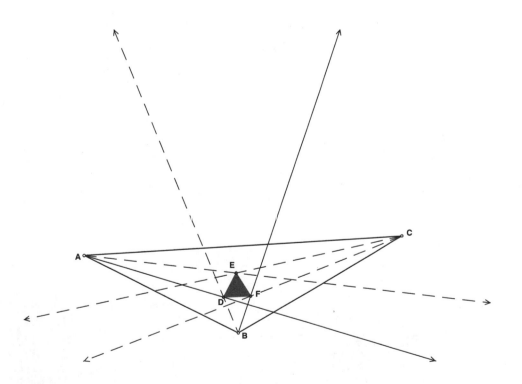

----

* Several proofs can be found in A. S. Posamentier and C. T. Salkind, *Challenging Problems in Geometry* (New York: Dover, 1996), pp. 158–161.

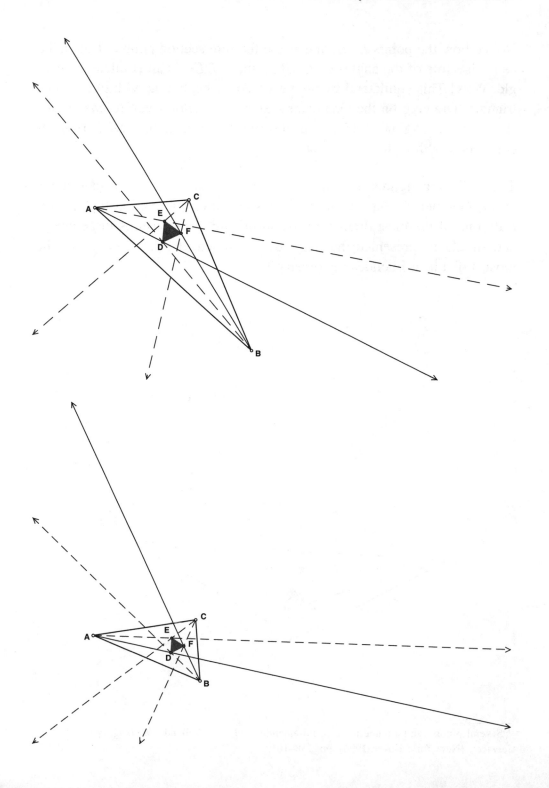

5.10 Napoleon's Theorem

At the beginning of the typical high school geometry course, things don't get interesting until students get to establish (and, of course, *prove*) triangles congruent. Even then, most of the exercises are rather dry and routine. There is, however, one relationship that can be proved with the barest minimum of geometry knowledge, yet appears to be deceptively difficult to prove. This may sound like a contradiction, but you will see what it entails. It's actually rewarding to prove and the result of the proof, that is, the theorem that is established, is extraordinarily powerful, with lots of extensions. In other words, to do the proof can be fun (or at least generate a feeling of accomplishment), but the real nice "stuff" comes once we can work with the results.

The theorem bears the name of Napoleon, but today's historians instead credit one of Napoleon's military engineers.

The theorem states that *the segments joining each vertex of a given triangle (of any shape) with the remote vertex of the equilateral triangle (drawn externally on the opposite side of the given triangle) are congruent.*

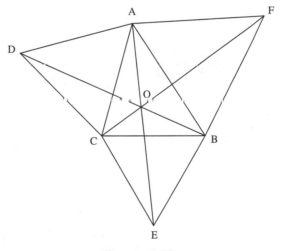

Figure 5.10a

That is, when $\triangle ADC$, $\triangle BCE$, and $\triangle ABF$ are equilateral, $\overline{AE}$, $\overline{BD}$, and $\overline{CF}$ are congruent to one another (Figure 5.10a). Your students should take note of the unusual nature of this situation, since we started with *any* triangle and still this relationship holds true. If each of your students were to draw an original triangle, each would come up with the same conclusion. Either straight edge and compasses or the Geometer's Sketchpad would be fine for this; however, the latter would be better.

Before we embark on the adventures that this theorem holds, it may be helpful to give your students a hint as to how to prove this theorem. The trick is to identify the proper triangles to prove congruent. They are not easy to identify. One pair of these triangles is shown in Figure 5.10b. These two congruent triangles will establish the congruence of $\overline{AE}$ and $\overline{BD}$. The other segments can be proved congruent in a similar way with another pair of congruent triangles, embedded in the figure as these are.

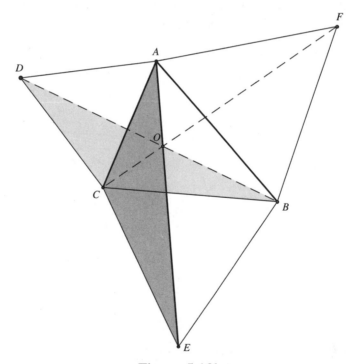

Figure 5.10b

There are quite a few most unusual properties in this figure. For example, your students probably paid little attention to the notion that the three segments $\overline{AE}$, $\overline{BD}$, and $\overline{CF}$ are also concurrent. This concept is not explored much in the typical high school geometry course. Yet, they ought not take this for granted. It must be proved, but for our purposes we shall accept it without proof.*

Not only is point O a common point for the three segments, but it is also the only point in the triangle where the sum of the distances to the vertices of the original triangle is a minimum. This is often called the *minimum distance point* of the triangle ABC.

As if this weren't enough, this point, O, is the only point in the triangle where the sides subtend equal angles (Figure 5.10c). That is, $m\angle AOC = m\angle COB = m\angle BOA = 120°$.

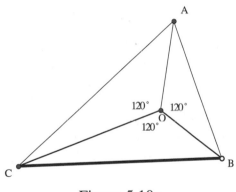

Figure 5.10c

There is more! Have your students locate the center of each of the three equilateral triangles. They can do this in a variety of ways: Find the point of intersection of the three altitudes, medians, or angle bisectors. Joining these center points reveals that an equilateral triangle appears (see Figure 5.10d). Remember, we began with just any randomly drawn triangle and now all of these lovely properties appear.

---

* For a proof of this theorem and its extensions, see A. S. Posamentier, *Advanced Euclidean Geometry: Excursions for Secondary Teachers and Students* (Emeryville, CA: Key College Press, 2002), Chapter 4.

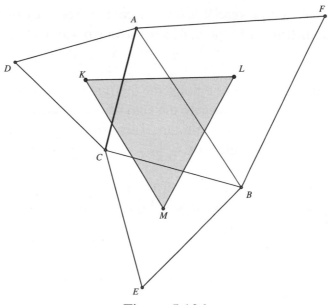

Figure 5.10d

With a computer geometry program, such as the Geometer's Sketchpad, you can see that, regardless of the shape of the original triangle, the above relationships all hold true. The question you might ask your students is what would they expect to happen if point C were to be on $\overline{AB}$, thereby collapsing the original triangle. See Figure 5.10e.

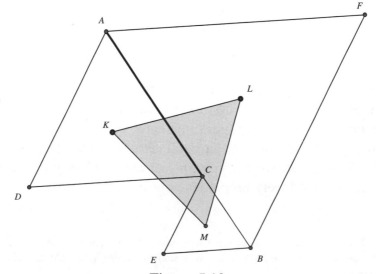

Figure 5.10e

Lo and behold, our equilateral triangle is preserved. Perhaps even more astonishing (if anything could be) is the generalization of this theorem. That is, suppose we constructed similar triangles, appropriately placed on the sides of our randomly drawn triangle, and joined their centers (this time we must be consistent as to which "centers" we choose to use—centroid, orthocenter, incenter, etc.). The resulting figure will be similar to the three similar triangles.

With the aid of a computer drawing program, students can see that all that we said above about triangles drawn *externally* on the sides of our randomly selected triangle can be extended to triangles drawn *internally* as well.

5.11 The Golden Rectangle

When we talk about the beauty of mathematics, we could talk about that which most artists think is the most beautiful rectangle. This rectangle, often called the Golden Rectangle, has been shown by psychologists to be the most aesthetically pleasing rectangle. It is often used in architecture and art. For example, the Parthenon in Athens is based on the shape of a Golden Rectangle. If we outline many figures in classical art, the Golden Rectangle will predominate.

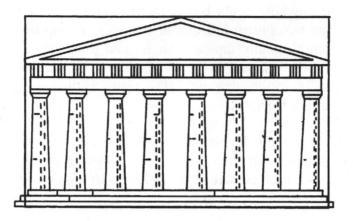

Have students try to find some Golden Rectangles in their environment.

To construct a Golden Rectangle, begin with a square (see Figure 5.11a). Locate the midpoint M of one side and make a circular arc with center at M and radius length ME. Call the point D where the arc intersects $\overleftrightarrow{AF}$. Then erect a perpendicular to $\overline{AD}$ at D to meet $\overleftrightarrow{BE}$ at C. Rectangle $ABCD$ is a Golden Rectangle. This can be done with straightedge and compasses, or students may be adept at using the Geometer's Sketchpad and then ought to be encouraged to use it.

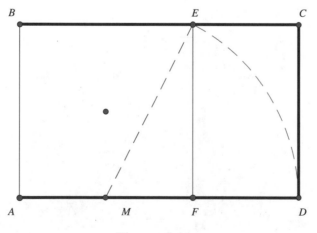

Figure 5.11a

Here is a nice extension of the Golden Rectangle. If we continuously construct squares in the Golden Rectangle, as shown below (Figure 5.11b), each resulting rectangle is a Golden Rectangle; that is, it is similar to the original rectangle, since all Golden Rectangles are similar.

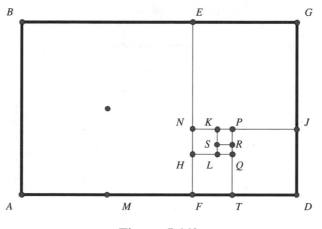

Figure 5.11b

Remove square *ABEF* from Golden Rectangle *ABGD* to get Golden Rectangle *EGDF*.

Remove square *EGJN* from Golden Rectangle *EGDF* to get Golden Rectangle *JDFN*.

Remove square *PJDT* from Golden Rectangle *JDFN* to get Golden Rectangle *TFNP*.

Remove square *TFHQ* from Golden Rectangle *TFNP* to get Golden Rectangle *HNPQ*.

Remove square *HNKL* from Golden Rectangle *HNPQ* to get Golden Rectangle *KPQL*.

Remove square *KPRS* from Golden Rectangle *KPQL* to get Golden Rectangle *SRQL*.

And so on.

Notice that each time a square is taken from a Golden Rectangle the resulting rectangle is also a Golden Rectangle.

Once they have drawn the above figure, students ought to be encouraged to draw quarter circular arcs, as shown in Figure 5.11c. The resulting figure approximates a logarithmic spiral.

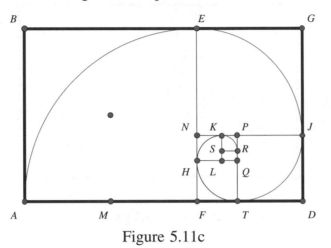

Figure 5.11c

We can locate the vanishing point of the spiral by drawing the diagonals of the two largest Golden Rectangles, as shown in Figure 5.11d.

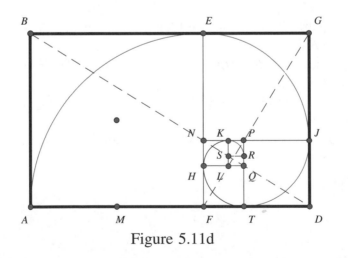

Figure 5.11d

Students who construct this figure accurately will see that $\overline{BD}$ and $\overline{GF}$ contain the diagonals of the other Golden Rectangles as well. Moreover, $\overline{BD} \perp \overline{GF}$.

A similar spiral can be drawn by locating the centers of each of the squares in succession from largest to smallest and drawing (see Figure 5.11e).

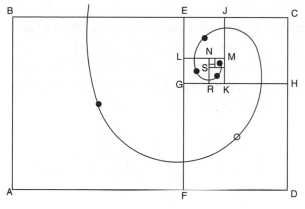

Figure 5.11e

There is no end to the beauty of this rectangle!

5.12 The Golden Section Constructed by Paper Folding

There are many things in mathematics that are "beautiful," yet sometimes the beauty is not apparent at first sight. This is not the case with the Golden Section, which ought to be beautiful at first sight, regardless of the form in which it is presented. The Golden Section refers to the proportion in which a line segment is divided by a point.

Simply, for the segment $\overline{AB}$, the point P partitions (or divides) it into two segments, $\overline{AP}$ and $\overline{PB}$, such that

$$\frac{AP}{PB} = \frac{PB}{AB}$$

This proportion, apparently already known to the Egyptians and the Greeks, was probably first named the "Golden Section" or "sectio aurea" by Leonardo da Vinci, who drew geometric diagrams for Fra Luca Pacioli's book, *De Divina Proportione* (1509), which dealt with this topic.

There are probably endless beauties involving this Golden Section. One of these is the relative ease with which one can construct the ratio by merely folding a strip of paper.

Simply have your students take a strip of paper, say about 1–2 inches wide, and make a knot. Then very carefully flatten the knot as shown in the next figure. Notice the resulting shape appears to be a regular pentagon, that is, a pentagon with all angles congruent and all sides the same length.

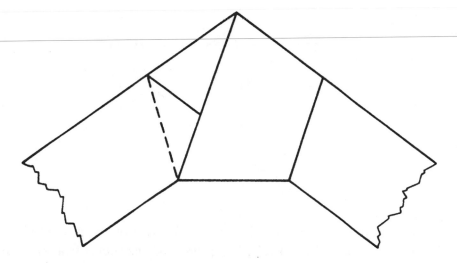

If the students use relatively thin translucent paper and hold it up to a light, they ought to be able to see the pentagon with its diagonals. These diagonals intersect each other in the Golden Section (see below).

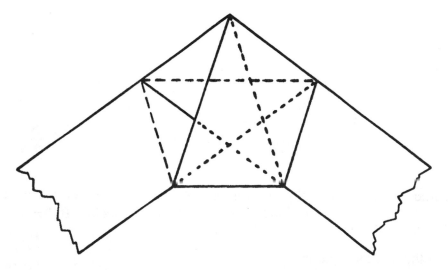

Let's take a closer look at this pentagon (Figure 5.12a). Point D divides $\overline{AC}$ into the Golden Section, since

$$\frac{DC}{AD} = \frac{AD}{AC}$$

We can say that the segment of length AD is the mean proportional between the lengths of the shorter segment (DC) and the entire segment (AC).

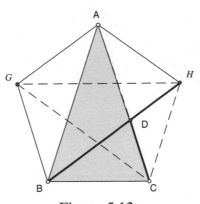

Figure 5.12a

For some student audiences, it might be useful to show what the value of the Golden Section is. To do this, begin with the isosceles triangle *ABC*, whose vertex angle has measure 36°. Then consider the bisector $\overline{BD}$ of ∠*ABC* (Figure 5.12b).

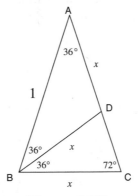

Figure 5.12b

We find that $m\angle DBC = 36°$. Therefore, $\triangle ABC \sim \triangle BCD$. Let $AD = x$ and $AB = 1$. However, since $\triangle ADB$ and $\triangle DBC$ are isosceles, $BC = BD = AD = x$.

From the similarity above,

$$\frac{1-x}{x} = \frac{x}{1}$$

This gives us

$$x^2 + x - 1 = 0 \quad \text{and} \quad x = \frac{\sqrt{5}-1}{2}$$

(The negative root cannot be used for the length of $\overline{AD}$.)

We recall that

$$\frac{\sqrt{5}-1}{2} = \frac{1}{\phi}$$

The ratio for $\triangle ABC$ of

$$\frac{\text{side}}{\text{base}} = \frac{1}{x} = \phi$$

We therefore call this a *Golden Triangle*.

5.13 The Regular Pentagon That Isn't

One of the more difficult constructions to do using unmarked straightedge and compasses is the regular pentagon. There are many ways to do this construction, none particularly easy. Your students might try to develop a construction on their own, realizing that the Golden Section is very much involved here.

For years, engineers have been using a method for drawing what appears to be a regular pentagon; yet careful inspection will show that the construction is a tiny bit irregular.* This method, which we will provide below, was developed in 1525 by the famous German artist, Albrecht Dürer.

We refer to Fig 5.13a on page 162. Beginning with a segment AB, five circles of radius AB are constructed as follows:

1. Circles with centers at A and B are drawn and intersect at Q and N.
2. Then the circle with center Q is drawn to intersect circles A and B at points R and S, respectively.
3. $\overline{QN}$ intersects circle Q at P.
4. $\overrightarrow{SP}$ and $\overrightarrow{RP}$ intersect circles A and B at points E and C, respectively.
5. Draw the circles with centers at E and C with radius AB to intersect at D.
6. The polygon $ABCDE$ is (supposedly) a regular pentagon.

---

* For a discussion of where the error lies, see A. S. Posamentier and H. A. Hauptman, *101 Great Ideas for Introducing Key Concepts in Mathematics* (Thousand Oaks, CA: Corwin Press, 2001), pp. 141–146.

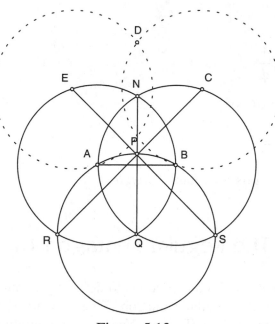

Figure 5.13a

Joining the points in order, we get the pentagon *ABCDE* in Figure 5.13b.

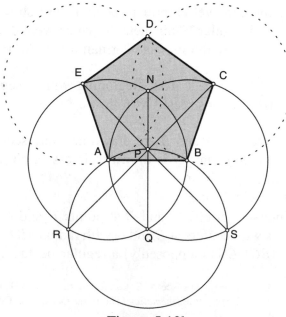

Figure 5.13b

Although the pentagon "looks" regular, the $m\angle ABC$ is about $\frac{22}{60}$ of a degree too large. That is, for *ABCDE* to be a regular pentagon, each angle must measure 108°; instead, we have that $m\angle ABC \approx 108.3661202°$. You might try to draw this with the Geometer's Sketchpad or simply on the chalkboard. It ought to be easy to draw this artwork, following the instructions provided.

5.14 Pappus's Invariant

One of the lovely relationships in geometry occurs when something remains true regardless of the shape of the figure. That is, we can draw something from instructions given over the telephone, where the appearance of the figure drawn will vary with each individual, but one part of it will be common to all drawings. We call this an *invariant*. Such a situation has been handed down to us by Pappus of Alexandria (ca. A.D. 300–350) from his book, *Collection*, which is a compilation of most of what was known in geometry at that time. Let us look at what he presents* and just marvel at it.

You ought to try this with your class. Have students independently draw the figure described below and then have them compare their resulting diagrams.

Consider any two lines, each with three points located anywhere on the lines. Then connect the points of the first line to those on the second line, but do not connect the corresponding points. That is, don't connect the rightmost point on one line to the rightmost point on the other line or don't connect the two middle points.

---

* It is listed in the *Collection* as Lemma 13, proposition 139.

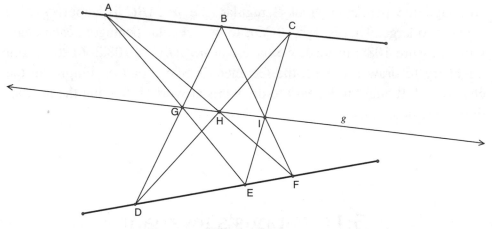

Figure 5.14

In Figure 5.14 we did just that. We marked the three points of intersection *G*, *H*, and *I*. Now here is the amazing part: Regardless of how you drew the original lines or where you located the points on the lines, the points *G*, *H*, and *I* are always collinear (i.e., they lie on the same straight line)!**

You might have your students either do their drawings on an overhead transparency or on a computer drawing program so that the rest of the class can see each student's drawing.

** For a proof of Pappus's theorem, see A. S. Posamentier, *Advanced Euclidean Geometry: Excursions for Secondary Teachers and Students* (Emeryville, CA: Key College Press, 2002).

5.15 Pascal's Invariant

This unit is analogous to the unit on Pappus' invariant in that it presents a common feature to a rather liberally drawn figure (but holding to the instructions). That is, students can draw something from instructions given over the telephone, where the appearance of the figure drawn will vary with each individual, but one part of it will be common to all drawings. We call this an *invariant*. This invariant also has an interesting history.

In 1640, at the age of 16, the famous mathematician Blaise Pascal published a one-page paper titled *Essay Pour les Coniques*, which presents us with a most insightful theorem. What he called *mysterium hexagrammicum* states that **the intersections of the opposite sides of a hexagon inscribed in a conic section are collinear**.* We shall use the most common conic section, a circle.

Consider the hexagon *ABCDEF* inscribed in the circle (i.e., all its vertices are on the circle). You might have your class try this independently, either on paper or on a computer geometry program. The trick is to draw the hexagon shape that will allow you to get intersections of opposite sides— so don't make the opposite sides parallel.

See Figure 5.15a to identify the pairs of opposite sides (extended) and their intersections:

$\overline{AB}$ and $\overline{DE}$ intersect at point *I*.
$\overline{BC}$ and $\overline{EF}$ intersect at point *H*.
$\overline{DC}$ and $\overline{FA}$ intersect at point *G*.

---

* For a proof of Pascal's theorem, see A. S. Posamentier, *Advanced Euclidean Geometry: Excursions for Secondary Teachers and Students* (Emeryville, CA: Key College Press, 2002).

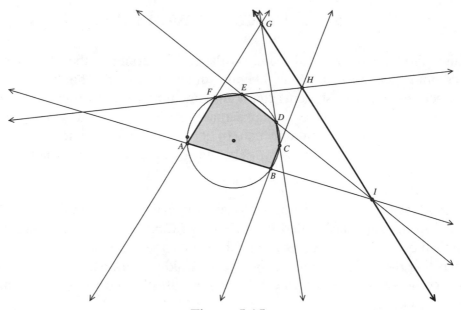

Figure 5.15a

Here is a different-shaped hexagon inscribed in a circle (see Figure 5.15b). Again notice that, regardless of the shape, the points of intersection of the opposite sides of the hexagon meet at three points on a straight line (i.e., they are collinear).

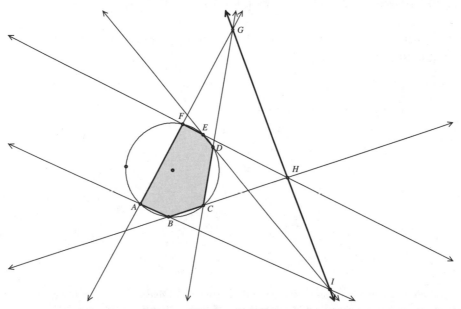

Figure 5.15b

If you do it on a computer, say, using the Geometer's Sketchpad, you can actually see how, by changing the shape of the hexagon, the points G, H, and I always remain collinear. The amazing thing about this situation is that it is independent of the shape of the hexagon. You can even distort the hexagon so that it doesn't look like a polygon anymore, and as long as you keep track of what were the opposite sides, the above collinearity will remain intact. Again, this is very easily and very dramatically demonstrated with the Geometer's Sketchpad.

In Figure 5.15c, you can identify the original hexagon only by referring to the sides of the original one. The pairs of opposite sides and their intersections are

$\overline{AB}$ and $\overline{DE}$ intersect at point I.
$\overline{BC}$ and $\overline{EF}$ intersect at point H.
$\overline{DC}$ and $\overline{FA}$ intersect at point G.

These intersection points, G, H, and I, are still collinear.

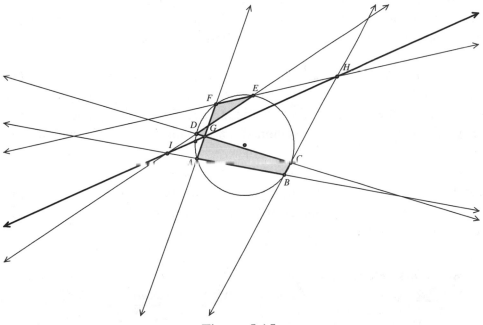

Figure 5.15c

This truly amazing relationship can give us motivation to look into why this behaves as it appears in the above illustrations.

5.16 Brianchon's Ingenius Extension
of Pascal's Idea

This unit should be shown right after the previous one on Pascal's invariant since it is related to it by a relationship called *duality*. This may be a new concept for most students, but is very easy to understand and lots of fun to work with. It will be described a bit later in this unit. First, a bit of history.

In 1806, at the age of 21, a student at the École Polytechnique, Charles Julien Brianchon (1785–1864), published an article in the *Journal de L'École Polytechnique* that was to become one of the fundamental contributions to the study of conic sections in projective geometry. His development led to a restatement of the somewhat forgotten theorem of Pascal and its extension, after which Brianchon stated a new theorem, which later bore his name. Brianchon's theorem,* which states "In any hexagon circumscribed about a conic section, the three diagonals cross each other in the same point,"** bears a curious resemblance to Pascal's theorem, which we presented in the preceding unit on Pascal's invariant.

To fully appreciate the relationship between Pascal's theorem and what Brianchon discovered, it is best to first appreciate what the concept of duality in mathematics is. Two statements are duals of one another when all of the key words in the statements are replaced by their dual words. For example, point and line are dual words, collinearity and concurrency are duals, inscribed and circumscribed are duals, sides and vertices are duals, and so on. You might have your students practice with a few simple statements. Here is an example of the duality relationship. Notice how the terms "point" and "line" have been interchanged.

> Two *points* determine a <u>*line*</u>.
> Two <u>*lines*</u> (intersecting, of course) determine a <u>*point*</u>.

---

* For a proof of Brianchon's theorem, see A. S. Posamentier, *Advanced Euclidean Geometry: Excursions for Secondary Teachers and Students* (Emeryville, CA: Key College Press, 2002).
** *Source Book in Mathematics*, edited by D. E. Smith (New York: McGraw–Hill, 1929), p. 336.

Below you will see Pascal's theorem restated and next to it Brianchon's theorem. Notice that the underlined words in Pascal's statement are replaced by their duals forming Brianchon's statement. Thus, they are, in fact, duals of one another.

Pascal's Theorem	**Brianchon's Theorem**
The points of intersection of the opposite sides of a hexagon inscribed in a conic section are collinear.	*The lines joining the opposite vertices of a hexagon circumscribed about a conic section are concurrent.*

In Figure 5.16a, the hexagon *ABCDEF* is circumscribed about the circle. As with Pascal's theorem, we shall consider only the conic section that is a circle. According to Brianchon's statement, the lines containing opposite vertices are concurrent. Your students can easily experiment with different-shaped circumscribed hexagons to verify that it is true. Again, we see that the simplicity of this figure and its result makes for its beauty.

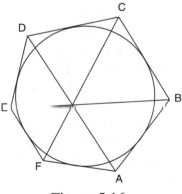

Figure 5.16a

Right after stating his theorem, he suggested that if points *A*, *F*, and *E* were to be moved so that they would be collinear, with vertex *F* becoming a point of tangency, and thereby forming a pentagon, the same statement could be made. That is, since pentagon *ABCDE* is circumscribed about a circle, then $\overline{CF}$, $\overline{AD}$, and $\overline{BE}$ are concurrent (see Figure 5.16b).

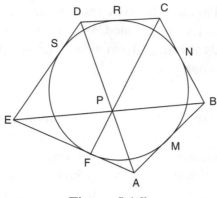

Figure 5.16b

You are encouraged to demonstrate this wonderful relationship with the Geometer's Sketchpad to get the full dramatic effect.

5.17 A Simple Proof of the Pythagorean Theorem

One of the most celebrated relationships in mathematics is the Pythagorean theorem. Why is this so much in the minds of adults, who usually remember this above all else learned in school mathematics? Could this be because we usually refer to the theorem with the first three letters of the alphabet, and it is like learning your ABCs? Whatever makes it popular, it still requires a proof for us to be able to accept it as a theorem. This unit presents a very simple proof that you might want to use instead of the one usually provided in the textbook. Because it is rather simple, you may want to present it out of context a bit earlier than usual. You must be cautioned that it does depend on a theorem about the chord of a circle that must be presented first.

Clearly, the Pythagorean theorem is the basis for much of geometry and all of trigonometry. For this reason, be careful about discovering a new proof to make sure that it is not based on a relationship established by the Pythagorean theorem itself. Such is the case with trigonometry. No proof of the Pythagorean theorem can use trigonometric relationships because they are based on the Pythagorean theorem—a clear case of circular reasoning. Students should be clear on what is meant by circular reasoning.

Now to the proof. It is very simple, but it is based on a theorem that states that *when two chords intersect in the circle, the product of the segments of one chord is equal to the product of the segments of the other chord.* In the figure below, this would mean that for the two intersecting chords: $p \cdot q = r \cdot s$.

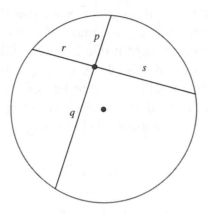

Now consider the circle with diameter $\overline{AB}$ perpendicular to chord $\overline{CD}$:

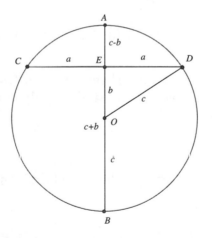

From the theorem stated above, $(c - b)(c + b) = a^2$. Then $c^2 - b^2 = a^2$ and, therefore, $a^2 + b^2 = c^2$. The Pythagorean theorem is proved again. Although there have been many proofs after its publication, a nice collection of 370 proofs of the Pythagorean theorem is by Elisha S. Loomis.[*] This is a lovely resource for all mathematics teachers.

---

[*] A classic source for 370 proofs of the Pythagorean theorem is E. S. Loomis, *The Pythagorean Proposition* (Reston, VA: NCTM, 1968).

5.18 Folding the Pythagorean Theorem

You are now about to embark on a unit that will surely win favor among your students. They ought to appreciate this if for no other reason than they will be able to "see" the Pythagorean theorem before them. After all the struggles students go through to prove the Pythagorean theorem, imagine that we will now prove this famous theorem by simply folding a piece of paper. Your first thought might be, why didn't my teachers ever show me this when I was in school? A good question, but perhaps that is one of the reasons many adults need to be convinced that mathematics is beautiful and holds many delights. So here is an opportunity to show your students a beauty they are not likely to forget.

We can extend from the statement of the Pythagorean theorem:

The sum of the squares on the legs of a right triangle is equal to the square on the hypotenuse of the triangle.

By replacing the word "squares" with "areas of similar polygons," to read:

The sum of the areas of similar polygons on the legs of a right triangle is equal to the area of the similar polygon on the hypotenuse of the triangle.

This replacement can be shown to be correct and holds true for any similar polygons appropriately (correspondingly) placed on the right triangle's sides.

Consider the following right triangle with altitude $\overline{CD}$. Figure 5.18a shows this with three triangular flaps folded over the $\triangle ABC$. The flaps are $\triangle ABC$, $\triangle ADC$, and $\triangle BDC$. Each student should be working along with you as you develop this demonstration.

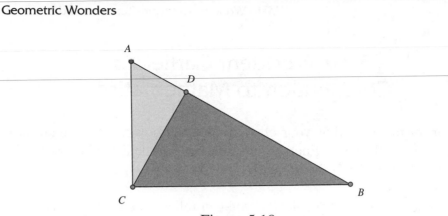

Figure 5.18a

Notice that $\triangle ADC \sim \triangle CDB \sim \triangle ACB$. In Figure 5.18a, $\triangle ADC$ and $\triangle CDB$ are folded over $\triangle ACB$. So clearly Area $\triangle ADC +$ Area $\triangle CDB =$ Area $\triangle ACB$. If we unfold the triangles (including the $\triangle ACB$ itself), we get the following (see Figure 5.18b) that shows that the relationship of the similar polygons (here right triangles) is the extension of the Pythagorean theorem:

The sum of the areas of similar *right triangles* on the legs of a right triangle is equal to the area of the similar *right triangle* on the hypotenuse of the triangle.

This essentially "proves" the Pythagorean theorem by paper folding!

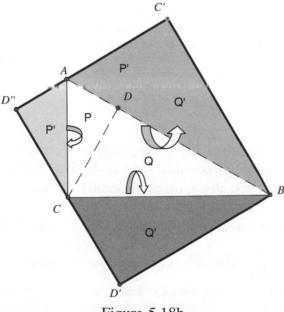

Figure 5.18b

5.19 President Garfield's Contribution to Mathematics

You can begin by asking your class what the following three men have in common: Pythagoras, Euclid, and James A. Garfield (1831–1881), the 20th president of the United States.

After some moments of perplexity, you can relieve the class of their frustration by telling them that all three fellows proved the Pythagorean theorem. The first two bring no surprise, but President Garfield? He wasn't a mathematician. He didn't even study mathematics. As a matter of fact, his only study of geometry, some 25 years before he published his proof of the Pythagorean theorem, was informal and alone.*

While a member of the House of Representatives, Garfield, who enjoyed "playing" with elementary mathematics, came upon a cute proof of this famous theorem. It was subsequently published in the *New England Journal of Education* after being encouraged by two professors (Quimby and Parker) at Dartmouth College, where he went to give a lecture on March 7, 1876. The text begins with

> In a personal interview with General James A. Garfield, Member of Congress from Ohio, we were shown the following demonstration of the pons asinorum,** which he had hit upon in some mathematical amusements and discussions with other M.C.'s. We do not remember to have seen it before, and we think it something on which the members of both houses can unite without distinction of party.

By this time, students are probably motivated to see what a nonmathematician U.S. president could possibly have done with this famous theorem. Garfield's proof is actually quite simple and therefore can be considered "beautiful." We begin the proof by placing two congruent right triangles ($\triangle ABE \cong \triangle DCE$) so that points B, C, and E are collinear, as

---

* In October 1851, he noted in his diary that "I have today commenced the study of geometry alone without class or teacher."

** This would appear to be a wrong reference, since we usually consider the proof that the base angles of an isosceles triangle are congruent as the pons asinorum, or "bridge of fools."

shown in Figure 5.19, and that a trapezoid is formed. Notice also that since $m\angle AEB + m\angle CED = 90°$, $m\angle AED = 90°$, making $\triangle AED$ a right triangle.

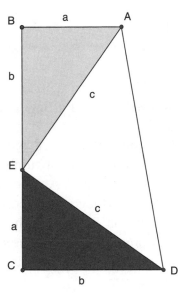

Figure 5.19

The area of the trapezoid $= \dfrac{1}{2}$(sum of bases)(altitude)

$$= \frac{1}{2}(a + b)(a + b)$$

$$= \frac{1}{2}a^2 + ab + \frac{1}{2}b^2$$

The sum of the areas of the three triangles (also the area of the trapezoid)

$$= \frac{1}{2}ab + \frac{1}{2}ab + \frac{1}{2}c^2$$

$$= ab + \frac{1}{2}c^2$$

We now equate the two expressions for the area of the trapezoid

$$\frac{1}{2}a^2 + ab + \frac{1}{2}b^2 = ab + \frac{1}{2}c^2$$

$$\frac{1}{2}a^2 + \frac{1}{2}b^2 = \frac{1}{2}c^2$$

which is the familiar $a^2 + b^2 = c^2$, the **Pythagorean theorem**.

There are more than 400 proofs* of the Pythagorean theorem available today; many are ingenious, yet some are a bit cumbersome. However, none will ever use trigonometry. Why is this? An astute student will tell you that there can be no proof of the Pythagorean theorem using trigonometry, since trigonometry depends (or is based) on the Pythagorean theorem. Thus, using trigonometry to prove the very theorem on which it depends would be circular reasoning. Encourage your students to discover a new proof of this most famous theorem.

5.20 What Is the Area of a Circle?

Students are often "told" that the area of a circle is found by the formula $A = \pi r^2$. Too often, they are not given an opportunity to discover where this formula may have come from or how it relates to other concepts they have learned. It is not only entertaining, but also instructionally sound, to have the formula evolve from previously learned concepts. Assuming that the students are aware of the formula for finding the area of a parallelogram, this unit presents a nice justification for the formula for the area of a circle.

---

* A classic source for 370 proofs of the Pythagorean theorem is E. S. Loomis, *The Pythagorean Proposition* (Reston, VA: NCTM, 1968).

Begin by drawing a conveniently sized circle on a piece of cardboard. Divide the circle into 16 equal arcs. This may be done by marking off consecutive arcs of 22.5° or by consecutively dividing the circle into two parts, then four parts, then bisecting each of these quarter arcs, and so on.

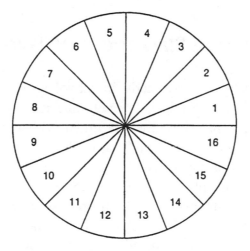

These sectors, shown above, are then cut apart and placed in the manner shown in the figure below.

This placement suggests that we have a figure that approximates a parallelogram. That is, were the circle cut into more sectors, then the figure would look even more like a true parallelogram. Let us assume it is a parallelogram. In this case, the base would have length $\frac{1}{2}C$, where $C = 2\pi r$ (r is the radius). The area of the parallelogram is equal to the product of its base and altitude (which here is r). Therefore, the area of the parallelogram is $(\frac{1}{2}C)r = \frac{1}{2}(2\pi r)(r) = \pi r^2$, which is the commonly known formula for the area of a circle. This should certainly impress your students to the point where this area formula begins to have some intuitive meaning.

5.21 A Unique Placement of Two Triangles

Most of the geometry that we study in school is not dependent on the placement of the figures. Students are not concerned with where two triangles are placed; rather they are concerned with their relative shape: congruent, similar, or equal in area. That is, they can be placed anywhere on the plane (a sheet of paper) as long as their relationship is held intact. Usually where they are placed in relation to other figures is not considered. There is a very important relationship that we will inspect since it has some remarkable results. This relationship actually forms the basis for a branch of geometry called projective geometry and was discovered in 1648 by Gérard Desargues (1591–1661).

We are going to consider two triangles, whose "corresponding vertices" we will designate with the same letter and that will also determine their corresponding sides. This is important to keep in mind as we move along. The two triangles are going to be situated in a very specific manner, and their shape (or relative shape) is of no real concern to us. This is quite different from the kind of thinking used in the high school study of geometry.

We will be placing any two triangles in a position that will enable the three lines joining corresponding vertices to be concurrent. Remarkably enough, when this is achieved, the pairs of corresponding sides meet in three collinear points. Let's see how this looks in a more formal setting.

Desargues's Theorem *If $\triangle A_1B_1C_1$ and $\triangle A_2B_2C_2$ are situated so that the lines joining the corresponding vertices, $\overleftrightarrow{A_1A_2}$, $\overleftrightarrow{B_1B_2}$, and $\overleftrightarrow{C_1C_2}$, are concurrent, then the pairs of corresponding sides intersect in three collinear points.*

In Figure 5.21, the lines joining the corresponding vertices, $\overleftrightarrow{A_1 A_2}$, $\overleftrightarrow{B_1 B_2}$, and $\overleftrightarrow{C_1 C_2}$, all meet at P. The extensions of the corresponding sides meet at points A', B', and C' as follows:

Lines $\overleftrightarrow{B_2 C_2}$ and $\overleftrightarrow{B_1 C_1}$ meet at A'.
Lines $\overleftrightarrow{A_2 C_2}$ and $\overleftrightarrow{A_1 C_1}$ meet at B'.
Lines $\overleftrightarrow{B_2 A_2}$ and $\overleftrightarrow{B_1 A_1}$ meet at C'.

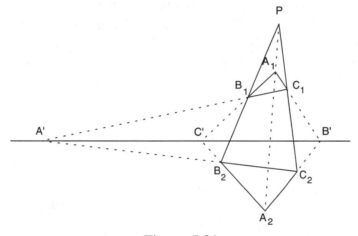

Figure 5.21

This is truly remarkable, but to make it even more astonishing, the converse is also true. Namely, *if* $\triangle A_1 B_1 C_1$ *and* $\triangle A_2 B_2 C_2$ *are situated so that the pairs of corresponding sides intersect in three collinear points, then the lines joining the corresponding vertices,* $\overleftrightarrow{A_1 A_2}$, $\overleftrightarrow{B_1 B_2}$, *and* $\overleftrightarrow{C_1 C_2}$, *are concurrent.* For the teacher who wishes to pursue this theorem further, it is useful to know that it is a self-dual. That is, the dual* of the theorem is the converse.**

---

* See Unit 5.16 for a review of duality.
** The proof of the theorem can be found in A. S. Posamentier, *Advanced Euclidean Geometry: Excursions for Secondary Teachers and Students* (Emeryville, CA: Key College Press, 2002).

5.22 A Point of Invariant Distance in an Equilateral Triangle

Equilateral triangles are the most symmetric triangles. The angle bisectors, the altitudes, and the medians are all the same line segments. No other triangle can boast this property. Their point of intersection is the center of the inscribed and circumscribed circles, again a unique property. These ought to be well-known properties. What is not well known is that if any point is chosen in an equilateral triangle, the sum of the distances to the sides of the triangle is constant. As a matter of fact, this sum is equal to the length of the altitude of the triangle. Rather than simply present this fact to your students, it would be advisable for them to experiment with several points in an equilateral triangle. They should measure the distances (perpendicular, of course) to each of the sides. They should notice that the sum of the distances is the same for each selected point. Then by measuring the length of the altitude of the triangle, they will find that these distance sums are equal to the length of the altitude.

A very elegant (or somewhat sophisticated) method for verifying this is by taking an "extreme" point. By taking "any point" to be at a vertex, this can be easily established. Then the sum of the distances to two of the sides is 0, leaving the distance to the third side as the sum. This distance to the third side is simply the altitude.

We can show this in a number of more traditional ways.

We seek to prove: *The sum of the distances from any point in the interior of an equilateral triangle to the sides of the triangle is constant* (*the length of the altitude of the triangle*).

Here you can see an example of this with actual measurements (see Figure 5.22a).

$$m\overline{PF} = 3.38 \text{ cm}$$

$$m\overline{PD} = 0.88 \text{ cm}$$

$$m\overline{PE} = 1.39 \text{ cm}$$

$$m\overline{PF} + m\overline{PD} + m\overline{PE} = 5.65 \text{ cm}$$

$$m\overline{BG} = 5.65 \text{ cm}$$

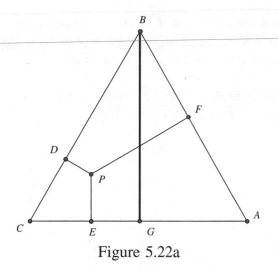

Figure 5.22a

Two proofs of this interesting property are provided here. The first compares the length of each perpendicular segment to a portion of the altitude, and the second involves area comparisons.

Proof I In equilateral $\triangle ABC$, $\overline{PR} \perp \overline{AC}$, $\overline{PQ} \perp \overline{BC}$, $\overline{PS} \perp \overline{AB}$, and $\overline{AD} \perp \overline{BC}$. Draw a line through P parallel to $\overline{BC}$, meeting $\overline{AD}$, $\overline{AB}$, and $\overline{AC}$ at G, E, and F, respectively (see Figure 5.22b).

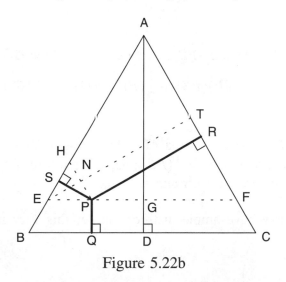

Figure 5.22b

Since $PGDQ$ is a rectangle, $PQ = GD$. Draw $\overline{ET} \perp \overline{AC}$. Since $\triangle AEF$ is equilateral, $\overline{AG} \cong \overline{ET}$ (all the altitudes of an equilateral triangle are congruent). Draw $\overline{PH} \parallel \overline{AC}$, meeting $\overline{ET}$ at N. $\overline{NT} \cong \overline{PR}$. Since $\triangle EHP$

is equilateral, altitudes $\overline{PS}$ and $\overline{EN}$ are congruent. Therefore, we have shown that $PS + PR = ET = AG$. Since $PQ = GD$, $PS + PR + PQ = AG + GD = AD$, a constant for the given triangle.

Proof II In equilateral $\triangle ABC$, $\overline{PR} \perp \overline{AC}$, $\overline{PQ} \perp \overline{BC}$, $\overline{PS} \perp \overline{AB}$, and $\overline{AD} \perp \overline{BC}$. Draw $\overline{PA}$, $\overline{PB}$, and $\overline{PC}$ (see Figure 5.22c).

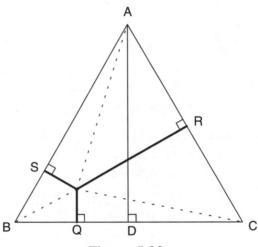

Figure 5.22c

$$\text{Area } \triangle ABC = \text{Area } \triangle APB + \text{Area } \triangle BPC + \text{Area } \triangle CPA$$

$$= \frac{1}{2}(AB)(PS) + \frac{1}{2}(BC)(PQ) + \frac{1}{2}(AC)(PR)$$

Since $AB = BC = AC$, the area of $\triangle ABC = \frac{1}{2}(BC)[PS + PQ + PR]$. However, the area of $\triangle ABC = \frac{1}{2}(BC)(AD)$. Therefore, $PS + PQ + PR = AD$, a constant for the given triangle.

Your students now have ample justification for this very interesting phenomenon.

5.23 The Nine-Point Circle

Perhaps one of the true joys in geometry is to observe how some seemingly unrelated points are truly related to each other. We begin with the very important notion that any three noncollinear points determine a circle. When a fourth point also emerges on the same circle, it is quite noteworthy. Yet when nine points all end up being on the same circle, that is phenomenal! These nine points, for any given triangle, are

- The midpoints of the sides
- The feet of the altitudes
- The midpoints of the segments from the orthocenter to the vertices

Have your students do the necessary construction to locate each of these nine points. Careful construction will allow them to be on the same circle. This circle is called the *nine-point circle* of the triangle. Unmarked straightedge and compasses or the Geometer's Sketchpad computer program would be fine for this activity.

In 1765, Leonhard Euler showed that six of these points, the midpoints of the sides and the feet of the altitudes, determine a unique circle. Yet not until 1820, when a paper* published by Brianchon and Poncelet appeared, were the remaining three points (the midpoints of the segments from the orthocenter to the vertices) found to be on this circle. The paper contains the first complete proof of the theorem and uses the name "the nine-point circle" for the first time.

Theorem *In any triangle, the midpoints of the sides, the feet of the altitudes, and the midpoints of the segments from the orthocenter to the vertices lie on a circle.*

Proof To simplify the discussion of this proof, we shall consider each part with a separate diagram. Bear in mind, though, that each of the Figures 5.23b–5.23e is merely an extraction from Figure 5.23a, which is the complete diagram.

---

* *Recherches sur la détermination d'une hyperbole équilatèau moyen de quartes conditions données* (Paris, 1820).

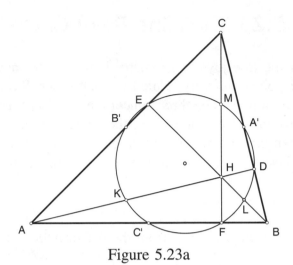

Figure 5.23a

In Figure 5.23b, points A', B', and C' are the midpoints of the three sides of $\triangle ABC$ opposite the respective vertices. $\overline{CF}$ is an altitude of $\triangle ABC$. Since $\overline{A'B'}$ is a midline of $\triangle ABC$, $\overline{A'B'} \parallel \overline{AB}$. Therefore, quadrilateral $A'B'C'F$ is a trapezoid. $\overline{B'C'}$ is also a midline of $\triangle ABC$, so that $B'C' = \frac{1}{2}BC$. Since $\overline{A'F}$ is the median to the hypotenuse of right $\triangle BCF$, $A'F = \frac{1}{2}BC$. Therefore, $B'C' = A'F$ and trapezoid $A'B'C'F$ is isosceles.

You will recall that when the opposite angles of a quadrilateral are supplementary, as in the case of an isosceles trapezoid, the quadrilateral is cyclic. Therefore, quadrilateral $A'B'C'F$ is cyclic.*

So far, we have four of the nine points on one circle.

To avoid any confusion, we redraw $\triangle ABC$ (see Figure 5.23a) and include altitude $\overline{AD}$. Using the same argument as before, we find that quadrilateral $A'B'C'D$ is an isosceles trapezoid and therefore cyclic. So we now have five of the nine points on one circle (i.e., points A', B', C', F, and D).

By repeating the same argument for altitude $\overline{BE}$, we can then state that points D, F, and E lie on the same circle as points A', B', and C'. These six points are as far as Euler got with this configuration.

---

* A cyclic quadrilateral is one whose four vertices lie on the same circle.

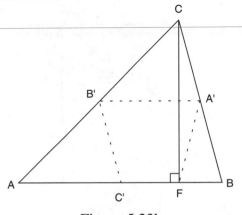

Figure 5.23b

With H as the orthocenter (the point of intersection of the altitudes), M is the midpoint of $\overline{CH}$ (see Figure 5.23d). Therefore, $\overline{B'M}$, a midline of $\triangle ACH$, is parallel to $\overline{AH}$, or altitude $\overline{AD}$. Since $\overline{B'C'}$ is a midline of $\triangle ABC$, $\overline{B'C'} \parallel \overline{BC}$. Therefore, since $\angle ADC$ is a right angle, $\angle MB'C'$ is also a right angle. Thus, quadrilateral $MB'C'F$ is cyclic (opposite angles are supplementary). This places point M on the circle determined by points B', C', and F. We now have a seven-point circle.

We repeat this procedure with point L, the midpoint of $\overline{BH}$ (see Figure 5.23e). As before, $\angle B'A'L$ is a right angle, as is $\angle B'EL$. Therefore, points B', E, A', and L are concyclic (opposite angles are supplementary). We now have L as an additional point on our circle, making it an eight-point circle.

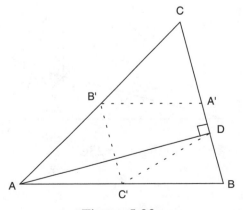

Figure 5.23c

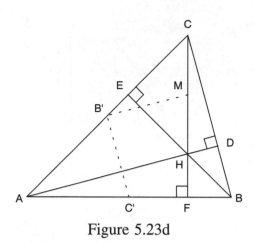

Figure 5.23d

To locate our final point on the circle, consider point K, the midpoint of $\overline{AH}$. As we did earlier, we find $\angle A'B'K$ to be a right angle, as is $\angle A'DK$. Therefore, quadrilateral $A'DKB'$ is cyclic and point K is on the same circle as points B', A', and D. We have therefore proved that **nine specific points** lie on this circle. This is not to be taken lightly; it is quite spectacular!

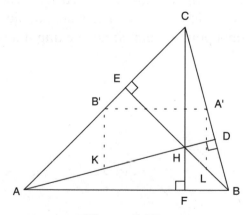

Figure 5.23e

5.24 Simson's Invariant

One of the great injustices in the history of mathematics involves a theorem originally published by William Wallace in Thomas Leybourn's *Mathematical Repository* (1799–1800), which through careless misquotes has been attributed to Robert Simson (1687–1768), a famous English interpreter of Euclid's *Elements*. To be consistent with the historic injustice, we shall use the popular reference and call it *Simson's theorem*.

The beauty of this theorem lies in its simplicity. Begin by having your students all draw a triangle with its vertices on a circle (something that is always possible, since any three noncollinear points determine a circle) and then they should select a point on the circle that is not at a vertex of the triangle. From that point, they should draw a perpendicular line to each of the three sides. The three points where these perpendiculars intersect the sides (points X, Y, and Z in Figure 5.24 on the next page) are always collinear (i.e., they lie on a straight line). Each accurate student drawing should reflect this fact. The line that these three points determine is often called the *Simson line* (further "injustice"!).

This can be more formally stated as follows.

Simson's Theorem *The feet of the perpendiculars drawn from any point on the circumcircle of a triangle to the sides of the triangle are collinear.*

In Figure 5.24, point P is on the circumcircle of $\triangle ABC$. $\overleftrightarrow{PY} \perp \overleftrightarrow{AC}$ at Y, $\overleftrightarrow{PZ} \perp \overleftrightarrow{AB}$ at Z, and $\overleftrightarrow{PX} \perp \overleftrightarrow{BC}$ at X. According to Simson's (i.e., Wallace's) theorem, points X, Y, and Z are collinear. This line is usually referred to as the *Simson line*.

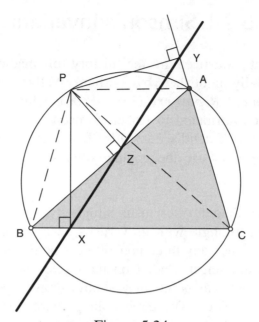

Figure 5.24

Because of the unconventional nature of the proof of this theorem, it is offered here.

Proof *   Since $\angle PYA$ is supplementary to $\angle PZA$, quadrilateral $PZAY$ is cyclic.** Draw $\overline{PA}$, $\overline{PB}$, and $\overline{PC}$.

Therefore,

$$m\angle PYZ = m\angle PAZ \qquad \text{(I)}$$

Similarly, since $\angle PYC$ is supplementary to $\angle PXC$, quadrilateral $PXCY$ is cyclic, and

$$m\angle PYX = m\angle PCB \qquad \text{(II)}$$

However, quadrilateral $PACB$ is also cyclic, since it is inscribed in the given circumcircle, and therefore

$$m\angle PAZ = m\angle PCB \qquad \text{(III)}$$

---

* For other proofs of Simson's theorem, see A. S. Posamentier and C. T. Salkind, *Challenging Problems in Geometry* (New York: Dover, 1996), pp. 43–45.
** A quadrilateral whose opposite angles are supplementary is cyclic; that is, its vertices all lie on the same circle.

From (I)–(III), $m\angle PYZ = m\angle PYX$, and thus points X, Y, and Z are collinear.

This invariant is beautifully demonstrated with the Geometer's Sketchpad. There students would draw the figure and then, by moving the point on the circle to various positions, they can observe how the collinearity is preserved under all positions of the point P. Dynamic geometry of this kind can go a long way to impress your students and win them over toward a love for mathematics.

5.25 Ceva's Very Helpful Relationship

One of the most neglected topics in high school geometry is the concept of concurrency. In many cases, it is taken for granted. Oftentimes, we just "know" that the altitudes of a triangle are concurrent; that is, they contain a common point of intersection. Similarly, we often take for granted that the medians of a triangle are concurrent, or the same for the angle bisectors of a triangle. The topic of concurrency of lines in a triangle deserves more attention than it usually gets in an elementary geometry course. To put these assumptions to rest, we must establish an extremely useful relationship. This will be done with the help of the famous theorem first published* by the Italian mathematician Giovanni Ceva (1647–1734) and which now bears his name.

In simple terms, the relationship that Ceva established says that if you have three concurrent line segments ($\overline{AL}$, $\overline{BM}$, and $\overline{CN}$), joining a vertex of a triangle with a point on the opposite side, then the products of the alternate segments along the sides are equal. In Figure 5.25a, you can see this, noting that the products of the alternate segments along the sides of the triangle are equal: $AN \cdot BL \cdot CM = NB \cdot LC \cdot MA$.

---

* *De lineis se invicem secantibus statica constructio* (Milan, 1678).

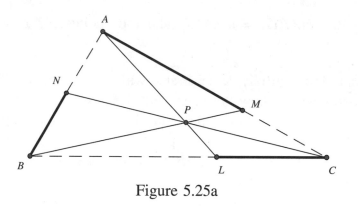

Figure 5.25a

This can be more formally stated as follows.

Ceva's Theorem[*] *The three lines containing the vertices A, B, and C of △ABC and intersecting the opposite sides at points L, M, and N, respectively, are concurrent if and only if*

$$\frac{AN}{NB} \cdot \frac{BL}{LC} \cdot \frac{CM}{MA} = 1$$

or AN · BL · CM = NB · LC · MA.

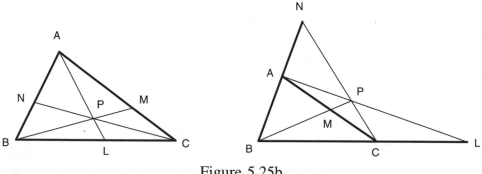

Figure 5.25b

There are two possible situations in which the three lines drawn from the vertices may intersect the sides and still be concurrent (see Figure 5.25b).

---

[*] The proof of Ceva's Theorem is beyond the focus of this book, but can be found in A. S. Posamentier *Advanced Euclidean Geometry* (Emeryville, CA: Key College Publishing, 2002), pp. 27–31.

It is perhaps easier to understand the left side diagram, and verify the theorem with the right side diagram.

Now having "accepted" this theorem for use, let's see how simple it is to prove some of the earlier mentioned relationships.

We shall begin with the task of proving that the medians of a triangle are concurrent. Normally (i.e., without the help of Ceva's theorem), this would be a very difficult proof to do, and therefore it is often omitted from the typical high school course. Now observe how simple it is to prove this concurrency.

Proof   In $\triangle ABC$, (Figure 5.25c) $\overline{AL}$, $\overline{BM}$, and $\overline{CN}$ are medians. Therefore, $AN = NB$, $BL = LC$, and $CM = MA$. Multiplying these equalities gives us

$$(AN)(BL)(CM) = (NB)(LC)(MA) \qquad \text{or} \qquad \frac{AN}{NB} \cdot \frac{BL}{LC} \cdot \frac{CM}{MA} = 1$$

Thus, by Ceva's theorem, $\overline{AL}$, $\overline{BM}$, and $\overline{CN}$ are concurrent.

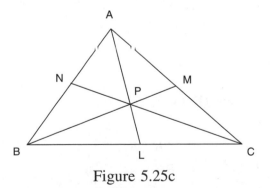

Figure 5.25c

Again, it would be advisable to compare the conventional proof (that presented in the context of elementary geometry) for the concurrency of the altitudes of a triangle to the following proof, using Ceva's theorem.

We will prove that the altitudes of a triangle are concurrent using Ceva's theorem.

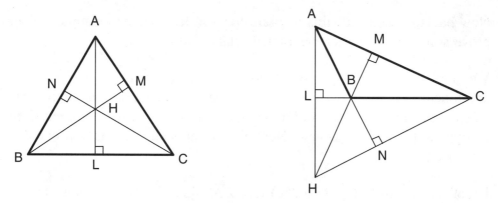

Figure 5.25d

Proof In $\triangle ABC$, (Figure 5.25d) $\overline{AL}$, $\overline{BM}$, and $\overline{CN}$ are altitudes. You may follow this proof for both of the above diagrams, since the same proof holds true for both an acute and an obtuse triangle.

$$\triangle ANC \sim \triangle AMB, \qquad \text{so that} \qquad \frac{AN}{MA} = \frac{AC}{AB} \tag{I}$$

$$\triangle BLA \sim \triangle BNC, \qquad \text{so that} \qquad \frac{BL}{NB} = \frac{AB}{BC} \tag{II}$$

$$\triangle CMB \sim \triangle CLA, \qquad \text{so that} \qquad \frac{CM}{LC} = \frac{BC}{AC} \tag{III}$$

Multiplying (I), (II), and (III) gives us

$$\frac{AN}{MA} \cdot \frac{BL}{NB} \cdot \frac{CM}{LC} = \frac{AC}{AB} \cdot \frac{AB}{BC} \cdot \frac{BC}{AC} = 1$$

This indicates that the altitudes are concurrent (by Ceva's theorem).

Students should become familiar with this very powerful theorem, as it can prove quite helpful in other similar situations.

5.26 An Obvious Concurrency?

A fascinating point of concurrency in a triangle was first established by Joseph-Diaz Gergonne (1771–1859), a French mathematician. Gergonne reserved a distinct place in the history of mathematics as the initiator (1810) of the first purely mathematical journal, *Annales des mathématiques pures et appliqués*. The journal appeared monthly until 1832 and was known as *Annales del Gergonne*. During the time of its publication, Gergonne published about 200 papers, mostly on geometry. Gergonne's *Annales* played an important role in the establishment of projective and algebraic geometry as it gave some of the greatest minds of the times an opportunity to share information. We will remember Gergonne for a rather simple theorem that can be shown as follows.

Begin by having the students construct a circle inscribed in a given triangle. This can be done by first locating the center of the circle, which is the point of intersection of the angle bisectors of the triangle, and then finding the perpendicular distance from the center to one of the sides. This gives them the radius. Then fortified with the center of the circle and the length of the radius, they can draw the inscribed circle. They now have a triangle with a circle inscribed in it. The line segments joining the vertices of the triangle with the three points of tangency should then be drawn, and, lo and behold, they are concurrent.

To prove this relationship involving concurrency of lines in a triangle, we can use Ceva's theorem (see 5.25, p. 189).

Gergonne's Theorem *The lines containing a vertex of a triangle and the point of tangency of the opposite side with the inscribed circle are concurrent.*

This point of concurrency is known as the *Gergonne point* of the triangle.

Proof In Figure 5.26, circle O is tangent to sides $\overline{AB}$, $\overline{AC}$, and $\overline{BC}$ at points N, M, and L, respectively. It follows that $AN = AM$, $BL = BN$, and $CM = CL$. These equalities may be written as

$$\frac{AN}{AM} = 1 \qquad \frac{BL}{BN} = 1 \qquad \frac{CM}{CL} = 1$$

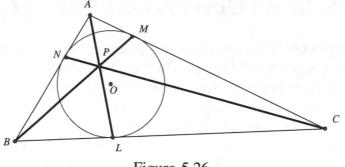

Figure 5.26

By multiplying these three fractions, we get

$$\frac{AN}{AM} \cdot \frac{BL}{BN} \cdot \frac{CM}{CL} = 1$$

Therefore,

$$\frac{AN}{BN} \cdot \frac{BL}{CL} \cdot \frac{CM}{AM} = 1$$

which, as a result of Ceva's theorem (see Unit 5.25), implies that $\overline{AL}$, $\overline{BM}$, and $\overline{CN}$ are concurrent. This point is the Gergonne point of $\triangle ABC$.

Neat and (relatively) simple! Yet a fact not well known. These easy-to-understand relationships make geometry fun.

5.27 Euler's Polyhedra

We often see geometric shapes in our daily comings and goings. Leonhard Euler, in the 18th century, discovered a lovely relationship among the vertices, faces, and edges of polyhedra (which are basically geometric solids).

You might begin by having students find various polyhedra and count the number of vertices (V), faces (F), and edges (E), make a chart of these findings, and then search for a pattern. They ought to discover that for all these figures the following relationship holds true: $V + F = E + 2$.

In the complete cube, the relationship holds true as $8 + 6 = 12 + 2$.

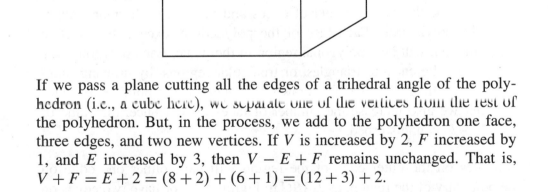

If we pass a plane cutting all the edges of a trihedral angle of the poly-hedron (i.e., a cube here), we separate one of the vertices from the rest of the polyhedron. But, in the process, we add to the polyhedron one face, three edges, and two new vertices. If V is increased by 2, F increased by 1, and E increased by 3, then $V - E + F$ remains unchanged. That is, $V + F = E + 2 = (8 + 2) + (6 + 1) = (12 + 3) + 2$.

We can obtain a similar result for any polyhedral angle. The new poly-hedron will have a new face with the same number of vertices as edges. Since we lose one vertex but gain one face, there is no change in the expression $V - E + F$.

We know the Euler formula applies to a tetrahedron (a "cut-off pyramid": $V + F = E + 2$ here is $4 + 4 = 6 + 2$). From the above argument, we can conclude that it applies to any polyhedron that can be derived by passing a plane that cuts off a vertex of a tetrahedron a finite number of times. However, we would like it to apply to all simple polyhedra. In the proof, we need to show that in regard to the value of the expression $V - E + F$, any polyhedron agrees with the tetrahedron. To do this, we need to discuss a new branch of mathematics called *topology*.

Topology is a very general type of geometry. Establishment of Euler's formula is a topological problem. Two figures are topologically equivalent if one can be made to coincide with the other by distortion, shrinking, stretching, or bending, but not by cutting or tearing. A teacup and a doughnut are topologically equivalent. The hole in the doughnut becomes the inside of the handle of the teacup. Have students give other examples of topologically equivalent objects.

Topology has been called "rubber-sheet geometry." If a face of a polyhedron is removed, the remaining figure is topologically equivalent to a region of a plane. We can deform the figure until it stretches flat on a plane. The resulting figure does not have the same shape or size, but its boundaries are preserved. Edges will become sides of polygonal regions. There will be the same number of edges and vertices in the plane figure as in the polyhedron. Each face of the polyhedron, except the one that was removed, will be a polygonal region in the plane. Each polygon not a triangle can be cut into triangles, or triangular regions, by drawing diagonals. Each time a diagonal is drawn, we increase the number of edges by 1 but we also increase the number of faces by 1. Hence, the value of $V - E + F$ is undisturbed.

Triangles on the outer edge of the region will have either one edge on the boundary of the region, as $\triangle ABC$ in Figure 5.27, or have two edges on the boundary, as $\triangle DEF$. We can remove triangles like $\triangle ABC$ by removing the one boundary side. In the figure, this is $\overline{AC}$. This decreases the faces by 1 and the edges by 1. Still, $V - E + F$ is unchanged. If we remove the other kind of boundary triangle, such as $\triangle DEF$, we decrease the number of edges by 2, the number of faces by 1, and the number of vertices by 1. Again, $V - E + F$ is unchanged. This process can be continued until one triangle remains.

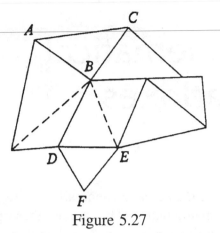

Figure 5.27

The single triangle has three vertices, three edges, and one face. Hence, $V - E + F = 1$. Consequently, $V - E + F = 1$ in the plane figure obtained from the polyhedron by distortion. Since one face had been eliminated, we conclude that for the polyhedron

$$V - E + F = 2$$

This procedure applies to any simple polyhedron, even if it is not convex. Can you see why it cannot be applied to a nonsimple polyhedron?

An alternate to the approach of distorting the polyhedron to a plane after a face has been eliminated can be called "shrinking a face to a point." If a face is replaced by a point, we lose the n edges of the face and the n vertices of the face, and we lose a face and gain a vertex (the point that replaces the face). This leaves $V - E + F$ unchanged. This process can be continued until only four faces remain. Then any polyhedron has the same value for $V - E + F$ as does a tetrahedron. The tetrahedron has four faces, four vertices, and six edges: $4 - 6 + 4 = 2$.

This unit will give students a widely enriched outlook into geometric shapes in three dimensions.

6 Mathematical Paradoxes

A paradox or fallacy in mathematics generally results from a violation of some rule or law of mathematics. This makes these paradoxes excellent vehicles for presenting these rules, for their violation leads to some rather "curious" results, such as $1 = 2$, or $1 = 0$, just absurd! They are clearly entertaining since they very subtly lead the student to an impossible result. Often the student becomes frustrated by the fact that every step to this weird result seemed correct. This is quite motivating and will make the conclusion that much more impressive.

Again, it is a fine source for investigating mathematical boundaries. Why isn't division by 0 permissible? Why isn't the product of the radicals always equal to the radical of the product? These are just a few of the questions that this chapter entertainingly investigates. The "funny" results are entertaining to expose and high in instructional value. Students are not apt to violate rules that lead to some of these fallacies but they usually make a lasting impression.

6.1 Are All Numbers Equal?

The title of this charmer is clearly preposterous! But as you will see from the demonstration below, such may not be the case. Present this demonstration line by line and let students draw their own conclusions.

We shall begin with the easily accepted equation:

$$\frac{x-1}{x-1} = 1$$

Each succeeding row can be easily justified with elementary algebra. There is nothing wrong with the algebra. See if your students can find the flaw.

	For $x = 1$
$\dfrac{x-1}{x-1} = 1$	$\dfrac{0}{0} = 1$
$\dfrac{x^2-1}{x-1} = x+1$	$\dfrac{0}{0} = 1+1 = 2$
$\dfrac{x^3-1}{x-1} = x^2+x+1$	$\dfrac{0}{0} = 1+1+1 = 3$
$\dfrac{x^4-1}{x-1} = x^3+x^2+x+1$	$\dfrac{0}{0} = 1+1+1+1 = 4$
$\vdots$	
$\dfrac{x^n-1}{x-1} = x^{n-1}+x^{n-2}+\cdots+x^2+x+1$	$\dfrac{0}{0} = 1+1+1+\cdots+1 = n$

When $x = 1$, the numbers $1, 2, 3, 4, \ldots, n$ are each equal to $\frac{0}{0}$, which would make them all equal to each other. Of course, this cannot be true. For this reason, we define $\frac{0}{0}$ to be meaningless. To define something to make things meaningful or consistent is what we do in mathematics to avoid ridiculous statements, as was the case here. Be sure to stress this point with your students before leaving this unit.

6.2 −1 Is Not Equal to +1

Your students should be aware of the notion that $\sqrt{6} = \sqrt{2} \cdot \sqrt{3}$, and then they might conclude that $\sqrt{ab} = \sqrt{a} \cdot \sqrt{b}$.

From this, have your students multiply and simplify: $\sqrt{-1} \cdot \sqrt{-1}$.

Some students will do the following to simplify this expression: $\sqrt{-1} \cdot \sqrt{-1} = \sqrt{(-1)(-1)} = \sqrt{+1} = 1$.

Other students may do the following with the same request: $\sqrt{-1} \cdot \sqrt{-1} = \left(\sqrt{-1}\right)^2 = -1$.

If both groups of students were correct, then this would imply that $1 = -1$, since both are equal to $\sqrt{-1} \cdot \sqrt{-1}$. Clearly, this can't be true!

What could be wrong? Once again, a "fallacy" appears when we violate a mathematics rule. Here (for obvious reasons) we define that $\sqrt{ab} = \sqrt{a} \cdot \sqrt{b}$ is only valid when at least one of a or b is nonnegative. This would indicate that the first group of students who got $\sqrt{-1} \cdot \sqrt{-1} = \sqrt{(-1)(-1)} = \sqrt{+1} = 1$ was wrong.

6.3 Thou Shalt Not Divide by 0

Every math teacher knows that division by 0 is forbidden. As a matter of fact, on the list of commandments in mathematics, this is at the top. But why is division by 0 not permissible? We in mathematics pride ourselves on the order and beauty in which everything in the realm of mathematics falls neatly into place. When something arises that could spoil that order, we simply *define* it to suit our needs. This is precisely what happens with division by 0. You give students a much greater insight into the nature of mathematics by explaining why "rules" are set forth. So let's give this "commandment" some meaning.

Consider the quotient $\frac{n}{0}$, with $n \neq 0$. Without acknowledging the division-by-zero commandment, let us speculate (i.e., guess) what the quotient might be. Let us say it is p. In that case, we could check by multiplying $0 \cdot p$ to see if it equals n, as would have to be the case for the division to be correct. We know that $0 \cdot p \neq n$, since $0 \cdot p = 0$. So there is no number p that can take on the quotient to this division. For that reason, we define division by 0 to be invalid.

A more convincing case for defining away division by 0 is to show students how it can lead to a contradiction of an accepted fact, namely, that $1 \neq 2$. We will show them that were division by 0 acceptable, then $1 = 2$, clearly an absurdity!

Here is the "proof" that $1 = 2$:

$$\text{Let } a = b$$
$$\text{Then } a^2 = ab \qquad \text{(multiplying both sides by } a\text{)}$$
$$a^2 - b^2 = ab - b^2 \qquad \text{(subtracting } b^2 \text{ from both sides)}$$
$$(a - b)(a + b) = b(a - b) \qquad \text{(factoring)}$$
$$a + b = b \qquad \text{[dividing by } (a - b)\text{]}$$
$$2b = b \qquad \text{(replacing } a \text{ by } b\text{)}$$
$$2 = 1 \qquad \text{(dividing both sides by } b\text{)}$$

In the step where we divided by $(a - b)$, we actually divided by 0, because $a = b$, so $a - b = 0$. That ultimately led us to an absurd result, leaving us with no option other than to prohibit division by 0. By taking the time to explain this rule about division by 0 to your students, they will have a much better appreciation for mathematics.

6.4 All Triangles Are Isosceles

George Pólya, one of the great mathematicians of our time, said, "Geometry is the science of correct reasoning on incorrect figures." We will demonstrate below that making conclusions based on "incorrect" figures can lead us to impossible results. Even the statements of the fallacies sound absurd. However, students will find the demonstration of proving something that is absurd to be either frustrating or enchanting, depending on the spin the teacher puts on it. Nevertheless, follow each statement of the "proof" and see if you can detect the mistake. It rests on something that Euclid in his *Elements* would not have been able to resolve because of a lack of a definition.

The Fallacy   *Any scalene triangle (a triangle with three unequal sides) is isosceles (a triangle having two equal sides).*

To prove that scalene $\triangle ABC$ is isosceles, we must draw a few auxiliary line segments. Draw the bisector of $\angle C$ and the perpendicular bisector of $\overline{AB}$. From their point of intersection, G, draw perpendiculars to $\overleftrightarrow{AC}$ and $\overleftrightarrow{CB}$, meeting them at points D and F, respectively.

It should be noted that there are four possibilities for the above description for various scalene triangles:

Figure 6.1, where $\overleftrightarrow{CG}$ and $\overleftrightarrow{GE}$ meet inside the triangle.

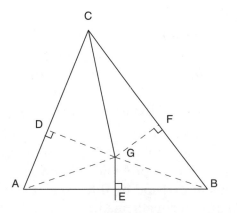

Figure 6.1

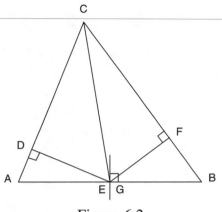

Figure 6.2

Figure 6.2, where $\overline{CG}$ and $\overline{GE}$ meet on $\overline{AB}$.

Figure 6.3, where $\overline{CG}$ and $\overline{GE}$ meet outside the triangle, but the perpendiculars $\overline{GD}$ and $\overline{GF}$ fall on $\overline{AC}$ and $\overline{CB}$.

Figure 6.4, where $\overline{CG}$ and $\overline{GE}$ meet outside the triangle, but the perpendiculars $\overline{GD}$ and $\overline{GF}$ meet $\overrightarrow{CA}$ and $\overrightarrow{CB}$ outside the triangle.

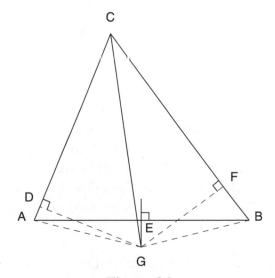

Figure 6.3

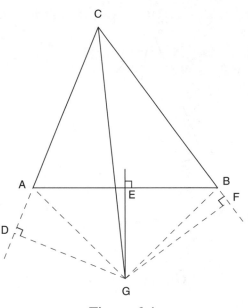

Figure 6.4

The "proof" of the fallacy can be done with any of these figures. Follow the "proof" on any (or all) of these figures.

Given   △*ABC* is scalene.

Prove   *AC* = *BC* (or △*ABC* is isosceles).

Proof   Since ∠*ACG* ≅ ∠*BCG* and right ∠*CDG* ≅ right ∠*CFG*, △*CDG* ≅ △*CFG* (SAA). Therefore, *DG* = *FG* and *CD* = *CF*. Since *AG* = *BG* (a point on the perpendicular bisector of a line segment is equidistant from the endpoints of the line segment) and ∠*ADG* and ∠*BFG* are right angles, △*DAG* ≅ △*FBG* (hypotenuse leg). Therefore, *DA* = *FB*. It then follows that *AC* = *BC* (by addition in Figures 6.1–6.3 and by subtraction in Figure 6.4).

At this point, you may be somewhat disturbed, wondering where the error was committed that permitted this fallacy to occur. By rigorous construction, you will find a subtle error in the figures:

a. The point *G must* be outside the triangle.
b. When perpendiculars meet the sides of the triangle, one will meet a
   side *between* the vertices, while the other will not.

In the general terms used by Euclid, this dilemma would remain an
enigma, since the concept of *betweenness* was not defined in his *Elements*. In the following discussion, we shall prove that errors exist in the
fallacious proof above. Our proof uses Euclidean methods, but assumes a
definition of betweenness.

Begin by considering the circumcircle of △*ABC* (see Figure 6.5).

The bisector of ∠*ACB* must contain the midpoint *G*, of $\overset{\frown}{AB}$ (since ∠*ACG*
and ∠*BCG* are congruent inscribed angles). The perpendicular bisector of
$\overline{AB}$ must bisect $\overset{\frown}{AB}$ and therefore pass through *G*. Thus, the bisector of
∠*ACB* and the perpendicular bisector of $\overline{AB}$ intersect *outside* the triangle
at *G*. This eliminates the possibilities illustrated in Figures 6.1 and 6.2.

Now consider inscribed quadrilateral *ACBG*. Since the opposite angles
of an inscribed (or cyclic) quadrilateral are supplementary, *m*∠*CAG* +
m∠*CBG* = 180°. If ∠*CAG* and ∠*CBG* are right angles, then $\overline{CG}$ would

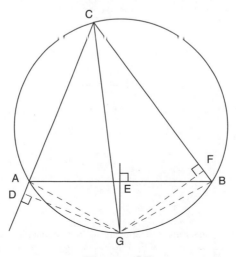

Figure 6.5

be a diameter and $\triangle ABC$ would be isosceles. Therefore, since $\triangle ABC$ is scalene, $\angle CAG$ and $\angle CBG$ are not right angles. In this case, one must be acute and the other obtuse. Suppose $\angle CBG$ is acute and $\angle CAG$ is obtuse. Then in $\triangle CBG$ the altitude on $\overline{CB}$ must be *inside* the triangle, while in obtuse $\triangle CAG$, the altitude on $\overline{AC}$ must be *outside* the triangle. (This is usually readily accepted without proof, but can be easily proved.) The fact that one and only one of the perpendiculars intersects a side of the triangle between the vertices destroys the fallacious "proof."

This rather thorough discussion of this famous geometric fallacy will give the teacher lots of options as to how to best present it to a class. It must be presented in an entertaining way and yet the explanation must be tailored to the particular class. Some may require a rigorous explanation, while others will be satisfied with one less formal.

6.5 An Infinite-Series Fallacy

Here is one that will leave many students somewhat baffled. Yet the "answer" is a bit subtle and may be beyond the reach of some students to whom you may be tempted to show this.

By ignoring the notion of a convergent series,* we get the following dilemma:

Let

$$
\begin{aligned}
S &= 1 - 1 + 1 - 1 + 1 - 1 + 1 - 1 + \cdots \\
&= (1 - 1) + (1 - 1) + (1 - 1) + (1 - 1) + \cdots \\
&= 0 + 0 + 0 + 0 + \cdots \\
&= 0
\end{aligned}
$$

---

* In simple terms, a series converges if it appears to be approaching a specific finite sum. For example, the series $1 + \frac{1}{2} + \frac{1}{4} + \frac{1}{8} + \frac{1}{16} + \frac{1}{32} + \cdots$ converges to 2, while the series $1 + \frac{1}{2} + \frac{1}{3} + \frac{1}{4} + \frac{1}{5} + \frac{1}{6} + \cdots$ does not converge to any finite sum, but continues to grow indefinitely.

However, were we to group this differently, we would get the following:

Let

$$S = 1 - 1 + 1 - 1 + 1 - 1 + 1 - 1 + \cdots$$
$$= 1 - (1 - 1) - (1 - 1) - (1 - 1) - \cdots$$
$$= 1 - 0 - 0 - 0 - \cdots$$
$$= 1$$

Therefore, since $S = 1$ and $S = 0$, it would follow that $1 = 0$. What's wrong with this argument?

If this hasn't upset you enough, consider the following argument:

Let

$$S = 1 + 2 + 4 + 8 + 16 + 32 + 64 + \cdots \tag{1}$$

Here S is clearly positive.

Also,

$$S - 1 = 2 + 4 + 8 + 16 + 32 + 64 + \cdots \tag{2}$$

Now, by multiplying both sides of (1) by 2, we get

$$2S = 2 + 4 + 8 + 16 + 32 + 64 + \cdots \tag{3}$$

Substituting (2) into (3) gives us

$$2S = S - 1$$

from which we can conclude that $S = -1$.

This would have us conclude that -1 is positive, since we established earlier that S was positive. What should students make of this weird result?

Have them look back to see if there was any obvious error made. Actually, the flaw here has to do with convergence.

To clarify the last fallacy, you might want students to compare the following correct form of a convergent series:

Let

$$S = 1 + \frac{1}{2} + \frac{1}{4} + \frac{1}{8} + \frac{1}{16} + \cdots$$

We then have

$$2S = 2 + 1 + \frac{1}{2} + \frac{1}{4} + \frac{1}{8} + \frac{1}{16} + \cdots$$

Then $2S = 2 + S$, and $S = 2$, which is true. The difference lies in the notion of a convergent series, as this last one is. What we did above for a divergent series was not permissible.

6.6 The Deceptive Border

Have you ever been frustrated by a map book that forced you to turn to the next map page, when the town you were searching for was "just off the map?" Most of these map books, in order to appear attractive, place a border around the map on each page. Have you ever wondered how much space these borders take up?

It probably would be an eye-opener for students to discover this, but, more important, it will make them more alert about the quantitative world around them. Let us consider a map book that has dimensions of 8 inches by 10 inches. A modest border might be $\frac{1}{2}$ inch in width and not be considered obtrusive. Let us inspect that situation.

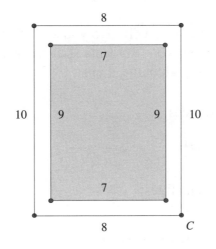

The area of the entire page is 80 square inches and the area of the map is 63 square inches. Therefore, the area of the border region is $80 - 63 = 17$ square inches. This happens to be

$$\frac{17}{80} = 0.2125 = 21.25\%$$

or more than one-fifth of the area of the page! Wouldn't it be nice if the "useless" borders did not take up over 20% of the map book? There would then be fewer pages, and perhaps even a lower cost. But above all, you wouldn't have to turn the page to find your town that just got cut off by the border.

What is essential here is to make students alert to the quantitative world around them. There are lots of examples in everyday life that could provoke this kind of astonishment.

6.7 Puzzling Paradoxes

Paradoxes are fun to observe and yet have a very important message embedded within them. There is much to be learned through this entertainment.

Here are some paradoxes that will give you something to think about and that will initially perplex your students. Let them ponder the difficulty, when it arises, before enlightening them.

$$2 \text{ pounds} = 32 \text{ ounces}$$
$$\frac{1}{2} \text{ pound} = 8 \text{ ounces}$$

By multiplying these equalities:

$$\left(2 \cdot \frac{1}{2}\right) \text{ pounds} = (32 \cdot 8) \text{ ounces}$$

or

$$1 \text{ pound} = 256 \text{ ounces!}$$

This paradox lies in the fact that the units were not treated properly and can be best answered by considering the following example:

$$2 \text{ feet} = 24 \text{ inches}$$
$$\frac{1}{2} \text{ foot} = 6 \text{ inches}$$

By multiplying, we get

$$1 \text{ square foot} = 144 \text{ square inches}$$

Another paradox is seen below:

$$1 \cdot 0 = 2 \cdot 0$$

And we know that

$$0 = 0$$

Dividing these equalities, gives us

$$1 = 2$$

Here, of course, we see the familiar rule, not allowing us to divide by zero, being broken and thus leading us to an absurd result.

The messages of each of these paradoxes should remain clear for your students.

6.8 A Trigonometric Fallacy

The basis for trigonometry is the Pythagorean theorem. In trigonometry, it often manifests itself as $\cos^2 x + \sin^2 x = 1$. Students should know that if a right triangle has sides of lengths $\sin x$, $\cos x$, and 1, then the trigonometric functions hold and the Pythagorean theorem yields $\cos^2 x + \sin^2 x = 1$.

From this, we can show that $4 = 0$. It is to be assumed that your students know this cannot be true. So it is up to them to find the fallacy as it is made. Don't expose it until they reach the end of the unit.

The Pythagorean identity can be written as

$$\cos^2 x = 1 - \sin^2 x$$

If they take the square root of each side of this equation, they get

$$\cos x = (1 - \sin^2 x)^{1/2}$$

Tell them to add 1 to each side of the equation to get

$$1 + \cos x = 1 + (1 - \sin^2 x)^{1/2}$$

Then they are to square both sides:

$$(1 + \cos x)^2 = \left[1 + (1 - \sin^2 x)^{1/2}\right]^2$$

Ask them to find the value of this when $x = 180°$:

$$\cos 180° = -1 \qquad \text{and} \qquad \sin 180° = 0$$

Substituting into the above equation gives them:

$$(1 - 1)^2 = \left[1 + (1 - 0)^{1/2}\right]^2$$

Then

$$0 = (1 + 1)^2 = 4$$

Since $0 \neq 4$, there must be some error. Where is it? Here is a hint you can give them:

When $x^2 = p^2$, then $x = +p$ and $x = -p$.

Students should realize that a quadratic equation must have two roots. Sometimes a root is rejected in context since it may lead to an absurd result.

6.9 Limits with Understanding

The concept of a limit is not to be taken lightly. It is a very sophisticated concept that can be easily misinterpreted. Sometimes the issues surrounding the concept are quite subtle. Misunderstanding of these can lead to some curious (or humorous, depending on your viewpoint) situations. This can be nicely exhibited with the following two illustrations. Consider them separately and then notice their connection.

Illustration 1   It is simple to see that the sum of the lengths of the bold segments (the "stairs") is equal to $a + b$.

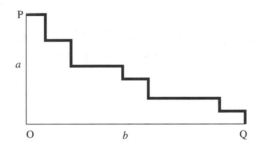

The sum of the bold segments ("stairs"), found by summing all the horizontal and all the vertical segments, is $a + b$. If the number of stairs increases, the sum is still $a + b$. The dilemma arises when we increase the stairs to a "limit," so that the set of stairs appears to be a straight line, in this case the hypotenuse of $\triangle POQ$. It would then appear that $\overline{PQ}$ has length $a + b$. Yet we know from the Pythagorean theorem that $PQ = \sqrt{a^2 + b^2}$ and *not* $a + b$. So what's wrong?

Nothing is wrong! While the set consisting of the stairs does indeed approach closer and closer to the straight line segment PQ, it does *not* therefore follow that the *sum* of the bold (horizontal and vertical) lengths approaches the length of $\overline{PQ}$, contrary to intuition. There is no contradiction here, only a failure on the part of our intuition.

Another way to "explain" this dilemma is to argue the following. As the "stairs" get smaller, they increase in number. In an extreme situation, we have zero-length dimensions (for the stairs) used an infinite number of times, which then leads to considering $0 \cdot \infty$, which is meaningless!

A similar situation arises with the following example.

Illustration 2   In the figure below, the smaller semicircles extend from one end of the large semicircle's diameter to the other.

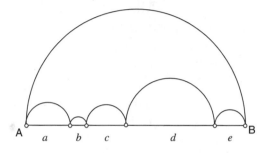

It is easy to show that the sum of the arc lengths of the smaller semicircles is equal to the arc length of the larger semicircle. That is, the sum of the smaller semicircles

$$= \frac{\pi a}{2} + \frac{\pi b}{2} + \frac{\pi c}{2} + \frac{\pi d}{2} + \frac{\pi e}{2} = \frac{\pi}{2}(a + b + c + d + e) = \frac{\pi}{2}(AB)$$

which is the arc length of the larger semicircle. This may not "appear" to be true, but it is! As a matter of fact, as we increase the number of smaller semicircles (where, of course, they get smaller), the sum "appears" to be approaching the length of the segment AB, but, in fact, does not!

Again, the set consisting of the semicircles does indeed approach the length of the straight line segment AB. It does *not* follow, however, that the *sum* of the semicircles approaches the *length* of the limit, in this case AB.

This "apparent limit sum" is absurd, since the shortest distance between points A and B is the length of segment AB, not the semicircle arc AB (which equals the sum of the smaller semicircles). This is an important concept to present to students, best done with the help of these motivating illustrations, so that future misinterpretations can be avoided.

7 Counting and Probability

In today's world, mathematically sophisticated ways of counting are becoming an important aspect of what youngsters are expected to learn in their mathematics instruction. Concepts of probability are being infused into the curriculum more than ever before. Both of these have an entertaining side as well. It is that which we will savor here.

For example, did you know that the 13th of the month is most likely to fall on a Friday, or have you considered the probability of two people in your class sharing the same birthday? Perhaps one of the most controversial topics for discussion several years ago was the ideal strategy that a contestant on the TV show "Let's Make a Deal" should use. These are just a few of the topics presented in this chapter. It is short and sweet and, we hope, also entertaining.

7.1 Friday the 13th!

The number 13 is usually associated with being an unlucky number. Buildings with more than 13 stories typically will omit the number 13 from the floor numbering. This is immediately noticeable in the elevator, where there is sometimes no button for 13. You might ask your students for other examples where the number 13 is associated with bad luck. They ought to stumble on the notion that when the 13th of a month turns up on a Friday, then it is particularly bad. This may derive from the belief that there were *13* people present at the Last Supper, which resulted in the crucifixion on a *Friday*.

Ask your students if they think that the 13th comes up on a Friday with equal regularity as on the other days of the week. They will be astonished that, lo and behold, the 13th comes up more frequently on Friday than on any other day of the week.

This fact was first published by B. H. Brown.* He stated that the Gregorian calendar follows a pattern of leap years, repeating every 400 years. The number of days in one 4-year cycle is $3 \cdot 365 + 366$. So in 400 years there are $100(3 \cdot 365 + 366) - 3 = 146{,}097$ days. Note that the century year, unless divisible by 400, is not a leap year; hence the deduction of 3. This total number of days is exactly divisible by 7. Since there are 4,800 months in this 400-year cycle, the 13th comes up 4,800 times according to the following table. Interestingly enough, the 13th comes up on a Friday more often than on any other day of the week. Students might want to consider how this can be verified.

Day of the week	Number of 13s	Percentage
Sunday	687	14.313
Monday	685	14.271
Tuesday	685	14.271
Wednesday	687	14.313
Thursday	684	14.250
Friday	*688*	*14.333*
Saturday	684	14.250

---

* "Solution to Problem E36," *American Mathematical Monthly*, Vol. 40, 1933, p. 607.

7.2 Think Before Counting

Very often a problem situation seems so simple that we plunge right in without first thinking about a strategy to use. This impetuous beginning for the solution often leads to a less elegant solution than one that results from a bit of forethought. Here are two examples of simple problems that can be made even simpler by thinking before working on them.

Find all pairs of prime numbers whose sum equals 999.

Many students will begin by taking a list of prime numbers and trying various pairs to see if they obtain 999 for a sum. This is obviously very tedious as well as time consuming, and students would never be quite certain that they had considered all the prime number pairs.

Let's use some logical reasoning to solve this problem. In order to obtain an odd sum for two numbers (prime or otherwise), exactly one of the numbers must be even. Since there is only one even prime, namely 2, there can be only one pair of primes whose sum is 999, and that pair is 2 and 997. That, now, seems so simple.

A second problem where preplanning, or some orderly thinking, makes sense is as follows:

A palindrome is a number that reads the same forward and backward, such as 747 or 1,991. How many palindromes are there between 1 and 1,000 inclusive?

The traditional approach to this problem would be to attempt to write out all the numbers between 1 and 1,000 and then see which ones are palindromes. However, this is a cumbersome and time-consuming task at best, and one could easily omit some of them.

Let's see if we can look for a pattern to solve the problem in a more direct fashion.

Range	Number of palindromes	Total number
1–9	9	9
10–99	9	18
100–199	10	28
200–299	10	38
300–399	10	48
·	·	·
·	·	·
·	·	·

There is a pattern. There are exactly 10 palindromes in each group of 100 numbers (after 99). Thus, there will be 9 sets of 10, or 90, plus the 18 from numbers 1 to 99, for a total of 108 palindromes between 1 and 1,000.

Another solution to this problem would involve organizing the data in a favorable way. Consider all the single-digit numbers (self-palindromes), which number 9. The two-digit palindromes (two same digits) also number 9. The three-digit palindromes have 9 possible "outside digits" and 10 possible "middle digits," so there are 90 of these. In total, there are 108 palindromes between 1 and 1,000, inclusive.

Clever counting can often make work much easier. The motto is: Think first, then begin a solution!

7.3 The Worthless Increase

Present the following situation to your students.

> **Suppose you had a job where you received a 10% raise. Because business was falling off, the boss was soon forced to give you a 10% cut in salary. Will you be back to your starting salary?**

The answer is a resounding (and very surprising) *No!*

Telling students this little story is quite disconcerting, since one would expect that with the same percentage increase and decrease you should be back to where you started. This is intuitive thinking, but wrong. Let students convince themselves of this by choosing a specific amount of money and trying to follow the instructions.

Begin with $100. Calculate a 10% increase on the $100 to get $110. Now take a 10% decrease of this $110 to get $99—$1 less than the beginning amount.

Students may wonder whether the result would have been different if we had first calculated the 10% decrease and then the 10% increase. Using the same $100 basis, we first calculate a 10% decrease to get $90. Then the 10% increase yields $99, the same as before. So order apparently makes no difference.

A similar situation, one that is deceptively misleading, can be faced by a gambler. Have your students consider the following situation. They may want to even simulate it with a friend to see if their intuition bears out.

> **You are offered a chance to play a game. The rules are simple. There are 100 cards, face down. Fifty-five of the cards say "win" and 45 of the cards say "lose." You begin with a bankroll of $10,000. You must bet one-half of your money on each card turned over, and you either win or lose that amount based on what the card says. At the end of the game, all cards have been turned over. How much money do you have at the end of the game?**

The same principle as above applies here. It is obvious that you will win 10 times more than you will lose, so it appears that you will end with more than $10,000. What is obvious is often wrong, and this is a good example. Let's say that you win on the first card; you now have $15,000. Now you lose on the second card; you now have $7,500. If you had first lost and then won, you would still have $7,500. So every time you win one and lose one, you lose one-fourth of your money. So you end up with

$$10,000 \cdot \left(\frac{3}{4}\right)^{45} \cdot \left(\frac{3}{2}\right)^{10}$$

This is $1.38 when rounded off. Surprised? What reaction might you get from your students?

7.4 Birthday Matches

This charmer presents one of the most surprising results in mathematics. It is best that you present it to your class with as much "drama" as you can. This unit will win converts to probability as no other example can, since it combats the students' intuition quite dramatically.

Let us suppose you have a class with about 35 students. Begin by asking the class what they think the chances (or probability) are of two classmates having the same birth date (month and day only) in their class of about 30+ students. Students usually begin to think about the likelihood of two people having the same date out of a selection of 365 days (assuming no leap year). Perhaps 2 out of 365?

Ask them to consider the "randomly" selected group of the first 35 presidents of the United States. They may be astonished that there are two with the same birth date:

the 11th President, James K. Polk (November 2, 1795)
the 29th President, Warren G. Harding (November 2, 1865)

The class will probably be surprised to learn that for a group of 35 the probability that two members will have the same birth date is greater than 8 out of 10, or 80%.

Students may wish to try their own experiment by visiting 10 nearby classrooms to check on date matches. For groups of 30, the probability that there will be a match is greater than 7 out of 10, or in 7 of these 10 rooms there ought to be a match of birth dates. What causes this incredible and unanticipated result? Can this be true? It seems to go against our intuition.

To relieve students of their curiosity, guide them as follows:

First, ask what the probability is that one selected student matches his own birth date? Clearly, *certainty*, or 1. This can be written as $\frac{365}{365}$.

The probability that another student does *not* match the first student is

$$\frac{365 - 1}{365} = \frac{364}{365}$$

The probability that a third student does *not* match the first and second students is

$$\frac{365 - 2}{365} = \frac{363}{365}$$

The probability of all 35 students *not* having the same birth date is the product of these probabilities:

$$p = \frac{365}{365} \cdot \frac{365 - 1}{365} \cdot \frac{365 - 2}{365} \cdot \ldots \cdot \frac{365 - 34}{365}$$

Since the probability (q) that two students in the group *have* the same birth date and the probability (p) that two students in the group do *not* have the same birth date is a certainty, the sum of those probabilities must be 1. Thus, $p + q = 1$.

In this case,

$$q = 1 - \frac{365}{365} \cdot \frac{365 - 1}{365} \cdot \frac{365 - 2}{365} \cdot \ldots \cdot \frac{365 - 33}{365} \cdot \frac{365 - 34}{365}$$
$$\approx 0.8143832388747152$$

In other words, the probability that there will be a birth date match in a randomly selected group of 35 people is somewhat greater than $\frac{8}{10}$. This is quite unexpected when one considers there were 365 dates from which to choose. Students may want to investigate the nature of the probability function. Here are a few values to serve as a guide:

Number of people in group	Probability of a birth date match
10	0.1169481777110776
15	0.2529013197636863
20	0.4114383835805799
25	0.5686997039694639
30	0.7063162427192686
35	0.8143832388747152
40	0.891231809817949
45	0.9409758994657749
50	0.9703735795779884
55	0.9862622888164461
60	0.994122660865348
65	0.9976831073124921
70	0.9991595759651571

Students should notice how quickly almost-certainty is reached. With about 60 students in a room, the table indicates that it is almost certain (0.99) that two students will have the same birth date.

Were one to do this with the death dates of the first 35 presidents, one would notice that two died on March 8 (Millard Fillmore in 1874 and William H. Taft in 1930) and three presidents died on July 4 (John Adams and Thomas Jefferson in 1826 and James Monroe in 1831).

Above all, this astonishing demonstration should serve as an eye-opener about the inadvisability of relying entirely on intuition.

7.5 Calendar Peculiarities

The calendar holds many recreational ideas that can be exploited to turn students on to mathematics—or at least to explore number relationships.

Consider any calendar page, say, October 2002.

Sunday	Monday	Tuesday	Wednesday	Thursday	Friday	Saturday
		1	2	3	4	5
6	7	8	9	10	11	12
13	14	15	16	17	18	19
20	21	22	23	24	25	26
27	28	29	30	31		

Have students select a (3 by 3) square of any nine dates on the calendar. We will select those shaded above. Students should add 8 to the smallest number in the shaded region and then multiply by 9:

$$(9 + 8) \cdot 9 = 153$$

Then have students multiply the sum of the numbers of the middle row (51) of this shaded matrix by 3. Surprise! It is the same as the previously arrived at answer, 153. But why? Here are some clues: The middle number is the mean (or average) of the nine shaded numbers. The sum of the numbers in the middle column is one-third of the sum of the nine numbers. Their investigations will have favorable results.

Now that your students have an appreciation for the calendar, ask them what the probability is of 4/4,* 6/6, 8/8, 10/10, and 12/12 all falling on the same day of the week. More than likely the "knee-jerk reaction" will be about one-fifth. Wrong! The probability is 1, certainty! But why this surprising result? They are all exactly nine weeks apart. Such little known facts always draw an interest that otherwise would be untapped.

---

* 4/4 represents April 4, 6/6 represents June 6, and so on.

7.6 The Monty Hall Problem

("Let's Make a Deal")

"Let's Make a Deal" was a long-running television game show that featured a problematic situation. A randomly selected audience member would come on stage and be presented with three doors. He was asked to select one, hopefully the one behind which there was a car, and not one of the other two doors, each of which had a donkey behind it. There was only one wrinkle in this: After the contestant made his selection, the host, Monty Hall, exposed one of the two donkeys behind a not-selected door (leaving two doors still unopened) and the audience participant was asked if he wanted to stay with his original selection (not yet revealed) or switch to the other unopened door. At this point, to heighten the suspense, the rest of the audience would shout out "stay" or "switch" with seemingly equal frequency. The question is what to do? Does it make a difference? If so, which is the better strategy (i.e., the greater probability of winning) to use here?

You might have students speculate about what they think intuitively is the best strategy. Most will probably say that there is no difference, since at the end you have a one out of two chance of getting the car. Tell them they are wrong, and then you will have a very curious audience in front of you.

Let's look at this now step by step. The result gradually will become clear.

There are *two donkeys* and *one car* behind these doors.

You must try to get the car. You select Door 3.

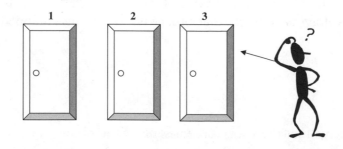

Monty Hall opens one of the doors that you *did not* select and exposes a donkey.

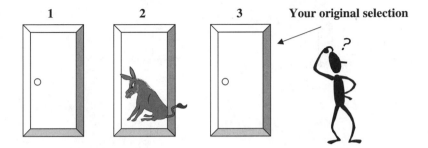

He asks, "Do you still want your first-choice door, or do you want to switch to the other closed door ?"

To help make a decision, consider an *extreme case*:

Suppose there were 1,000 doors instead of just three doors.

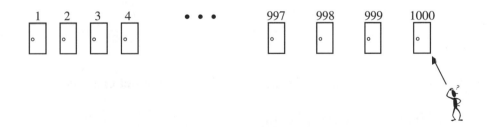

You choose Door 1,000. How likely is it that you chose the right door?

"Very unlikely," since the probability of getting the right door is $\frac{1}{1,000}$.

How likely is it that the car is behind one of the other doors?

"Very likely": $\frac{999}{1,000}$.

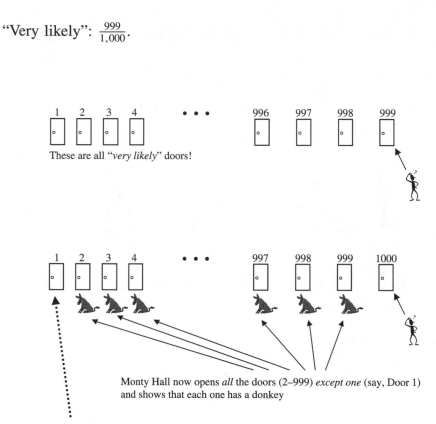

These are all *"very likely"* doors!

Monty Hall now opens *all* the doors (2–999) *except one* (say, Door 1) and shows that each one has a donkey

A *"very likely"* door is left: Door 1.

We are now ready to answer the question. Which is a better choice:

- Door 1,000 ("very unlikely" door)?
- Door 1 ("very likely" door)?

The answer is now obvious. We ought to select the "very likely" door, which means "switching" is the better strategy for the audience participant to follow.

In the extreme case, it is much easier to see the best strategy than had we tried to analyze the situation with the three doors. The principle is the same in either situation.

There is another way to look at this problem. Consider the three cases shown in the chart below.

Case	Door 1	Door 2	Door 3
1	Car	Donkey	Donkey
2	Donkey	Car	Donkey
3	Donkey	Donkey	Car

If you chose Door 1, your chances of having a car is $\frac{1}{3}$.

Monty Hall opens the door you selected and reveals a donkey. In cases 2 and 3, you should select a different door (only in case 1 should you select the same door). In other words, in 2 of the 3 cases, switching is better. Therefore, you are better off switching doors 2 out of 3 times.

You might want to mention to students that this problem has caused many an argument in academic circles, and was also a topic of discussion in the *New York Times* and other popular publications. John Tierney wrote in the *New York Times* (Sunday, July 21, 1991) that "perhaps it was only an illusion, but for a moment here it seemed that an end might be in sight to the debate raging among mathematicians, readers of *Parade* magazine, and fans of the television game show 'Let's Make a Deal.' They began arguing last September after Marilyn vos Savant published a puzzle in *Parade*. As readers of her 'Ask Marilyn' column are reminded each week, Ms. vos Savant is listed in the Guinness Book of World Records Hall of Fame for 'Highest I.Q.,' but that credential did not impress the public when she answered this question from a reader." She gave the right answer, but still many mathematicians argued.

7.7 Anticipating Heads and Tails

This lovely little unit will show you how some clever reasoning, along with algebraic knowledge of the most elementary kind, will help you solve a seemingly "impossibly difficult" problem.

Have your students consider the following problem.

> **You are seated at a table in a dark room. On the table there are 12 pennies, 5 of which are heads up and 7 are tails up. (You know where the coins are, so you can move or flip any coin, but because it is dark you will not know if the coin you are touching was originally heads up or tails up.) You are to separate the coins into two piles (possibly flipping some of them) so that when the lights are turned on there will be an equal number of heads in each pile.**

Their first reaction is likely to be: "You must be kidding! How can anyone do this task without seeing which coins are heads or tails up?" This is where a most clever (yet incredibly simple) use of algebra will be the key to the solution.

Let's "cut to the quick." You might actually want to have your students try it with 12 coins. Here is what you have them do. Separate the coins into two piles of five and seven coins, respectively. Then flip over the coins in the smaller pile. Now both piles will have the same number of heads! That's all! They will think this is magic. How did this happen? Well, this is where algebra helps to understand what was actually done.

Let's say that when they separate the coins in the dark room, h heads will end up in the seven-coin pile. Then the other pile, the five-coin pile, will have $5 - h$ heads and $5 - (5 - h) = h$ tails. When they flip all the coins in the smaller pile, the $5 - h$ heads become tails and the h tails become heads. Now each pile contains h heads! What an awed reaction you will get!

8 Mathematical Potpourri

All the topics that could not find a proper home in the first seven chapters of the book reside in this chapter. We have a mixture of delightful topics that are sure to interest your students in mathematics. Do not be fooled by their location; less important topics are not relegated to the last chapter (as may be the case with some textbooks). Quite the contrary.

Here you will see one of the most amazing magic squares, presented from its first appearance in Albrecht Dürer's *Melencolia I* to the plethora of properties that it has, above and beyond those of normal magic squares. You will be exposed to mathematical manifestations in nature and you will be presented ultimately with some famous unsolved problems (no, your students are not expected to solve problems that, for hundreds of years, have not been solved). It is quite likely that this last chapter could prove most entertaining, as it seems to cover a very wide range of topics, none of which allows itself to be categorized in the previous seven chapters. Perhaps we should have called this Chapter 1!

8.1 Perfection in Mathematics

What is perfect in mathematics, a subject where most think everything is already perfect? Over the years, various authors have been found to name perfect squares, perfect numbers, perfect rectangles, and perfect triangles. You might ask your students to try to add to the list of "perfection." What other mathematical things may be worthy of the adjective "perfect"?

Begin with the **perfect squares.** They are well known: 1, 4, 9, 16, 25, 36, 49, 64, 81, 100, ... They are numbers whose square roots are natural numbers: 1, 2, 3, 4, 5, 6, 7, 8, 9, 10, ...

A **perfect number** is one having the property that the sum of its factors (excluding the number itself) equals the number. The first four perfect numbers are

    6 $(1 + 2 + 3)$
    28 $(1 + 2 + 4 + 7 + 14)$
    496 $(1 + 2 + 4 + 8 + 16 + 31 + 62 + 124 + 248)$
    8,128 (have your students find the sum of the factors)

They were already known to the ancient Greeks (*Introductio Arithmeticae* by Nichomachus, ca. 100 C.E.). Interestingly, the Greeks felt that there was exactly one perfect number for each digit group of numbers. The first four perfect numbers seemed to fit this pattern; namely, among the single-digit numbers, the only perfect number is 6, among the two-digit numbers, there is only 28, then 496 is the only three-digit perfect number, and 8,128 is the only four-digit perfect number. Try asking your students to predict the number of digits in the next larger perfect number. No doubt, they will say it must be a five-digit number. Furthermore, if you ask your students to make other conjectures about perfect numbers, they may conclude that perfect numbers must end in a 6 or an 8 alternately.

As a matter of fact, there is no five-digit perfect number at all. This should teach students to be cautious about making predictions with relatively little evidence. The next larger perfect number has eight digits: 33,550,336. Then we must take a large leap to the next perfect number: 8,589,869,056.

Here we also see that our conjecture (although reasonable) of getting alternate final digits of 6 and 8 is false.* This is a good lesson about drawing inductive conclusions prematurely.

Perfect rectangles are those whose areas are numerically equal to their perimeters. There are only two perfect rectangles, namely, one having sides of length 3 and 6, and the other with sides of lengths 4 and 4.

There are also **perfect triangles.**** These are defined as triangles whose areas are numerically equal to their perimeters. Students should be able to identify the right triangles that fit that pattern by simply setting the area and perimeter formulas equal to each other. Among the right triangles, there are only two triangles, one with sides of lengths 6, 8, and 10, and the other with sides of lengths 5, 12, and 13.

Among the non–right triangles, there are only three whose areas are numerically equal to their perimeters. They are

6, 25, 29
7, 15, 20
9, 10, 17

These three cases can be verified using Heron's formula:

$$\text{Area} = \sqrt{s(s-a)(s-b)(s-c)}$$

where a, b, and c are the lengths of the sides and s is the semiperimeter.

What does this do for us? Very little, except to allow us to appreciate the "perfection" in mathematics. Students ought to be encouraged to find other candidates for perfection.

---

* The formula for a perfect number is that if $2^k - 1$ is a prime number ($k > 1$), then $2^{k-1}(2^k - 1)$ is an even perfect number.
** See M. V. Bonsangue, G. E. Gannon, E. Buchman, and N. Gross, "In Search of Perfect Triangles," *The Mathematics Teacher*, Vol. 92, No. 1, January 1999, pp. 56–61.

8.2 The Beautiful Magic Square

There are entire books written about magic squares* of all kinds. There
is one magic square, however, that stands out from the rest for its origin
and the many properties it has beyond those required for a square matrix
of numbers to be considered "magic." This magic square even comes to
us through art and not through the usual mathematical channels. It is
depicted in the background of the famous engraving produced in 1514 by
the renowned German artist Albrecht Dürer (1471–1528), who lived in
Nürnberg, Germany.

---

* See W. H. Benson and O. Jacoby, *New Recreations with Magic Squares* (New York: Dover, 1976)
and W. S. Andrews, *Magic Squares and Cubes* (New York: Dover, 1960). A concise treatment
can be found in A. S. Posamentier and J. Stepelman, *Teaching Secondary School Mathematics:
Techniques and Enrichment Units*, 6th ed. (Upper Saddle River, NJ: Prentice Hall/Merrill, 2002),
pp. 240–244.

A magic square is a square matrix of numbers, where the sum of the numbers in each of its columns, rows, and diagonals is the same. Just for practice, you might have your students try to construct a 3-by-3 magic square. Here is the solution (for your convenience).

4	9	2
3	5	7
8	1	6

You might then ask them to construct a 4-by-4 magic square.* After they have had ample time to construct this magic square, begin the discussion of the Dürer square. Most of Dürer's works were signed by him with his initials, one over the other, with the year in which the work was made included there. Here we find it near the lower right side of the picture. We notice that it was made in the year 1514. Astute students may notice that the two center cells of the bottom row depict the year as well. Let us look at this magic square more closely.

16	3	2	13
5	10	11	8
9	6	7	12
4	15	14	1

First, let's make sure that it is a magic square. The sums of all the rows, all the columns, and the two diagonals must be equal. Well, they are, each having a sum of 34. So that is all that would be required for this square matrix of numbers to be considered a "magic square." However, this Dürer magic square has lots more properties that other magic squares do not have. We shall list some here.

- The four corner numbers have a sum of 34:

$$16 + 13 + 1 + 4 = 34$$

---

* A 4-by-4 magic square is usually constructed by writing the numbers from 1 to 16 in proper order, row by row, and then striking out the numbers in the two diagonals. Each of these struck-out numbers is then replaced by its complement, that is, the number which when added to it yields a sum of 17 (one greater than the number of cells). However, the Dürer square interchanged the two middle columns to get the date of the etching in the two bottom center cells.

- Each of the four corner 2-by-2 squares has a sum of 34:

$$16 + 3 + 5 + 10 = 34$$
$$2 + 13 + 11 + 8 = 34$$
$$9 + 6 + 4 + 15 = 34$$
$$7 + 12 + 14 + 1 = 34$$

- The center 2-by-2 square has a sum of 34:

$$10 + 11 + 6 + 7 = 34$$

- The sum of the numbers in the diagonal cells equals the sum of the numbers in the cells not in the diagonals:

$$16 + 10 + 7 + 1 + 4 + 6 + 11 + 13$$
$$= 3 + 2 + 8 + 12 + 14 + 15 + 9 + 5 = 68$$

- The sum of the squares of the numbers in the diagonal cells equals the sum of the squares of the numbers not in the diagonal cells:

$$16^2 + 10^2 + 7^2 + 1^2 + 4^2 + 6^2 + 11^2 + 13^2$$
$$= 3^2 + 2^2 + 8^2 + 12^2 + 14^2 + 15^2 + 9^2 + 5^2 = 748$$

- The sum of the cubes of the numbers in the diagonal cells equals the sum of the cubes of the numbers not in the diagonal cells:

$$16^3 + 10^3 + 7^3 + 1^3 + 4^3 + 6^3 + 11^3 + 13^3$$
$$= 3^3 + 2^3 + 8^3 + 12^3 + 14^3 + 15^3 + 9^3 + 5^3 = 9{,}248$$

- The sum of the squares of the numbers in the diagonal cells equals the sum of the squares of the numbers in the first and third rows:

$$16^2 + 10^2 + 7^2 + 1^2 + 4^2 + 6^2 + 11^2 + 13^2$$
$$= 16^2 + 3^2 + 2^2 + 13^2 + 9^2 + 6^2 + 7^2 + 12^2 = 748$$

- The sum of the squares of the numbers in the diagonal cells equals the sum of the squares of the numbers in the second and fourth rows:

$$16^2 + 10^2 + 7^2 + 1^2 + 4^2 + 6^2 + 11^2 + 13^2$$
$$= 5^2 + 10^2 + 11^2 + 8^2 + 4^2 + 15^2 + 14^2 + 1^2 = 748$$

- The sum of the squares of the numbers in the diagonal cells equals the sum of the squares of the numbers in the first and third columns:

$$16^2 + 10^2 + 7^2 + 1^2 + 4^2 + 6^2 + 11^2 + 13^2$$
$$= 16^2 + 5^2 + 9^2 + 4^2 + 2^2 + 11^2 + 7^2 + 14^2 = 748$$

- The sum of the squares of the numbers in the diagonal cells equals the sum of the squares of the numbers in the second and fourth columns:

$$16^2 + 10^2 + 7^2 + 1^2 + 4^2 + 6^2 + 11^2 + 13^2$$
$$= 3^2 + 10^2 + 6^2 + 15^2 + 13^2 + 8^2 + 12^2 + 1^2 = 748$$

- Notice the following beautiful symmetries:

$$2 + 8 + 9 + 15 = 3 + 5 + 12 + 14 = 34$$
$$2^2 + 8^2 + 9^2 + 15^2 = 3^2 + 5^2 + 12^2 + 14^2 = 374$$
$$2^3 + 8^3 + 9^3 + 15^3 = 3^3 + 5^3 + 12^3 + 14^3 = 4{,}624$$

- The sum of each adjacent upper and lower pair of numbers (vertically) produces a pleasing symmetry:

$16 + 5 = 21$	$3 + 10 = 13$	$2 + 11 = 13$	$13 + 8 = 21$
$9 + 4 = 13$	$6 + 15 = 21$	$7 + 14 = 21$	$12 + 1 = 13$

- The sum of each adjacent upper and lower pair of numbers (horizontally) produces a pleasing symmetry:

$16 + 3 = 19$	$2 + 13 = 15$
$5 + 10 = 15$	$11 + 8 = 19$
$9 + 6 = 15$	$7 + 12 = 19$
$4 + 15 = 19$	$14 + 1 = 15$

Can your students find some other patterns in this beautiful magic square?

8.3 Unsolved Problems

This may come as a shock to some of your students, but who says that all mathematical problems get solved? Unsolved problems have a very important role in mathematics. Attempts to solve them oftentimes lead to very important findings of other sorts. Yet an unsolved problem—one not yet solved by the world's most brilliant minds—tends to pique our interest by quietly asking us if we can solve it, especially when the problem itself is exceedingly easy to understand. We shall look at some unsolved problems to get a better understanding of the history of mathematics. Twice in recent years, mathematics has made newspaper headlines, each time with the solution to a long-time unsolved problem.

The four-color problem dates back to 1852, when Francis Guthrie, while trying to color the map of counties of England, noticed that four colors sufficed. He asked his brother Frederick if it was true that *any* map can be colored using four colors in such a way that adjacent regions (i.e., those sharing a common boundary segment, not just a point) receive different colors. Frederick Guthrie then communicated the conjecture to the famous mathematician, Augustus DeMorgan. In 1977, the four-color-map problem was solved by two mathematicians, K. Appel and W. Haken, who, using a computer, considered all possible maps and established that it was never necessary to use more than four colors to color a map so that no two territories sharing a common border would be represented by the same color.

More recently, on June 23, 1993, Andrew Wiles, a Princeton University mathematics professor, announced that he solved the 350-year-old Fermat's Last Theorem. It took him another year to fix some errors in the proof, but it puts to rest a nagging problem that occupied scores of mathematicians for centuries. The problem, which Pierre de Fermat wrote (ca. 1630) in the margin of a mathematics book (Diophantus' *Arithmetica*) he was reading, was not discovered by his son until after his death. In addition to the statement of the theorem, Fermat stated that his proof was too long to fit the margin, so he effectively left to others the job of proving his statement.

Fermat's theorem $x^n + y^n = z^n$ has no nonzero integer solutions for $n > 2$.

During this time, speculation began about other unsolved problems, of which there are still many. Two of them are very easy to understand but apparently exceedingly difficult to prove. Neither has yet been proved.

Christian Goldbach (1690–1764), a Prussian mathematician, in a 1742 letter to the famous Swiss mathematician, Leonhard Euler, posed the following problem, which to this day has yet to be solved.

Goldbach's conjecture *Every even number greater than 2 can be expressed as the sum of two prime numbers.*

Even numbers greater than 2	Sum of two prime numbers
4	$2 + 2$
6	$3 + 3$
8	$3 + 5$
10	$3 + 7$
12	$5 + 7$
14	$7 + 7$
16	$5 + 11$
18	$7 + 11$
20	$7 + 13$
$\vdots$	$\vdots$
48	$19 + 29$
$\vdots$	$\vdots$
100	$3 + 97$

Can you find some more examples of this?

Goldbach's second conjecture *Every odd number greater than 5 is the sum of three primes.*

Let us consider the first few odd numbers:

Odd numbers greater than 5	Sum of three prime numbers
7	$2 + 2 + 3$
9	$3 + 3 + 3$
11	$3 + 3 + 5$
13	$3 + 5 + 5$
15	$5 + 5 + 5$
17	$5 + 5 + 7$
19	$5 + 7 + 7$
21	$7 + 7 + 7$
$\vdots$	$\vdots$
51	$3 + 17 + 31$
$\vdots$	$\vdots$
77	$5 + 5 + 67$
$\vdots$	$\vdots$
101	$5 + 7 + 89$

Your students may wish to see if there is a pattern here and generate other examples.

8.4 An Unexpected Result

Present your class with the following sequence and ask them to tell you the next number: **1, 2, 4, 8, 16.**

When the next number is given as 31 (instead of the expected 32), cries of "wrong!" are usually heard. Just tell your students that this is a correct answer, and that **1, 2, 4, 8, 16, 31** can be a legitimate sequence.

You must now convince your students of the legitimacy of this sequence. It would be nice if it could be done geometrically, as that would give convincing evidence of a physical nature. Let us first find the succeeding number in this "curious sequence."

We shall set up a table of differences (i.e., a chart showing the differences between terms of a sequence), beginning with the given sequence up to 31, and then work backward once a pattern is established (here at the third difference).

Original sequence	1		2		4		8		16		31
First difference		1		2		4		8		15	
Second difference			1		2		4		7		
Third difference				1		2		3			
Fourth difference					**1**		**1**				

With the fourth differences forming a sequence of constants, we can reverse the process (turn the table upside down), and extend the third differences a few more steps with 4 and 5.

Fourth difference				1		1		1		1					
Third difference			1		2		3		**4**		**5**			
Second difference		1		2		4		7		**11**		**16**		
First difference	1		2		4		8		**15**		**26**		**42**	
Original sequence	1		2		4		8		16		**31**		**57**		**99**

The boldface numbers are those that were obtained by working backward from the third-difference sequence. Thus, the next numbers of the given sequence are 57 and 99. The general term is a fourth-power expression since we had to go to the third differences to get a constant. The general term (n) is

$$\frac{n^4 - 6n^3 + 23n^2 - 18n + 24}{24}$$

One should not think that this sequence is independent of others parts of mathematics. Consider the Pascal triangle:

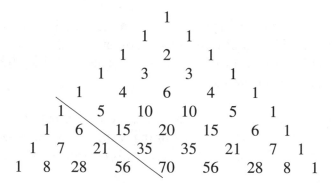

Consider the horizontal sums of the rows of the Pascal triangle to the right of the bold line drawn: 1, 2, 4, 8, 16, 31, 57, 99, 163. This is again our newly developed sequence.

A geometric interpretation can help convince students of the beauty and consistency inherent in mathematics. To do this, we shall make a chart of the number of regions into which a circle can be partitioned by joining points on the circle. This ought to be done by the class. Just make sure that no three lines meet at one point, or else you will lose a region.

Number of points on the circle	Number of regions into which the circle is partioned
1	1
2	2
3	4
4	8
5	16
6	31
7	57
8	99

Now that students can see that this unusual sequence appears in various other fields, a degree of satisfaction may be setting in. Remind them of their initial disbelief.

8.5 Mathematics in Nature

The famous Fibonacci numbers, a sequence of numbers that was the direct result of a problem posed by Leonardo of Pisa in his book *Liber abaci* (1202), regarding the regeneration of rabbits (see Unit 1.18), has many other applications in nature. At first sight, it may appear that these applications are coincidental, but eventually you will be amazed at the vastness of the appearance of this famous sequence of numbers.

The original problem posed by Fibonacci asks for the number of pairs of rabbits accumulating each month and leads to the sequence: 1, 1, 2, 3, 5, 8, 13, 21, 34, 55, 89, 144, ...

Before you enchant your students with the many applications of the Fibonacci numbers, you ought to have them bring to class various species of pine cones, a pineapple, a plant (see below), and, if possible, other spiral examples in nature (e.g., a sunflower).

Have students divide each number in the Fibonacci sequence by its right-hand partner to see what sequence develops. They will get a series of fractions:

$$\frac{1}{1}, \frac{1}{2}, \frac{2}{3}, \frac{3}{5}, \frac{5}{8}, \frac{8}{13}, \frac{13}{21}, \frac{21}{34}, \frac{34}{55}, \frac{55}{89}, \frac{89}{144}, \ldots$$

Ask students if they can determine a relationship between these numbers and the leaves of a plant (have a plant on hand). From the standpoint of the Fibonacci numbers, one may observe two items: (1) the number of leaves it takes to go (rotating about the stem) from any given leaf to the next one "similarly placed" (i.e., above it and in the same direction) on the stem and (2) the number of revolutions as one follows the leaves in going from one leaf to another one "similarly placed." In both cases, these numbers turn out to be the Fibonacci numbers.

In the case of leaf arrangement, the following notation is used: $\frac{3}{8}$ means that it takes three revolutions and eight leaves to arrive at the next leaf "similarly placed." In general, if we let r equal the number of revolutions and s equal the number of leaves it takes to go from any given leaf to one "similarly placed," then $\frac{r}{s}$ will be the *phyllotaxis* (the arrangement of leaves in plants). Have students look at the figure below and try to find the plant ratio. Draw a diagram on the board and, if possible, provide a live plant.

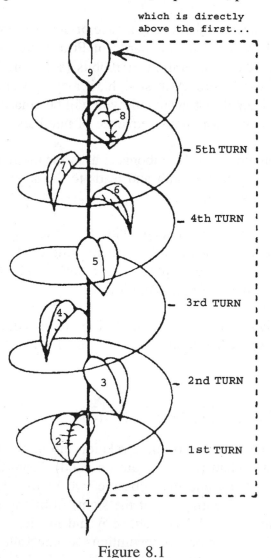

Figure 8.1

In this figure, the plant ratio is $\frac{5}{8}$.

The pine cone also presents a Fibonacci application. The bracts on the cone are considered to be modified leaves compressed into smaller space. Upon observation of the cone, one can notice two spirals, one to the left (clockwise) and the other to the right (counterclockwise). One spiral increases at a sharp angle, while the other spiral increases more gradually. Have students consider the steep spirals and count them, as well as the spirals that increase gradually. Both numbers should be Fibonacci numbers. For example, a white pine cone has five clockwise spirals and eight counterclockwise spirals. Other pine cones may have different Fibonacci ratios. Later, have students examine the daisy or sunflower to see where the Fibonacci ratios apply to them.

We noticed that the ratios of consecutive Fibonacci numbers approach the Golden Section ratio (or Golden Ratio). See Unit 1.18.

If we look closely at the ratios of consecutive Fibonacci numbers, we can approximate their decimal equivalents. The early Fibonacci ratios are

$$\frac{2}{3} = 0.666667$$

$$\frac{3}{5} = 0.600000$$

Then, as we go further along the sequence of Fibonacci numbers, the ratios begin to approach ϕ:

$$\frac{89}{144} - 0.618056$$

$$\frac{144}{233} = 0.618026$$

The Golden Ratio $\phi = 0.6180339887498948482045868343 6564 \ldots.$

Geometrically, point B in Figure 8.2 divides line $\overline{AC}$ into the Golden Ratio:

$$\frac{AB}{BC} = \frac{BC}{AC} \approx 0.618034$$

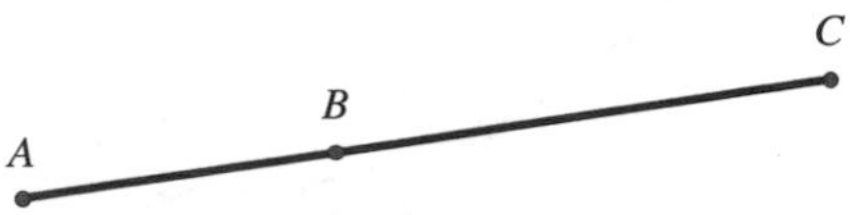

Figure 8.2

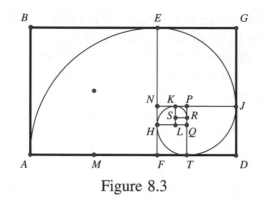

Figure 8.3

Now consider the series of Golden Rectangles (Figure 8.3), those whose dimensions are chosen so that the ratio of $\frac{\text{width}}{\text{length}}$ is the Golden Ratio $\frac{w}{l} = \frac{l}{w+l}$.

If the rectangle is divided by a line segment $(\overline{EF})$ into a square $(ABEF)$ and a Golden Rectangle $(EFDG)$, and if we keep partitioning each new Golden Rectangle in the same way, we can construct a "logarithmic spiral" in the successive squares (Figure 8.3). This type of curve is frequently found in the arrangements of seeds in flowers or in the shapes of seashells and snails. If possible, you ought to have students bring in illustrations to show these spirals (Figure 8.4).

Figure 8.4

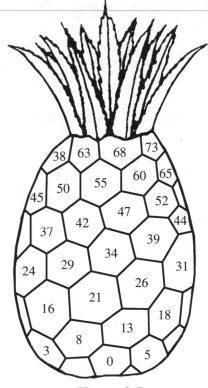

Figure 8.5

For another example of mathematics in nature, students should consider the pineapple. Here there are three distinct spirals of hexagons: a group of *5* spirals winding gradually in one direction, a second group of *13* spirals winding more steeply in the same direction, and a third group of *8* spirals winding in the opposite direction. Each group of spirals consists of a Fibonacci number. Each pair of spirals interacts to give Fibonacci numbers. Figure 8.5 shows a representation of the pineapple with the scales numbered in order. This order is determined by the relative distance each hexagon is from the bottom. That is, the lowest is numbered 0, the next higher one is numbered 1. Note hexagon 42 is slightly higher than hexagon 37.

See if students can note three distinct sets of spirals in Figure 8.5 that cross each other, starting at the bottom. One spiral is the 0, 5, 10, ... sequence, which increases at a slight angle. The second spiral is the 0, 13, 26, ...

sequence, which increases at a steeper angle. The third spiral has the 0, 8, 16, ... sequence, which lies in the opposite direction from the other two. Have students figure out the common difference between the numbers in each sequence. In this case, the differences are 5, 8, 13, all of which are Fibonacci numbers. Different pineapples may have different sequences.

Not to be cute, but to move these applications to a completely different venue, have students consider the regeneration of male bees. They must be told and accept that male bees hatch from unfertilized eggs, female bees from fertilized eggs. You should then guide students in tracing the regeneration of the male bees. The following pattern develops:

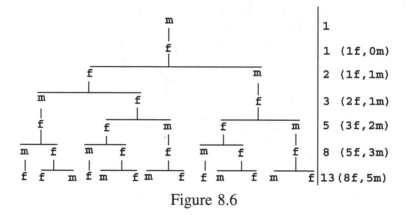

Figure 8.6

It should be obvious by now that this pattern is the Fibonacci sequence.

As was said earlier, there are endless applications of the Fibonacci numbers (sometimes through their relative, the Golden Ratio) in nature, architecture, art, and many other fields of interest. Impress upon your students the independence of these applications, as a part of the amazement these applications usually generate.

8.6 The Hands of a Clock

The clock can be an interesting source of mathematical applications. These can be applications in mathematics, and not in other disciplines as we usually find mathematics being applied.

Begin by asking your students to determine the *exact time* that the hands of a clock will overlap after 4:00 o'clock. Your students' first reaction to the solution to this problem will most likely be that the answer is simply 4:20.

When you remind them that the hour hand moves uniformly while the minute hand moves faster, they will begin to estimate the answer to be between 4:21 and 4:22. They should realize that the hour hand moves through an interval between minute markers every 12 minutes. Therefore, it will leave the interval 4:21–4:22 at 4:24. This, however, doesn't answer the original question about the exact time of this overlap.

You could show them a technique, once they realize that this is not the correct answer, since the hour hand does not remain stationary and moves when the minute hand moves. The trick: Simply multiply the 20 (the wrong answer) by $\frac{12}{11}$ to get $21\frac{9}{11}$, which yields the correct answer: $4:21\frac{9}{11}$.

One way to have students begin to understand the movement of the hands of a clock is by having them consider the hands traveling independently around the clock at uniform speeds. The minute markings on the clock (from now on referred to as "markers") will serve to denote distance as well as time. An analogy should be drawn here to the "uniform motion" of automobiles (a popular topic for verbal problems in an elementary algebra course). A problem involving a fast automobile overtaking a slower one would be analogous.

Experience has shown that the analogy might be helpful in guiding the class to find the distance necessary for a car traveling at 60 mph to overtake a car with a head start of 20 miles and traveling at 5 mph.

Now have the class consider 4 o'clock as the initial time on the clock. Our problem will be to determine exactly when the minute hand will overtake the hour hand after 4 o'clock. Consider the speed of the hour hand to be r; then the speed of the minute hand must be $12r$. We seek the distance, measured by the number of markers traveled, that the minute hand must travel to overtake the hour hand.

Let us refer to this distance as d markers. Hence, the distance that the hour hand travels is $d - 20$ markers, since it has a 20-marker head start over the minute hand.

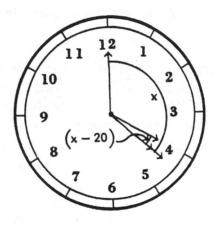

For this to take place, the times required for the minute hand, $\frac{d}{12r}$, and for the hour hand, $\frac{d-20}{r}$, are the same. Therefore,

$$\frac{d}{12r} = \frac{d - 20}{r}$$

and

$$d = \frac{12}{11} \cdot 20 = 21\frac{9}{11}$$

Thus, the minute hand will overtake the hour hand at exactly $4{:}21\frac{9}{11}$.

Consider the expression $d = \frac{12}{11} \cdot 20$. The quantity 20 is the number of markers that the minute hand had to travel to get to the desired position, if we assume the hour hand remained stationary. However, quite obviously, the hour hand does not remain stationary. Hence, we must multiply this quantity by $\frac{12}{11}$, since the minute hand must travel $\frac{12}{11}$ as far. Let us refer to this fraction, $\frac{12}{11}$, as the correction factor. You might wish to have the class verify this correction factor both logically and algebraically.

To begin to familiarize the students with use of the correction factor, choose some short and simple problems. For example, you may ask them to find the exact time when the hands of a clock overlap between 7 and 8 o'clock. Here the students would first determine how far the minute hand would have to travel from the "12" position to the position of the hour hand, assuming again that the hour hand remains stationary. Then by multiplying the number of markers, 35, by the *correction factor*, $\frac{12}{11}$, they will obtain the exact time, $7{:}38\frac{2}{11}$, that the hands will overlap.

To enhance students' understanding of this new procedure, ask them to consider a person checking a wristwatch against an electric clock and noticing that the hands on the wristwatch overlap every 65 minutes (as measured by the electric clock). Ask the class if the wristwatch is fast, slow, or accurate.

You may wish to have them consider the problem in the following way. At 12 o'clock the hands of a clock overlap exactly. Using the previously described method, we find that the hands will again overlap at exactly $1{:}05\frac{5}{11}$, and then again at exactly $2{:}10\frac{10}{11}$, and again at exactly $3{:}16\frac{4}{11}$, and so on. Each time there is an interval of $65\frac{5}{11}$ minutes between overlapping positions. Hence, the person's watch is inaccurate by $\frac{5}{11}$ of a minute. Have students now determine if the wristwatch is fast or slow.

There are many other interesting, and sometimes rather difficult, problems made simple by this correction factor. You may very easily pose your own problems. For example, you may ask your students to find the exact times when the hands of a clock will be perpendicular (or form a straight angle) between, say, 8 and 9 o'clock.

Again, you would have the students determine the number of markers that the minute hand would have to travel from the "12" position until it forms the desired angle with the stationary hour hand. Then have them multiply this number by the correction factor, $\frac{12}{11}$, to obtain the exact actual time. That is, to find the exact time that the hands of a clock are *first* perpendicular between 8 and 9 o'clock, determine the desired position of the minute hand when the hour hand remains stationary (here, on the 25-minute marker). Then multiply 25 by $\frac{12}{11}$ to get $8{:}27\frac{3}{11}$, the exact time when the hands are *first* perpendicular after 8 o'clock.

For students who have not yet studied algebra, you might justify the $\frac{12}{11}$ correction factor for the interval between overlaps in the following way:

Think of the hands of a clock at noon. During the next 12 hours (i.e., until the hands reach the same position at midnight), the hour hand makes one revolution, the minute hand makes 12 revolutions, and the minute hand coincides with the hour hand 11 times (including midnight, but not noon, starting just after the hands separate at noon).

Since each hand rotates at a uniform rate, the hands overlap each $\frac{12}{11}$ of an hour, or $65\frac{5}{11}$ minutes.

This can be extended to other situations.

Your students should derive a great sense of achievement and enjoyment as a result of employing this simple procedure to solve what usually appears to be a very difficult clock problem.

8.7 Where in the World Are You?

This is a popular riddle that has some very interesting extensions, seldom considered. It requires some "out of the box" thinking that can have some favorable lasting effects on students. Let's consider the question:

Where on earth can you be so that you can walk *1 mile south***, then** *1 mile east***, and then** *1 mile north* **and end up at the starting point?**

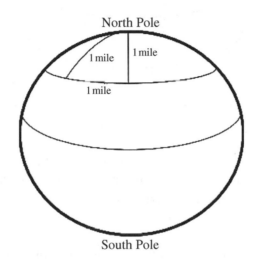

(Not drawn to scale, obviously!)

Mostly through guess and test, a clever student will stumble on the right answer: the North Pole. To test this answer, try starting from the North Pole and travel south 1 mile and then east 1 mile. This takes you along a latitudinal line that remains equidistant from the North Pole, 1 mile from it. Then travel 1 mile north to get you back to where you began, the North Pole.

Most people familiar with this problem feel a sense of completion. Yet we can ask: Are there other such starting points, where we can take the same three "walks" and end up at the starting point? The answer, surprising enough for most people, is *yes*.

One set of starting points is found by locating the latitudinal circle, which has a circumference of 1 mile and is nearest the South Pole. From this circle, walk 1 mile north (along a great circle, naturally) and form another latitudinal circle. Any point along this second latitudinal circle will qualify. Let's try it.

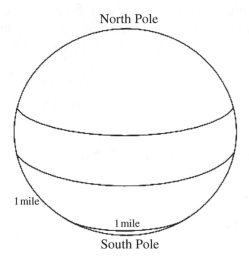

Begin on this second latitudinal circle (the one farther north). Walk 1 mile south (takes you to the first latitudinal circle), then 1 mile east (takes you exactly once around the circle), and then 1 mile north (takes you back to the starting point).

Suppose the first latitudinal circle, the one we would walk along, had a circumference of $\frac{1}{2}$ mile. We could still satisfy the given instructions, yet this time walking around the circle *twice*, and get back to our original starting point. If the first latitudinal circle had a circumference of $\frac{1}{4}$ mile, then we would merely have to walk around this circle *four* times to get back to the starting point on this circle and then go north 1 mile to the original starting point.

At this point, we can take a giant leap to a generalization that will lead us to many more points that satisfy the original stipulations, actually an infinite number of points! This set of points can be located by beginning with the latitudinal circle, located nearest the South Pole, which has a $\frac{1}{n}$th-mile circumference, so that the 1-mile walk east (which is composed of n circumnavigations) will take you back to the point on this latitudinal circle at which you began your walk. The rest is the same as before, that is, walking 1 mile south and then later 1 mile north. Is this possible with latitude circle routes near the North Pole? Yes, of course!

This unit will provide your students with some very valuable "mental stretches," not normally found in the school curriculum. You will not only entertain them, but you will be providing them with some excellent training in thinking logically.

8.8 Crossing the Bridges

The famous Königsberg Bridge Problem is a lovely application of a topological problem with networks. It is very nice to observe how mathematics used properly can put a practical problem to rest. Before we embark on the problem, we ought to become familiar with the basic concept involved. Toward that end, have students try to trace with a pencil each of the following configurations, without missing any part, without going over any part twice, and without lifting their pencils off the paper. Ask students to determine the number of arcs or line segments, which have an endpoint at each of the points A, B, C, D, and E.

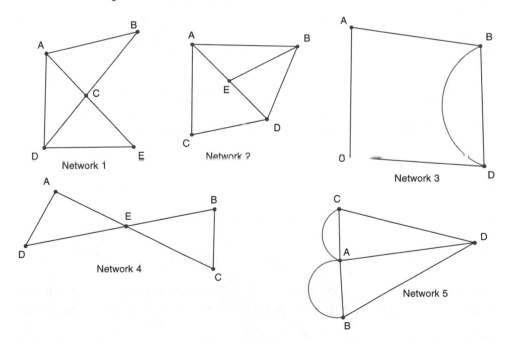

Configurations such as the five figures above, made up of line segments and/or continuous arcs, are called *networks*. The number of arcs or line segments that have an endpoint at a particular vertex is called the *degree* of the vertex.

After trying to trace these networks without taking their pencils off the paper and without going over any line more than once, students should notice two direct outcomes. The networks can be traced (or traversed) if they have (1) all even-degree vertices or (2) exactly two odd-degree vertices. The following two statements establish this.*

1. There is an even number of odd-degree vertices in a connected network.
2. A connected network can be traversed only if it has at most two odd-degree vertices.

Have students now draw both traversible and nontraversible networks (using these two theorems).

Network 1 has five vertices. Vertices *B*, *C*, and *E* are of even degree and vertices *A* and *D* are of odd degree. Since Network 1 has exactly two odd-degree vertices, as well as three even-degree vertices, it is traversible. If we start at *A*, then go down to *D*, across to *E*, back up to *A*, across to *B*, and down to *D*, we have chosen a desired route.

Network 2 has five vertices. Vertex *C* is the only even-degree vertex. Vertices *A*, *B*, *E*, and *D* are all of odd degree. Consequently, since the network has more than two odd vertices, it is not traversible.

Network 3 is traversible because it has two even vertices and exactly two odd-degree vertices.

Network 4 has five even-degree vertices and can be traversed.

Network 5 has four odd-degree vertices and *cannot* be traversed.

To generate interest among your students, present them with the famous Königsberg Bridge Problem. In the 18th century, the small Prussian city

---

* The proof of these two theorems can be found in A. S. Posamentier and J. Stepelman, *Teaching Secondary School Mathematics: Techniques and Enrichment Units*, 6th ed. (Columbus, OH: Merrill/Prentice Hall, 2002).

of Königsberg, located where the Pregel River divided into two branches, was faced with a recreational dilemma: Could a person walk over each of the seven bridges exactly once in a continuous walk through the city?

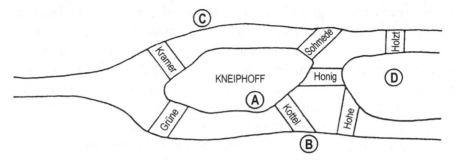

Network 6

In 1735, the famous mathematician Leonhard Euler (1707–1783) proved that this walk could not be performed. Indicate to students that the ensuing discussion will tie in their earlier work with networks to the solution of the Königsberg Bridge Problem.

Tell pupils to indicate the island by *A*, the left bank of the river by *B*, the right one by *C*, and the area between the two arms of the upper course by *D*. If we start at Holzt, walk to Sohmede, and then walk through Honig, through Hohe, through Kottel, through Grüne, we *will* never cross Kramer. On the other hand, if we start at Kramer and walk to Honig, through Hohe, through Kottel, through Sohmede, through Holzt, we will never travel through Grüne.

The Königsberg Bridge Problem is the same problem as the one posed in Network 5. Let's take a look at Networks 5 and 6 and note the similarity. There are seven bridges in Network 6 and there are seven lines in Network 5. In Network 5, each vertex is of odd degree. In Network 6, if we start at *D*, we have three choices: We could go to Hohe, Honig, or Holzt. If, in Network 5, we start at *D*, we have three line paths to choose from. In both networks, if we are at *C*, we have either three bridges we could go on or three lines. A similar situation exists for locations *A* and *B* in Network 6 and vertices *A* and *B* in Network 5. Emphasize that this network *cannot* be traversed.

By reducing the bridges and islands to a network problem, we can easily solve it. This is a clever tactic to solve problems in mathematics.

8.9 The Most Misunderstood Average

Most uninformed students, when asked to calculate the average speed for a round trip with a "going" average speed of 30 miles per hour and a "returning" average speed of 60 miles per hour, would think that their average speed for the entire trip is 45 miles per hour (calculated as $\frac{30+60}{2} = 45$). The first task is to convince the students that this is the wrong answer. For starters, you might ask the students if they believe it is fair to consider the two speeds with equal "weight." Some may realize that the two speeds were achieved for different lengths of time and therefore cannot get the same weight. This might lead someone to offer that the trip at the slower speed, 30 mph, took twice as long and, therefore, ought to get twice the weight in the calculation of the average round-trip speed. This would then bring the calculation to the following:

$$\frac{30 + 30 + 60}{3} = 40$$

which happens to be the correct average speed.

For those not convinced by this argument, try something a bit closer to "home." A question can be posed about the grade a student deserves who scored 100% on nine of ten tests in a semester and on one test scored only 50%. Would it be fair to assume that this student's performance for the term was 75% (i.e., $\frac{100+50}{2}$)? The reaction to this suggestion will tend toward applying appropriate weight to the two scores in consideration. The 100% was achieved nine times as often as the 50% and therefore ought to get the appropriate weight. Thus, a proper calculation of the student's average ought to be

$$\frac{9(100) + 50}{10} = 95$$

This clearly appears more just!

An astute student may now ask, "What happens if the rates to be averaged are not multiples of one another?" For the speed problem above, one could find the time "going" and the time "returning" to get the total time, and then, with the total distance, calculate the "total rate," which is, in fact, the average rate.

There is a more efficient way and that is the highlight of this unit. We are going to introduce a concept called the harmonic mean, which is the mean of a harmonic sequence. The name *harmonic* may come from the fact that one such harmonic sequence is $\frac{1}{2}, \frac{1}{3}, \frac{1}{4}, \frac{1}{5}, \frac{1}{6}, \frac{1}{7}, \frac{1}{8}$, and if one takes guitar strings of these relative lengths and strums them together, a harmonious sound results.

This frequently misunderstood mean (or average) usually causes confusion, but to avoid this, once we identify that we are to find the average of rates (i.e., the harmonic mean), then we have a lovely formula for calculating the harmonic mean for rates over the same base. In the above situation, the rates were for the same distance (round-trip legs).

The harmonic mean for two rates, a and b, is $\frac{2ab}{a+b}$, and for three rates, a, b, and c, the harmonic mean is $\frac{3abc}{ab+bc+ac}$.

You can see the pattern evolving, so that for four rates the harmonic mean is $\frac{4abcd}{abc+abd+acd+bcd}$.

Applying this to the above speed problem gives us

$$\frac{2 \cdot 30 \cdot 60}{30 + 60} = \frac{3,600}{90} = 40$$

Begin by posing the following problem:

> **On Monday, a plane makes a round-trip flight from New York City to Washington with an average speed of 300 miles per hour. The next day, Tuesday, there is a wind of constant speed (50 miles per hour) and direction (blowing from New York City to Washington). With the same speed setting as on Monday, this same plane makes the same round trip on Tuesday. Will the Tuesday trip require more time, less time, or the same time as the Monday trip?**

This problem should be slowly and carefully posed, so that students notice that the only thing that has changed is the "help and hindrance of the wind." All other controllable factors are the same: distances, speed regulation, airplane's conditions, etc. An expected response is that the two round-trip flights ought to be the same, especially since the same wind is helping and hindering two equal legs of a round-trip flight.

Realization that the two legs of the "wind trip" require different amounts of time should lead to the notion that the two speeds of this trip cannot be weighted equally as they were done for different lengths of time. Therefore, the time for each leg should be calculated and then appropriately apportioned to the related speeds.

We can use the harmonic mean formula to find the average speed for the "windy trip." The harmonic mean is

$$\frac{(2)(350)(250)}{250 + 350} = 291.667$$

which is slower than the no-wind trip.

What a surprise!

This topic is not only useful, but also serves to sensitize students to the notion of weighted averages.

8.10 The Pascal Triangle

Perhaps one of the most famous triangular arrangements of numbers is the Pascal triangle (named after Blaise Pascal, 1623–1662). Although used primarily in conjunction with probability, it has many interesting properties beyond that field. To better familiarize students with the Pascal triangle, have them construct it.

Begin with a 1, then beneath it 1, 1, and then begin and end each succeeding row with a 1 and get the other numbers in the row by adding the two numbers above them and to their right and left. So far, we would then have the following:

Continuing with this pattern, the next row would be $1-(1+3)-(3+3)-(3+1)-1$, or $1-4-6-4-1$.

A larger version of the Pascal triangle is shown below:

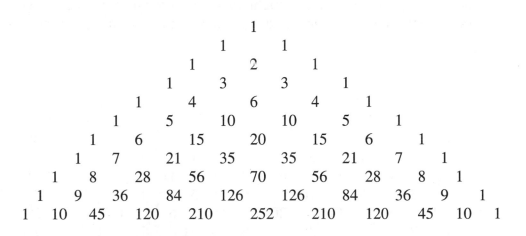

In probability, the Pascal triangle emerges from the following example. We will toss coins and calculate the frequency of each event.

Number of coins	Number of heads	Number of arrangements
1 coin	1 head	1
	0 heads	1
2 coins	2 heads	1
	1 head	2
	0 heads	1
3 coins	3 heads	1
	2 heads	3
	1 head	3
	0 heads	1
4 coins	4 heads	1
	3 heads	4
	2 heads	6
	1 head	4
	0 heads	1

Students should be encouraged to do some investigating of this result by flipping coins and tabulating their results.

What makes the Pascal triangle so truly outstanding is the many fields of mathematics it touches (or involves). In particular, there are many number relationships present in the Pascal triangle. For the sheer enjoyment of it, we shall consider some here. You might try to have your students see if they can locate some of these, perhaps after you show them a few such properties.

The sum of the numbers in the rows of the Pascal triangle are the powers of 2:

$$
\begin{array}{ccccccccccccc}
 & & & & & 1 & & & & & & & 2^0 \\
 & & & & 1 & & 1 & & & & & & 2^1 \\
 & & & 1 & & 2 & & 1 & & & & & 2^2 \\
 & & 1 & & 3 & & 3 & & 1 & & & & 2^3 \\
 & 1 & & 4 & & 6 & & 4 & & 1 & & & 2^4 \\
1 & & 5 & & 10 & & 10 & & 5 & & 1 & & 2^5 \\
\end{array}
$$

1   6   15   20   15   6   1 · · · · 2^6

1 7 21 35 35 21 7 1· · · 2^7

1 8 28 56 70 56 28 8 1 · · 2^8

1 9 36 84 126 126 84 36 9 1· 2^9

1 10 45 120 210 252 210 120 45 10 1 2^{10}

If we consider each row as a number, with the members of the row the digits, such as 1, 11, 121, 1,331, 14,641, etc. (until we have to regroup from the sixth row on), you will find the powers of 11.

					1	·		·	·	·		·	·	·	·	·	·	·	11^0
				1		1	·		·	·	·		·	·	·	·	·	·	11^1
			1		2		1	·	·		·	·		·	·	·	·	·	11^2
		1		3		3		1 ·		·	·	·	·		·	·	·		11^3
	1		4		6		4		1 ·		·	·	·	·		·	·		11^4

```
                    1   ·  ·  ·  ·  ·  ·  · · · · 11⁰
                  1   1  ·  ·  ·  ·  ·  · · · · 11¹
                1   2   1  ·  ·  ·  ·  · · · · 11²
              1   3   3   1 ·  ·  ·  · · · · 11³
            1   4   6   4   1 ·  ·  · · · · 11⁴
          1   5   10   10   5   1 ·  · · · · ·
        1   6   15   20   15   6   1 · · · · ·
      1   7   21   35   35   21   7   1 · · · ·
    1   8   28   56   70   56   28   8   1 · ·
  1   9   36   84   126   126   84   36   9   1 ·
1  10  45  120  210   252   210  120  45  10  1
```

The oblique path marked below indicates the natural numbers. Then to the right of it (and parallel to it), your students will notice the triangular numbers: 1, 3, 6, 10, 15, 21, 28, 36, 45, ...

From the triangle, the students ought to notice how the triangular numbers evolve from the sum of the natural numbers. That is, the sum of the natural numbers (listed to the left of the line) to a certain point may be found by simply looking to the number below and to the right of that point (e.g., the sum of the natural numbers from 1 to 7 is below and to the right, 28).

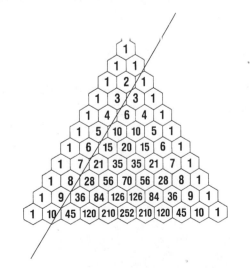

Students ought to be encouraged to look for the square numbers. They are embedded as the sum of two consecutive triangular numbers: $1 + 3 = 4$, $3 + 6 = 9$, $6 + 10 = 16$, $10 + 15 = 25$, $15 + 21 = 36$, etc.

They may also find the square numbers in groups of four: $1 + 2 + 3 + 3 = 9$, $3 + 3 + 6 + 4 = 16$, $6 + 4 + 10 + 5 = 25$, $10 + 5 + 15 + 6 = 36$, etc.

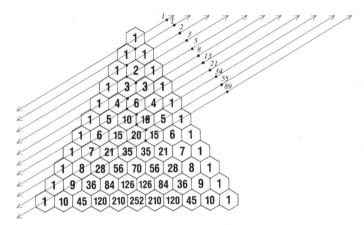

In the above Pascal triangle, your students should add the numbers along the lines indicated. They will be astonished to find that they have, in fact, located the Fibonacci numbers: 1, 1, 2, 3, 5, 8, 13, 21, 34, 55, 89, 144, ...

There are many more numbers embedded in the Pascal triangle. Students may wish to find the pentagonal numbers: 1, 5, 12, 22, 35, 51, 70, 92, 117, 145, ... The turf is fertile. The challenge to find more gems in this triangular arrangement of numbers is practically boundless!

8.11 It's All Relative

With this unit, your students will appreciate and no longer fear the concept of relativity. It will be discussed in a familiar setting, so students will not feel uncomfortable with this idea.

It is expected that the class will comprehend this concept at varying rates. As a matter of fact, it might be wise to present this unit and have students reflect on it at home, where they can do so at their own pace and without outside distractions.

Begin by presenting the following problem:

> **While rowing his boat upstream, David drops a cork overboard and continues rowing for 10 more minutes. He then turns around, chasing the cork, and retrieves it when the cork has traveled 1 mile downstream. What is the rate of the stream?**

Rather than approaching this problem by the traditional methods, common in an algebra course, consider the following. The problem can be made significantly easier by considering the notion of relativity. It does not matter if the stream is moving and carrying David downstream, or is still. We are concerned only with the separation and the coming together of David and the cork. If the stream were stationary, David would require as much time rowing to the cork as he did rowing away from the cork. That is, he would require $10 + 10 = 20$ minutes. Since the cork travels 1 mile during these 20 minutes, its (i.e., the stream's) rate of speed is 3 miles per hour.

Again, this may not be an easy concept to grasp for some students and is best left to them to ponder in quiet. It is a concept worth understanding, for it has many useful applications in everyday life thinking processes. This is, after all, one of the purposes for learning mathematics.

8.12 Generalizations Require Proof

It can be very tempting to let lots of consistent examples lead you to a generalization. Many times the generalization is correct, but it doesn't have to be. The famous mathematician Carl Friedrich Gauss was known to have used his brilliance at calculating and mentally processing number relationships to form some of his theories. Then he proved his conjectures, and these contributions to the field of mathematics have become legendary. Students must be cautious not to draw conclusions just because lots of examples fit a pattern. For example, there is the belief that every odd number greater than 1 can be expressed as the sum of a power of 2 and a prime number. So when we inspect the first few cases, it works.

$$3 = 2^0 + 2$$

$$5 = 2^1 + 3$$

$$7 = 2^2 + 3$$

$$9 = 2^2 + 5$$

$$11 = 2^3 + 3$$

$$13 = 2^3 + 5$$

$$15 = 2^3 + 7$$

$$17 = 2^2 + 13$$

$$19 = 2^4 + 3$$

$$\vdots$$

$$51 = 2^5 + 19$$

$$\vdots$$

$$125 = 2^6 + 61$$

$$127 = ?$$

$$129 = 2^5 + 97$$

$$131 = 2^7 + 3$$

This scheme worked for each number we tested, up to 126, but when we reached 127 there was no solution. Yet, then it continued to work. Thus, this cannot be generalized. Caution should be taken before jumping to conclusions, especially when no proof has been developed. This is a good example of drawing premature conclusions. Yet, above all, it is instructive.

8.13 A Beautiful Curve*

One of the most wonderful curves I can think of, and one that had a great influence on me in my youth, is called a *cycloid*, which is the locus** of a fixed point on the circumference of a circle as it rolls, without slipping, along a straight line (Figure 8.8). This curve has lots of amazing properties that will be revealed to you now.

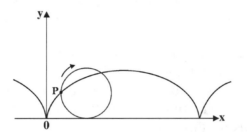

Figure 8.8   The cycloid. As the circle rolls along the line $0x$, the
point P, fixed on the circle, generates the cycloid.

We are going to focus on this curve, or arch, called a *cycloid*. Suppose we turn this arch upside down and place a weighted ball at the point on the vertical line Oy that is $4r$ units from O, where r is the radius of the circle generating the cycloid. Pretend that this vertical line is a string with the weighted ball and can swing as a pendulum. We see this in Figure 8.9, where A and B are the midpoints of the respective arches of the cycloid.

The cycloidal pendulum, also called the *isochronous* pendulum (from the Greek *isochrones*, occurring at equal intervals of time), invented by Christaan Huygens about 350 years ago, consists of a small mass P (we called it a weighted ball before) suspended from the point O by means of a string

---

* By Dr. Herbert A. Hauptman.

** This is the set of points that a fixed point on the rolling circle traces out as it moves along a straight line.

of length equal to the arc length *AO* (or *BO*) and free to oscillate between the inverted half-cycloidal arches *AO* and *BO* generated by a circle of radius *r*.

First, it turns out that the length of the pendulum is $4r$, precisely one-half the length of the full-cycloidal arch. Next, if the mass *P* swings from *A* to *B* (and in a sense, the pendulum string "wraps" itself onto the cycloidal arches *AO* and *BO* when it reaches an extreme), then *P* itself traces out a full cycloidal arch (of length $8r$) generated by a circle having the same radius, *r*, as the one which generated the half arcs *AO* and *BO*. This can be seen in Figure 8.9, where arch *APB* has length $8r$. Furthermore, and this was Huygens great discovery, the period of the oscillation is independent of the amplitude, in sharp contrast to the simple pendulum where the period increases with increasing amplitude. The cycloidal pendulum is therefore said to be isochronous.

Enough with the pendulum property of a cycloid. Let's look at the cycloid curve itself. Again, we will look at the inverted (i.e., upside down) curve. The cycloid is also said to be a *tautochrone* (from the Greek *tautos*, or identical, and *khronos*, or time). We will demonstrate a property of the cycloid that will justify this name.

The inverted cycloid (with a vertical axis) is the curve (see Figure 8.10) along which a particle *sliding* under the influence of gravity from a variable point *A* (*A′* or *A″*, for example) on the curve to the fixed point *B* on the curve will arrive at *B* at the same time no matter where the point *A* is chosen (for example at *A′* or *A″*, etc.). Now, you may find this hard to believe. You may be thinking, how could a point *A″*, far away from *B*, reach point *B* as quickly as a point *A* that is right next to *B*. Well,

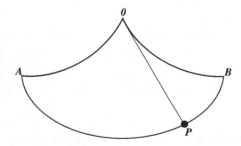

Figure 8.9   The cycloidal (isochronous) pendulum.

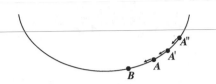

Figure 8.10   The cycloid as tautochrone.

it can and does. You can justify it to yourself, intuitively, by seeing that the cycloid curve has a much greater slope farther away from *B* than it does right next to *B*, accounting for the faster speed of the point *A* farther away from *B* than one close to *B*.

Finally, the cycloid is also said to be the *brachistochrone* (from the Greek *brakhistos*, or shortest, and *khronos*, or time) because it is the path of an object falling freely from the fixed point *A* to the fixed point *B* in the shortest possible time. In other words, among all curves joining *A* to *B* (including a straight line, which can also be considered a curve), it is the cycloid along which a body moves in the least possible time under the influence of gravity (Figure 8.11). This may seem hard to accept, but if you think of a straight line, which is an "extreme curve," then you will see that the initial slope of the cycloid is much greater than that of the straight line; this accounts for the faster speed along the cycloid.

A final property of the cycloid is that the area under the arch is precisely equal to three times the area of the generating circle; that is, the area under the curve (right side up, as it was originally) is $3\pi r^2$.

The cycloid is only one of an infinite variety of curves, some planar, others twisted, having a myriad of characteristic properties aptly described by Bertrand Russell as "sublimely beautiful" and capable of a stern perfection. The examples given here clearly show that the great book of mathematics lies ever open before our eyes and the true philosophy is written in it (to paraphrase Galileo); the reader is invited to open and enjoy it.

Figure 8.11   The cycloid as brachistochrone.

Epilogue

Now that you have reached the end of the book, you should have ample ammunition to convert your students into lovers of mathematics. This was, after all, the aim of this book. If we can convert students to have a very positive feeling of mathematics at school—the earlier the better—then we will be able to rid our society from the ever-popular notion that it is chic to claim weakness in mathematics. For no other school subject would anyone blatantly claim this deficit. We covered the spectrum of elementary mathematics, and for each area we have selected easily understood examples that would motivate your students to seek further entertainments in this most important subject.

Our goal was to make mathematics enticing for its own beauty and not because students are constantly told they must do well in mathematics or else they will have little chance for success in other subjects, most notably the sciences. When Gauss referred to mathematics as the queen of the sciences,* he had not intended that scientists from other disciplines would refer to mathematics as the handmaiden of the sciences; that is, they would judge its value by its usefulness to the other sciences. By this time in your reading of this book, you should get the feeling that there is much to admire in mathematics in its own right, and not that its primary appeal is its usefulness to other disciplines. Naturally, the latter point is one that keeps mathematics high on the list of important areas of study in our society, but it would be so much more effectively taught and maintained if its appeal could be one that rests only on its own inherent beauty.

---

 * Carl Friedrich Gauss (1777–1855), one of the greatest mathematicians of all time, actually said, "Mathematics is the Queen of the Sciences and Arithmetic the Queen of Mathematics. She often condescends to render service to astronomy and the other natural sciences, but under all circumstances the first place is her due."

The effort to show this beauty in mathematics was done through a variety of ways. First, there are the truly delightful, arithmetically clever processes that have become well-kept secrets and that we have attempted to expose for the purpose of exhibiting other ways of thinking. The quirks in our number system present us with some truly amazing number patterns or almost inexplicable phenomena, all presented to delight your students and to announce to them that there are some really nice things in mathematics. Further, the completely unexpected connections between various seemingly unrelated branches of mathematics always have great appeal. For example, the many fields of mathematics invaded by such topics as the Golden Ratio, the Fibonacci numbers, and the Pascal triangle show the interconnectedness of this rich discipline. While on the notion of the unexpected, the problems presented in Chapter 4 show how, with some out-of-the-box thinking, some problems lend themselves to very clever solutions—the kind of solutions that evoke a "gee-whiz" response and, hopefully, entice the student to search for other examples to try these unusual techniques.

The chapter on geometry is the one where we can see some visual beauty in mathematics. How surprisingly invariants appear. Of course, these can be best seen by using a computer program such as the Geometer's Sketchpad, where a dynamic presentation is possible. If your school doesn't have the program, then it would be advisable for you to get a copy of it. It is a most worthwhile computer application.

Where possible (and appropriate), historical notes have been provided so that you can put much of these wonderful ideas in historical context. There is always something appealing when the human element is infused into the discussion of mathematics. Students like to see that mathematics also has some history to it. This is too often missing from the instructional program. Teachers are not willing to give up valuable class time to present this "human side" of mathematics. This little investment of time (just as time taken to show some of the beauties in this book) can go a long way to motivate students, so that they will, in turn, be more receptive learners for the curriculum material.

You ought to begin to collect books on recreational mathematics, read them, and hold them for reference. There are many books on topics not usually taught in the schools. These could include books on the history of mathematics, books on problem solving (at various levels), and books on special topics (e.g., magic squares, mathematical entertainments). What has been provided in this book is merely a whetting of an appetite that you should have for motivating youngsters toward mathematics.

As an ongoing exercise, you might challenge yourself to make a list of suitable applications of mathematics in the daily newspapers. Of particular interest is finding mathematical errors and then showing them to your students. This will make them much more critical readers. Examples of these may be found in a journalist's reasoning, a summary of data presented, the slanting of a story by (mis)use of data, the calculation of data (sometimes incorrectly), geometrical mistakes, or the interpretation of data, which sometimes can be explained in a manner completely opposite to what the writer has done.

In 1987, as I was reading the *New York Times* with my daughter, we noticed a journalist's error regarding the Pythagorean theorem. She urged me to send a correction to the editors, which I did. This experience made me a much more vigilant reader of the newspaper. So whenever there are corrections or comments needed, I am quick to respond. As I mentioned in the Introduction, this book is the outgrowth of the almost 500 letters I received in response to my comments in the *New York Times* (Op-Ed) on January 2, 2002. I hope that others will also read the newspapers and comment where appropriate to keep the mathematics correct. Now fortified with this newly developed love for mathematics, this is the least one could expect for you to model for your students.

Acknowledgments

One picks up many cute ideas in mathematics from a variety of sources. Some ideas remain engrained in memory while others fade with time. I have dug deeply into my memory bank to find entertaining material for this book. It is impossible to cite the many hundreds of mathematics books I have read and where I probably got some of the ideas for this book. It is also not possible to properly acknowledge the many fine colleagues, and students from whom, over the past several decades, I may have gotten some of the ideas presented in this book. However, I would like to thank Dr. Ingmar Lehmann from the Humboldt University of Berlin for some enhancement ideas he so generously offered. Thanks are also extended to Jacob Cohen, David Linker, and Amir Dagan for helping with proofreading the manuscript, and technical assistance from Jan Siwanowicz. Naturally, sincere thanks are due to Barbara Lowin for her service as sample audience, as I tried to find the most motivating ideas and then put them into appropriately intelligible form. Finally, I appreciate the encouragement and assistance from my ASCD editors and support from Tina Burke at Technical Typesetting as we prepared this work for publication.

October 18, 2002

Index

About the Author

Alfred S. Posamentier is Professor of Mathematics Education and Dean of the School of Education of the City College of the City University of New York. He is the author and co-author of numerous mathematics books for teachers and secondary school students. As a guest lecturer, he favors topics that enrich the learning experience of youngsters, including mathematics problem solving and the introduction of uncommon topics that demonstrate the beauty of mathematics. Posamentier is also a frequent commentator in newspapers on topics relating to mathematics and its teaching. The development of this book reflects these penchants and grew out of his desire to bring some refreshing motivational ideas into the regular classroom instruction.

After completing his A.B. degree in mathematics at Hunter College of the City University of New York, he took a position as a teacher of mathematics at Theodore Roosevelt High School in the Bronx (New York), where he focused on improving the students' problem-solving skills and, at the same time, enriching their instruction far beyond what the traditional textbooks offered. Posamentier also developed the school's first mathematics teams (both at the junior and senior level). This endeavor resulted in the establishment of a special mathematics class designed to provide students with an opportunity to explore familiar topics from an unusual viewpoint and to study topics not a part of the secondary school curriculum yet eminently within the scope of an above-average high school student. He is involved in working with mathematics teachers, nationally and internationally, to help them maximize their effectiveness.

Immediately upon joining the faculty of the City College (after having received his masters' degree there), he began to develop in-service courses for secondary school mathematics teachers, including such special areas as recreational mathematics and problem solving in mathematics.

Posamentier received his Ph.D. from Fordham University (New York) in mathematics education and has since extended his reputation in mathematics education to Europe. He has been visiting professor at several European universities in Austria, England, Germany, and Poland, most recently at the University of Vienna and at the Technical University of Vienna. At the former, he was a Fulbright Professor in 1990.

In 1989, he was awarded as an Honorary Fellow at the South Bank University (London, England). In recognition of his outstanding teaching, the City College Alumni Association named him Educator of the Year in 1994 and had the day, May 1, 1994, named in his honor by the City Council President of New York City. In 1994, he was also awarded the Grand Mcdal of Honor from the Federal Republic of Austria, and, in 1999, upon approval of Parliament, the President of the Federal Republic of Austria awarded him the title of University Professor of Austria.

Now after 33 years on the faculty of the City College, Posamentier still seeks ways to make mathematics interesting to both teachers and students and sees this book as another medium to reach his objective.